Earl **rea**

Early Years Foundations Meeting the Challenge

Edited by
Janet Moyles

 Open University Press
Maidenhead

Open University Press
McGraw-Hill Education
McGraw-Hill House
Shoppenhangers Road
Maidenhead
Berkshire
England
SL6 2QL

email: enquiries@openup.co.uk
world wide web: www.openup.co.uk

and Two Penn Plaza, New York, NY 10121–2289, USA

First published 2007

A catalogue record of this book is available from the British Library

ISBN-10: 0335 223 494 (pb) 0335 223 486 (hb)
ISBN-13: 978 0335 223 497 (pb) 978 0335 223 497 (pb)

Library of Congress Cataloguing-in-Publication Data
CIP data applied for

Typeset by YHT Ltd, London
Printed in Poland by OZGraf S.A.
www.polskabook.pl

The McGraw·Hill Companies

Contents

Contributors

Deborah Albon is a Senior Lecturer in Early Childhood Studies at London Metropolitan University. Prior to this she worked for nearly 20 years as a nursery nurse, teacher and manager in a variety of early childhood settings, primarily in South-west London. Her main research interest is in children, food and eating, and she is currently engaged in research looking at food and drink practices in early childhood settings.

Pat Broadhead is Professor of Playful Learning at Leeds Metropolitan University where she and her colleagues have established the Centre for Research into Childhood (CRinCH). Previous to this appointment, Pat worked at the Universities of Northumbria, York and Leeds. She has worked in teacher education and as an early years teacher. Her main area of research is children's learning through play with peers in educational settings and the links with developing sociability and cooperation.

Liz Brooker a former early years teacher, is now Senior Lecturer in Early Childhood at the Institute of Education. Her research into the educational experiences of ethnic minority children stems from her own classroom teaching, and was the subject of the book, *Starting School: Young Children Learning Cultures* (2002). Liz is currently writing a book, *Supporting Transitions in the Early Years,* which explores the experiences of very young children as they move into group settings.

Naima Browne has worked in the field of early years and primary education for almost 30 years. During this time she has been a nursery and primary teacher, held a number of advisory posts and worked as a lecturer in several universities. She is currently a freelance consultant. Naima is an experienced researcher and has published a range of books, chapters and articles on early years education. She is particularly interested in equity issues.

Elizabeth Carruthers is head teacher of Redcliffe Children's Centre, Bristol. Formerly she has worked as an early years advisor and also as a numeracy consultant. She has taught for over 25 years both in England and the United States, mostly with children from 3–8 years. She is co-author of the book *Children's Mathematics: Making Marks, Making Meaning* (Paul Chapman, 2003).

Her present research interest is the pedagogy of children's mathematical graphics.

Tricia David is now retired but continues her involvement in the field of Early Childhood Education and Care, through writing, conference presentations, grandmothering, and so on. She was greatly honoured to be awarded the title of Emeritus Professor by Canterbury Christ Church and Sheffield Universities (the latter for three years). Having reached the age that her contemporaries, the Beatles, sang about, she is also happy to have time for 'doing the garden, digging the weeds'.

Dan Davies is Professor of Science and Technology Education, Head of Primary Education and Assistant Dean of Education at Bath Spa University. He taught in primary schools in London before moving into teacher education at Goldsmiths College, University of London. He has published widely in the fields of primary science and design & technology education.

Jackie Eyles was initially a teacher and then Head Teacher of two primary and nursery schools. She then became a university lecturer involved in undergraduate and post-graduate work including the development of Early Years modules for the MA programme. Latterly, she has been involved in the mentor teacher programme for Worcestershire LEA, supporting early years settings, a subject which was part of her doctorate. Professional activities also include research, consultancy and membership of TACTYC (Training, Advancement and Co-operation in Teaching Young Children) and of PUG (Primary Umbrella Group).

Hilary Fabian is Head of Education and Childhood Studies at the North East Wales Institute. She has taught young children in London, Buckinghamshire, Shropshire and with the Service Children's Education Authority in Germany, and has worked in Higher Education since 1991. Her MSc and PhD theses, books and journal publications reflect her interest in transitions, particularly children starting school, children transferring between schools and early years settings and the ways in which induction to new settings is managed.

Rose Griffiths is a Lecturer in Education at the University of Leicester where she is responsible for initial and in-service education in primary mathematics. Starting as a mathematics teacher with a particular interest in working with children who find maths difficult, she was head of mathematics at a comprehensive school, and later worked extensively with young children and their parents, including through Sure Start. Her publications include several books for parents and teachers and she also enjoys writing books for children.

The latter include the *Oxford First Book of Maths* (2003), *Simple Maths* (Priddy, 2005), and a series of books called *Number Connections* (Heinemann, 2005).

Alan Howe is a Senior Lecturer in Primary Education and Primary Science Co-ordinator at Bath Spa University. He taught in primary schools in London, Bristol and Bath before moving into teacher education. He has published widely in the fields of primary science and creativity in primary education. He is joint author of *Science 5–11: A Guide for Teachers* (2005), *Teaching Science and Design and Technology in the Early Years* (2002) and *Primary Design and Technology for the Future* (2006), all published by David Fulton.

Paulette Luff is a Senior Lecturer in Early Childhood Studies at Anglia Ruskin University. She is currently completing research exploring early years practitioners' uses of child observation, as a doctoral researcher in the Centre for Research in Education And Teaching (CREATe), founded by Professor Janet Moyles. She has worked in the field of early childhood for over 20 years, as a teacher, foster carer, school–home liaison worker and as a lecturer in further education.

Janet Moyles is Professor Emeritus at Anglia Ruskin University and an early years consultant. She has worked as an early teacher and head, and also run early years initial and in-service training courses for teachers on play and learning and effective/reflective pedagogy. She has directed several research projects including *Jills of All Trades?* (ATL, 1996), *Teaching Fledglings to Fly* (ATL, 1997), *Too Busy to Play?* (Leicester, 1997–2000), *SPEEL – Study of Pedagogical Effectiveness in Early Learning* (DfES, 2002), *Recreating the Reception Year* (ATL, 2004) and *Effective Leadership and Management* (OUP, 2007).

Theodora Papatheodorou is a Professor in Early childhood at Anglia Ruskin University. She has long and diverse teaching and research experience in the field of early childhood. Her work has been widely disseminated by publications and in international journals and presentations at conferences. She is the author of the book *Behaviour Problems in the Early Years* (Routledge, 2005).

Rod Parker-Rees was a nursery and reception teacher in Bristol before he joined the University of Plymouth where he is now co-ordinator of the Early Childhood Studies programmes. He is one of the editors of the TACTYC journal, *Early Years: An International Journal of Research and Development* and co-editor of *Early Childhood Studies: An Introduction to the Study of Children's Worlds and Children's Lives* (Learning Matters, 2004) and *Early Years Education: Major Themes in Education* (Routledge, 2005).

Emmie Short lives in the north-west of Cumbria and at present works part-time as a registered childminder. A graduate in Ancient History and Literature, she is the mother of four children, the oldest now at university and the youngest having just started in full-time education. She has served on nursery school committees and as a pre-school volunteer. Her particular concern about children's experience in their earliest years is the increasingly earlier formalization of education.

David Whitebread is a Senior Lecturer in Psychology and Education in the Faculty of Education, University of Cambridge, and a former director of the Early Years and Primary PGCE course. His research interests are concerned with learning in young children, including the role of play, thinking skills in young children, and the development of self-regulation and independent learning. His publications include *The Psychology of Teaching and Learning in the Primary School* (RoutledgeFalmer, 2000) and *Teaching and Learning in the Early Years* (2nd edition) (RoutledgeFalmer, 2003).

Marian Whitehead is the author of several standard texts on the development of language and literacy in the early years and co-editor of the international research journal *Early Years*. She was formerly a Senior Lecturer at Goldsmiths College, University of London, and now advises schools, children's centres, training providers and various publications on ways of working with families and communities to support young children's language and literacy learning.

Maulfry Worthington has taught in the full 3–8-year age range for 25 years. She has lectured on primary and early years mathematics pedagogy on B Ed and PGCE courses and was a National Numeracy consultant. She is co-author of *Children's Mathematics: Making Marks, Making Meaning* (Paul Chapman, 2003) and joint founder of the international *Children's Mathematics Network*. Maulfry is currently engaged in research on multi-modality and children's mathematical graphics for her doctorate (Free University, Amsterdam).

Introduction

Janet Moyles

There are so many challenges and issues facing Foundation Stage practitioners at the moment and continual dilemmas between doing what one knows is essentially 'right' for young children from all backgrounds and conforming to the demands made by government and policy-makers – not always a happy alliance. The early years, as we understand it today, is still a very 'young' field (forgive the pun): for example, many practitioners are still learning on-the-job, through the roles they fulfil daily, multi-disciplinary teams are learning to work and train together, managers are still learning how to be setting leaders and playful approaches still faze many practitioners in terms of supporting children's learning and development. Dealing with children from birth to 5 years from diverse backgrounds and cultures and with differential learning needs, remains a challenge for many practitioners and, politically, the government appears to have a long way to go to meet its own targets for 2020 in relation to *End Child Poverty* (ECPC 2005).

It will be many years before England effectively establishes its early years education and care systems within our multi-cultural, multi-racial and, essentially, still unequal society: as an example, many still find it difficult to work closely with parents from diverse backgrounds or to provide appropriate curriculum experiences for all our young children through play. Outdoor play, in particular, is in an early stage of development in many settings. We also have the issue of how the Early Years Foundation Stage (EYFS) will link (or otherwise) with Key Stage 1 of the National Curriculum and how the Early Years Practitioner role will be fully augmented and developed in the next few years. Indeed, one of the things I have discovered in researching this book is that while all the current initiatives are very laudable in principle, relating them one to the other can be extremely difficult. Overlaps do exist, of course, but it is actually nearly impossible to map one document on to another. This difficulty in linking different policy documents appears to indicate two things:

1   the vast scope of the task undertaken by the government in trying to amalgamate and extend a number of systems for children which have stood relatively independently for many years;

2   the complexity for early years practitioners in trying to make sense of all the legislation and policy documents *and* meet the requirements laid upon them.

How very disconcerting it must be for hard-working early years practitioners trying to implement the early years curriculum while remaining aware of all the underpinning legislation and policy directives. The need to be a reflective and analytical practitioner has clearly never been greater or more urgent.

While reflective practice is emphasized in the EYFS, how can this evolve and develop in a climate where governments insist on dictating everyday practices, essentially removing the onus of responsibility from practitioners? One example recently is the requirement that young children should be taught synthetic phonics when all those who know young children realize that all children learn differently and multi-methods are better employed. These are national challenges that have parallels in other parts of the world: China, for example, is just beginning to realize that children need to play and to be individually creative and that it is possible to provide a curriculum based on play that nonetheless enables children to achieve the kinds of outcomes desired by parents, practitioners and policy-makers and become creative individuals (DfCMS/DfES 2006). The issue of what constitutes a 'teacher' is still discussed internationally as so many countries have differently trained adults working in the early years. Many practitioners find it difficult to deal effectively with young children's identities and gender, and the changing cultural identities of children in the context of their first education and care experiences outside the home, especially in the first days at school. Issues such as bereavement or other traumatic events experienced by young children (see e.g. Adams and Moyles 2005) are avoided by many practitioners as being just too disturbing to consider.

Literacy is an ever-popular topic with increasing pressure being put on young children to 'learn to read and write' and to 'do' phonics (especially of the synthetic variety!), yet some children come to school without the basic speaking and listening skills upon which to build literacy development (see Palmer 2006): others come with a wealth of language experiences from different cultures and ethnic groups. Similarly with independence: some children come to school able to take a range of responsibilities, particularly for their own actions and behaviours, while others need continual support for the smallest task. Some of these children may well have very individualized needs and require a great deal of additional support to deal with their diverse or special circumstances. The assessment of children's abilities, capabilities and dispositions is a continual source of concern to early years practitioners, for effective assessment means that individual children's learning and development must be taken into account in developing plans for the next stages of learning and teaching. Indeed, the *Early Years Foundation Stage* (DfES

2006) emphasizes the uniqueness of each child and in the Foreword to the *Five Year Strategy for Children and Learners*, the Secretary of State for Education in the UK clearly states:

> the central characteristic of such a new system will be personalisation – so that the system fits to the individual rather than the individual having to fit to the system . . . a system which will genuinely give high standards for all . . . which builds a detailed picture of what each child already knows, and how they learn, to help them go further . . . a system that recognises individual aptitudes . . . the system must be both freer and more diverse – with more flexibility to help meet individual needs . . . so that there really are different and personalised opportunities available.
>
> (DfES 2004: 2)

This individualization and personalization require practitioners not only to be highly skilled but also to work together in multi-faceted teams which include parents and other carers. As in England, there are international issues around teams of differentially trained people working together and the roles of those with and without qualified teacher status. How far should roles like nursery nurse and teaching assistant emulate those of degree-level teachers: what is the likely outcome of the creation of Early Years Professional status? Should we aim for an all-graduate profession in the early years as has been the case in British primary education for over 30 years now? Teachers in England are currently being used as mentors for other early years practitioners as a form of training which is an innovative dimension to practitioner development. What can we learn from this approach? Is it sustainable?

These issues which face early years practitioners today will continue to do so well into the foreseeable future. The potential issues are many and varied and, clearly, a short book cannot incorporate every conceivable topic. But, using the new (draft) *Early Years Foundation Stage* (DfES 2006) principles as its basic framework, this exciting and original edited collection aims to support early years practitioners in thinking through their roles in meeting some of these challenges and dilemmas and dealing sensitively and professionally with the issues. Of necessity, many of the topics within EYFS overlap, as an example, how can one separate out child development from play and exploration or health and well-being from active learning and creativity?

It will be vital – as the book emphasizes – that practitioners personalize the requirements for each child and family who come within their sphere of responsibility. Each of the four sections – A Unique Child; Positive Relationships; Enabling Environments and Learning and Development – is preceded by a very short discussion and analysis by the editor of relevant background thinking and information which sets that focus in context and aims to present evidence and guidance upon which practitioners can establish their own views and reach their own decisions. (The Appendix indicates the areas covered by the various writers in relation to the EYFS.)

All the contributors are experienced writers and avid early years advocates who have written on topics about which they are both knowledgeable and passionate. They have all laid out their specific focus and outlined the challenges, issues and dilemmas within that focus facing practitioners in the UK and beyond. Each writer has provided a brief *abstract* at the start of the chapter so that readers can 'tune in' quickly to the contents. Writers then examine some of the *background issues* to each topic, offering opinions on why the situation is as it is and how it might move forward within the current Frameworks, e.g. *Every Child Matters, the Common Core, Children's Rights, the Early Years Foundation Stage, the Common Assessment Framework* and *Key Elements of Effective Practice* (pertinent to the topic). They offer *suggestions to practitioners* for dealing with the challenges faced in that particular focus and also include *questions for reflection* and suggested *discussion points* to encourage staff development opportunities. Recommended books, articles and websites are highlighted (in bold) in the *reference lists* which accompany each chapter.

Because of the complexities already highlighted, it was felt appropriate to begin the book with a thorough analysis of the current context of early years education and care provided by Liz Brooker. She writes about the opportunities and the challenges that the new early childhood 'landscape' presents and describes how the developments and legislation of the past ten years have brought about new ways of thinking and working which we need now to embrace in order effectively to 'promote the interests of young children and their families'.

So let's begin!

References

Adams, S. and Moyles, J. (2005) *Images of Violence: Responding to Children's Representations of Violence as They See It*. Lutterworth: Featherstone Publications.

DCMS (Department for Culture, Media and Sport)/DfES (Department for Education and Skills) (2006) *The Roberts Report: Nurturing Creativity in Young People*. London: The Stationery Office.

DfES (2006) *The Early Years Foundation Stage: Consultation on a Single Quality Framework for Services to Children from Birth to Five*. Nottingham: DfES Publications.

DfES (2004) *Five Year Strategy for Children and Learners*. London: Crown Copyright.

End Child Poverty Campaign (2005) Available online: http://www.ecpc.org.uk/index.php?id=1 (accessed 7 January 2007).

Palmer, S. (2006) *Toxic Childhood*. London: Orion.

1 Changing the landscape of early childhood

Liz Brooker

Abstract

All of us working in the early years field, whether as front-line practitioners with young children and families, or as academics and local authority personnel struggling to absorb and disseminate new knowledge, are aware of living through a period of rapid and dramatic changes to our practice. In the past few years we have faced a succession of challenges, including changing government policies towards children and families, changing understandings of teaching and learning, and a welter of new home-grown initiatives as well as some exciting initiatives that have come from overseas.

This chapter summarizes what lies behind our present situation. It explores the policy initiatives that have transformed the role and status of early childhood services, and examines both the challenges we are presented with and the opportunities we must seize to make early childhood provision a truly transformative service for young children and their families, now and in the future.

Introduction

The recent rapid pace of change in early years services has been awe-inspiring in every sense – both exhilarating and terrifying – for everyone involved in the field. Over the past ten years we have seen our profession transformed from a low-status service of 'care' for young children, widely viewed as an extension of women's family-based caring role, and hence a professional role based more on instinct and experience than on training and qualifications, to an instrument of social transformation that holds the key to creating a better society, and meeting both social and economic goals. This rapid change is in many ways gratifying. It is good to have recognition, at last, for the key role of early years professionals in supporting families, including those most disadvantaged; in creating inclusive and enlightened communities of learners; in intervening in young children's lives to safeguard and support their physical and intellectual development, and their growing identities and relationships. But at the same time it is challenging: every new initiative brings its own set of regulations and requirements, its new responsibilities, and only the most robust and resilient of us can remain entirely unshaken in our professional confidence. Our professional roles are changing too, as early years professionals from different fields of practice learn to work together in the interests of children and families; and as early years experts increasingly step outside the world of the nursery and take a leadership role in constructing social policy, and formulating a vision for society.

This chapter sets the scene for the rest of the book by examining both the opportunities and the challenges that the new early childhood 'landscape' presents. It describes the events of the past ten years which have brought us to the threshold of a new way of working – the developments and legislation which have brought us from the *Sure Start* programme to the *Foundation Stage* and from the *Every Child Matters* framework to the *Early Years Foundation Stage*. It summarizes the key challenges presented by this new landscape and the opportunities offered for working more creatively and more effectively to promote the interests of young children and their families.

There is another context for our work, however: the changing landscape of research evidence in young children's lives and learning – but how many busy practitioners can keep up with *that*? The past decade has provided an entirely new evidence base on the development of the brain in early infancy and through the pre-school years; on the most effective and appropriate forms of early education; on the impact of early experiences on life-long dispositions and attitudes; on the role of partnership working with parents; and on the importance of transitions in shaping young children's lives and the path their development will take. Sometimes, new policies and legislation appear to build on such research (although at other times they do not). But most people working with young children are aware of this 'new knowledge' which is filtering into, and transforming, our daily practice, and many of us are acutely aware of not knowing enough, of struggling to 'keep up'.

So, our dilemmas are many:

- how to hold fast to the underlying commitment to young children that we have developed through training and experience, while remaining open to new interpretations and new interventions;
- how to retain a close focus on the children in our immediate care, while keeping our eyes on the bigger, national and international picture which shapes that responsibility;
- how to retain our professional identity as 'educators', while understanding and accepting our new roles as jointly responsible for a much wider range of outcomes for children and families;
- how to combine our profession's traditionally modest, and local,

stance with the more assertive and more political role of leadership that is now required.

This chapter does not offer any simple answers to these dilemmas. But it does argue that, in order to make the most of the positive opportunities we are now offered, and to manage those aspects which may appear to be more challenging, we must keep an informed and open mind both about the beliefs and practices we know and trust, and about the new knowledge, and new ways of working, of our changing professional landscape. Like the young children we work with, we are undergoing transitions; like them, we may experience feelings of vulnerability, and a loss of confidence; like them, we need to use our own inner resilience, and the support of our colleagues, to ensure that these uncomfortable moments have positive outcomes in the longer term.

How did we get here? Policy changes and professional consequences

The ten years from the 1997 election which brought a Labour government to power were a period of unprecedented change in the early years' world. Underlying all the particular instances of new policies, new programmes, new curricula, new regulatory arrangements, new buildings, new job titles, lay a far bigger conception. It was the belief that the services provided by the state for children under 5 years and their families (including through its regulation of private providers), could have a wide-reaching and long-term impact on every single aspect of our society; that high quality services for young children could generate a better quality of life and better outcomes for those of all ages, individually and collectively.

The new government's agenda had several strands, but its over-riding commitment was to social inclusion and a more equal and just society. Social inclusion was addressed through a multitude of initiatives intended to redistribute wealth and improve health, end child poverty, reduce welfare dependency, halve the incidence of teenage pregnancy, tackle the lack of basic skills and raise overall educational achievements. All these mechanisms were linked by an unassailable chain of logic: better provision for young children, along with tax credits and other financial measures, would enable more young parents to study, train and work; as a result they would become both higher earners (and hence, higher tax-payers) and better parents; in the process they would become more integrated into society and feel more commitment to their communities and perhaps also to the national interest. At the same time, through high quality early experiences, their children would acquire the knowledge and skills, and the dispositions and commitment to be life-long learners (and earners) themselves. It appeared to be a win–win programme, with the single drawback that it would require massive investment in the short term in order for the long-term goals, and the pay-back, to be realized.

Ten years later, it is clear both that the programme has run into many difficulties and setbacks, but also that a great deal has been achieved. While this is not the place to evaluate specific targets – for redistribution, for child poverty, for school achievement, for teenage pregnancy – it is helpful to review some of the steps which have made up the transformation of services we now experience, and to identify some of the key changes to the profession. Figure 1.1 offers a timeline of some of these steps.

1997	National Early Excellence programme launched
1998	Sure Start Local programme initiative launched
1999	First round of Sure Start local programmes
2000	*Curriculum Guidance for the Foundation Stage*
2001	*Special Education Needs (revised) Code of Practice*
2002	*Birth-to-Three Matters Framework* Education Act DfES Sure Start Unit
2003	*Every Child Matters* (Green Paper) Children's Centres programme launched
2004	Children Act *Ten-year Childcare strategy: choice for parents, the best start for children*
2005	*Common Core of Skills and Knowledge for the Children's Workforce*
2006	*Early Years Foundation Stage* (consultation document) Childcare Act
2007	Revision of the EYFS following consultation
2008	*Early Years Foundation Stage* implemented

Figure 1.1 Landmarks in the new educational landscape

Integrated centres and integrated working practices

Integrated centres and family centres were not 'new' in 1997 – they had existed since the 1970s (Makins 1997) as isolated beacons in a world of fragmented and frequently poor quality provision. But from 1997 the National Early Excellence Centre programme made such centres a national priority rather than a local lottery: originally 25 were to be identified and funded, but as the programme grew it was recognized that the need was much greater than this, and over 100 were established in the next few years. The programme, it was argued at the time, would allow 'greater collaboration between providers to improve the coherence of services, extend opportunities, raise standards and promote good practice' (DfEE 1997: np).

As research continued to show the benefits (Pugh et al. 1994; Makins 1997), including the cost benefits, of investing in childhood services and in particular of providing a wider range of services for families in a 'one stop shop', integrated services became the model for all new initiatives. Sure Start local programmes, launched in six 'rounds' from 1999 (Sure Start Unit 2003) offered support for health, learning, childcare and parenting in relatively deprived communities. Over 500 local projects were developed, and the national evaluation (Melhuish et al. 2005) provided further evidence of what forms of provision were most effective. The government's Neighbourhood Nursery Initiative, commenced in 2000, was similarly targeted at the 20 per cent most deprived neighbourhoods in the country, and aimed to provide daycare from birth to school age in areas where none was available or accessible to families. All these strategies had both immediate and local goals in terms of the health and well-being of families and children, and longer-term goals of tackling poverty and social exclusion.

Curriculum matters

Within educational programmes similarly wide-reaching changes were under way. From 2000, the new Foundation Stage (QCA 2000) provided a curriculum underpinned by important principles about the nature of children's learning, about equality and inclusion, and about partnership with parents, while the *Birth-to-Three Matters* framework (Sure Start Unit 2002) re-emphasized the broad and multi-stranded nature of young children's development. Provision for under-3s was based on four aspects of the child – the 'strong' child, the skilful communicator, the competent learner and the healthy child. It was a logical next step, following the success of this framework and its popularity with practitioners, to integrate the birth–3 and the 3–5 frameworks into a single outline of good practice for birth–5, and the resulting consultation document for the *Early Years Foundation Stage* (DfES 2006) has also met with broad approval for its holistic view of the child, and its sound basis in research.

Every Child Matters

Meanwhile the 'bigger picture' in government policy continued to develop. The Green Paper *Every Child Matters* (DfES 2003) was the outcome of a lengthy process of policy development, in part, responding to Lord Laming's report on the circumstances leading to the death of Victoria Climbié. *The Children Act 2004* (HMG 2004) which enacted this legislation brought together all those working with children under a single framework of responsibility, and made them all responsible for working together towards five broad outcomes: staying safe, being healthy, enjoying and achieving, making a contribution, and avoiding poverty and hardship. The *Ten Year Strategy for Childcare* (HM Treasury 2004) made far-reaching requirements for universally available, accessible and affordable day care for parents who wanted or needed it. As the momentum gathered, the task of reforming the children's workforce resulted in the *Common Core of Skills and Knowledge* (DfES 2005a) and the publication of standards for the new role of *Early Years Professional* status (CWDC 2006).

The decision to draw together all those with responsibilities for children and families under the *Every Child Matters* outcomes framework was a bold one, and one which required all those involved to re-think their professional duties: 'challenges and issues', indeed. Teachers whose primary responsibility was always to 'teach' now have collective responsibility with their colleagues in other services for all aspects of a child's, and the family's, well-being. The outcomes targeted are wide-ranging, including reducing road deaths and household accidents, improving children's physical fitness, tackling bullying, avoiding undue financial pressure on parents, and above all being alert to signs that a child or family is experiencing stress or distress. This major transition in the lives of professionals occurred against a background of research evidence which also required all early years' practitioners to re-think their practice.

Reflection points

1   How do we feel when we hear about a new policy or initiative which requires us to think and act differently in our work with children and families?

2   Do we make the most of opportunities to share any feelings we may have – whether positive or negative – with colleagues and managers?

3   Can we make time in our settings for regular reflection and discussion on the changes in our professional responsibilities?

What do we know? Research findings to bring about 'change for children'

Research into the development of babies and young children, and the ways that this is shaped by early environments, has transformed our knowledge and understanding over recent years, and has helped to inform changes in practice. In the interests of promoting children's well-being and development, research findings from the scientific and psychological fields have been combined with those from sociology and economics, healthcare and education, to create a 'big picture' of the most favourable conditions for young children.

Neuroscience

Some of the most compelling new evidence comes from research into the human brain (Bruer 1999; Shonkoff and Phillips 2000). It is now clear that the brain grows at a faster rate before birth and during early infancy than at any subsequent time, and may reach its maximum capacity by the time a child is 8. Although there is still plenty of room for further growth later in life, there is no subsequent period when new knowledge can be constructed so efficiently and so effortlessly as it can in the pre-school years. This growth is stimulated by a range of experiences – emotional as well as sensory – and is supported by basic levels of health and nutrition. A favourable environment triggers the expansion of synaptic connections to create a vast and dense network of paths of meaning, which remain viable and effective so long as they remain in use, but may be slowly extinguished through adverse circumstances or through lack of use.

Fortunately for us all, this rapid growth, and the gradual extinction of synaptic connections do not depend on a highly-tuned, hot-house environment – Beethoven for breakfast, Latin for lunch, and so on – but simply on a modest amount of nutrition, affection, interest and stimulation, on 'good enough' parenting and on consistent levels of care and interaction. And, despite what was once taught about critical periods, we now know that children whose early environments are unfavourable have quite a good chance of making up for lost time when their circumstances improve. But there is no doubt that supporting children's early learning in every aspect – social and emotional, physical and creative, as well as cognitive and linguistic – is an endeavour that now has the strongest scientific foundations. As the UNICEF *State of the World's Children* report affirms, this endeavour is one which makes sense for societies as well as for individuals: 'Choices made and actions taken on behalf of children during this critical period affect not only how a child develops but also how a country progresses' (UNICEF 2006: 14).

Our own policy-makers have apparently taken this message to heart, despite the competition for investment from other government projects and priorities which have squeezed the necessary funding.

Effective pedagogy, appropriate practice

Since the 1980s, research into the ways in which early educational experiences shape children's careers as learners has steadily enhanced the evidence base for our understanding of good early years practice. Early investigations into the outcomes of pre-school (including from Schweinhart and colleagues, 1993, in the USA, and from Sylva and her colleagues, 1980, in the UK) prepared the ground for the spate of post-1997 studies which inform current policy. The Effective Provision of Pre-school Education (EPPE) project (Sylva et al. 2004) and the related *Researching Effective Pedagogy in the Early Years* (REPEY) project (Siraj-Blatchford et al. 2002) have shown an enormous range of causal factors which predict both short-term and long-term gains for children. These include:

- the integration of education and care in services for children under-5;
- well-qualified staff who understand the nature of children's development as well as having good subject knowledge and skills of their own;
- a combination of freely chosen child-initiated activities, and well-planned adult-initiated activities, including explicit instruction;
- opportunities for extended and thoughtful conversations – 'sustained shared thinking' – which allow children to co-construct meanings and understandings with adults and peers;
- environments which allow children to access resources to solve the problems which arise in their activities, and adult support in mastering new tools for learning;
- communities of learners who support the development of positive dispositions towards learning – including persistence and resilience.

Complementary findings from the Study of Pedagogical Effectiveness in Early Learning (SPEEL) project (Moyles et al. 2002) have offered additional examples of ways in which practitioners can develop children's enthusiasm for learning, and support them through the setbacks that occur as they acquire the knowledge and skills they need to move on to each stage. As a result, learning is now seen to be very much the outcome of relationships: between children and their friends and classmates, between children and the adults who care for them in every setting, and between the professional educators and the families and communities who have provided children's earliest experiences, long before they enter the classroom. For this reason, the KEEP (Key Elements of Effective Practice) framework is an important guide to practice. Its six principles emphasize the dependence of children's development and learning on the knowledge, skills and relationships of all the adults who teach and care for them, and its basis in research is clearly spelled out (DfES 2005b: 10).

Emotions, dispositions and early transitions

Growing awareness of the role of emotions in our lives and specifically in our learning (Goleman 1994) has filtered into our provision in many ways, and informs the underlying conception of the *Early Years Foundation Stage*: at last, the link between feelings of belonging, confidence and well-being, and the acquisition of knowledge, skills and dispositions for life-long learning, has been recognized and written into policy for young children. Goleman's significant contribution was to demonstrate, beyond doubt, the physical as well as the psychological impact of feelings of anxiety and unhappiness, or elation and euphoria, on our ability to function in everyday life. In tune with this new awareness, the *Early Years Foundation Stage*, like the earlier *Curriculum Guidance*, places personal, social and emotional development at the head of all areas of learning, but places a more explicit emphasis on emotional well-being than earlier documents. Practitioners are now expected to focus on children's emotional health more directly, enabling even the youngest children to understand and manage their feelings, to give names to their emotions, and to recognize the way that these impact on others in the setting (DfES 2006: 37–41). This emphasis on emotional well-being extends to work with families: in the *Every Child Matters* framework, practitioners need to understand the impact of parents' mental health problems on the functioning of families and on children's development, and to know who to consult if there are concerns about the child's home experience.

The EYFS is equally clear in its focus on 'dispositions and attitudes', another key theme in recent early years' research (Carr and Claxton 2002; Claxton and Carr 2004). Carr's important work in analysing the types of environment which foster (rather than extinguish) the disposition to learn, and make a child 'ready, willing and able' to tackle new experiences, is reflected in the EYFS as well as in the New Zealand Te Whaariki curriculum (Carr and May 2000). The document indicates the ways that practitioners can provide opportunities for children to develop and strengthen the disposition to become involved, persist with failure, collaborate with others, and become aware of their own learning (DfES 2006: 29–30).

Finally, the impact on children of the transitions they make in early childhood has become a major focus for national and international research (Fthenakis 1998; Margetts 2002; Dockett and Perry 2004a, 2005). The increase in children's participation in group care facilities, for under-3s as well as for Foundation Stage children, has prompted a widespread questioning of the number of horizontal, as well as vertical, transitions young children are making in the twenty-first century. The traditional model of a child 'at home in the family' until 5, and 'starting school' after their fifth birthday, is increasingly rare and children starting school may have experienced many other forms of group care in their first five years. As many practitioners are aware, the 'big' transition may now be the move from a Foundation Stage setting into Year 1, and so the recent focus is on the continuity and progression that can be offered to children at this point (Wood and Bennett 2001). Children's own voices are now much more frequently heard on this subject (Dunlop 2001; Dockett and Perry 2004a, b).

Reflection points

4   How much has evidence from recent research changed our views of children and their learning?
5   Is this new evidence really 'challenging' – or does it confirm and validate traditional early years' practice?

The agenda for change

The challenges of working towards all the outcomes of the *Every Child Matters* framework are enormous, and some of them will only become apparent as practitioners begin to work together to evaluate their own efforts. The opportunities, however, are very clear: the chance to be part of a coherent service which puts children's lives – rather than simply the academic curriculum – at the centre, and which views all aspects of these lives as inter-related. Early years practitioners have always known that children's development and learning were shaped by relationships within families, and relationships between parents and teachers; by their family's housing and income, and by the degree of social inclusion or exclusion they experience; and by the physical and mental health of the child and all those involved in his or her care. Now they have the opportunity, as well as the responsibility, to identify the entire spectrum of factors which can affect a child, and to work with colleagues in health, welfare and social care services to alleviate them where necessary.

What will this involve?

A timetable for change was included in The Children Act, requiring local authorities to develop partnerships, 'encourage integrated working', adopt the common assessment framework for children, and share information about children using their services, from 2005; by 2008 they are required to set up children's trusts and appoint a Director of Children's Services. In schools and settings, a number of new perspectives, and new roles, will be needed:

- a whole-school awareness of the outcomes for which the staff is responsible, and a whole-school policy and structure for meeting those outcomes;
- collaboration with a wide range of professionals, including listening respectfully and working constructively with people from different professional backgrounds, experiences and perspectives;
- new kinds of partnerships with families, to include offering information, advice and advocacy;
- new kinds of early years' leadership: leading from inside the early childhood education setting, and advocating for services outside the setting.

The ultimate aim of this agenda, in Pugh's words, is 'to improve outcomes for all children and narrow the gap between those who do well and those who do not, through reconfiguring services around children and families' (2005: 9). The Green Paper made it clear that providing good services for *all* children was the best way to safeguard the lives, and well-being, of those few children who may otherwise slip through the net of provision. Isn't this what early years educators have always tried to do?

The children's rights agenda

One other important context exists for the new agenda for children and families: it is our growing awareness of the implications for young children of the United Nations Convention on the Rights of the Child (UN 1989). Most of the follow-up research and monitoring for the Convention has focused on older children or those in adverse circumstances, but a recent addition to the Convention (General Comment 7: Implementing child rights in early childhood) has spelled out what it means to view children as rights-holders from birth, and to recognize that 'early childhood is a critical period for the realization of these rights' (UN 2006: 1).

Many of the points made in this 20-page 'comment' bear a close resemblance to the stance taken in the ECM framework. The document stresses the 'diversities in young children's circumstances, in the quality of their experiences and in the influences shaping their development' and 'the vulnerability of young children to poverty, discrimination, family breakdown and multiple other adversities' (2005: 2). It emphasizes that children are 'active members of families, communities and societies, with their own concerns, interests and points of view' and that they need 'time and space for social play, exploration and learning' (2005: 3). Above all, it encompasses some of the research findings discussed in this chapter, which lead us to view children as individuals whose rapid brain development, strong emotional attachments, and significant relationships with peers, should guide us in our efforts to safeguard their rights and identities through the provision we offer. Few children in the affluent Western world need us to safeguard their primary right to 'life, survival and development', but many of the other rights discussed in this paper may prompt us to review our practices as we implement the current children's agenda.

Conclusion

The landscape is changing, and change is hard for most of us, but if the changes help to safeguard the rights of the youngest children, we will do well to overcome the challenges and seek out the opportunities.

Points for discussion

- How can we ensure that the requirement to work with other key professionals is met in our own schools and settings?
- How different would our services look if we began our planning from a children's rights' perspective?
- Is it possible to reconcile the interests of parents (who need extended-day and year-round childcare) with the rights of young children to leisure, relaxation and share in family life?

References and further reading

Bruer, J. (1999) Neural connections: some you use, some you lose, *Phi Delta Kappan*, 81(4): 264–77.

Carr, M. and Claxton, G. (2002) Tracking the development of learning dispositions, *Assessment in Education*, 9: 9–37.

Carr, M. and May, H. (2000) Te Whaariki, in H. Penn (ed.) *Early Childhood Services*. Buckingham: Open University Press.

Children's Workforce Development Council (CWDC) (2006) *Early Years Professional Prospectus*. Leeds: CWDC.

Claxton, G. and Carr, M. (2004) A framework for teaching learning: the dynamics of dispositions, *Early Years*, 24(1): 87–97.

DfEE (Department for Education and Employment) (1997) *Standards for Early Excellence Centres*. London: HMSO.

DfES (Department for Education and Skills) (2003) *Every Child Matters* (Green Paper). London: HMSO.

DfES (2005a) *Common Core of Skills and Knowledge for the Children's Workforce*. Nottingham: DfES Publications.

DfES (2005b) *Key Elements of Effective Practice*. London: HMSO.

DfES (2006) *The Early Years Foundation Stage: Consultation on a Single Quality Framework for Services to Children from Birth to Five*. Nottingham: DfES Publications. Available online at: www.teachernet.gov.uk/publications (accessed 12 December 2006).

Dockett, S. and Perry, B. (2004a) You need to know how to play safe: children's experiences of starting school, *Contemporary Issues in Early Childhood*, 6(1): 4–18.

Dockett, S. and Perry, B. (2004b) Starting school: perspectives of Australian children, *Journal of Early Childhood Research*, 2(2): 171–89.

Dockett, S. and Perry, B. (2005) Starting school in Australia is 'a bit safer, a lot easier ...', *Early Years*, 25(3): 271–81.

Dunlop, A-W. (2001) Children's Thinking about Transitions to School, paper presented at EECERA annual conference, Alkmaar.

Fthenakis, W. (1998) Family transitions and quality in early childhood education, *European Early Childhood Education Research Journal*, 6(1): 5–18.

Goleman, D. (1994) *Emotional Intelligence: Why It Can Matter More than IQ*. New York: Bantam Books.

Her Majesty's Government (2004) *The Children Act 2004*. London: HMSO.

Her Majesty's Treasury/DfES/Department for Work and Pensions/Department of Trade and Industry (2004) *Choice for Parents, the Best Start for Children: A Ten-Year Strategy for Childcare*. London: HMSO.

Makins, V. (1997) *Not Just a Nursery*. London: National Children's Bureau.

Margetts, K. (2002) Transition to school – complexity and diversity, *European Early Childhood Education Research Journal*, 10(2): 103–14.

Melhuish, E. and Core Team (2005) *National Evaluation of Sure Start*. London: Institute for the Study of Children, Families and Social Issues, Birkbeck, University of London (and see www.ness.bbk.ac.uk) (accessed 30 November 2006).

Moyles, J., Adams, S. and Musgrove, A. (2002) *SPEEL: Study of Pedagogical Effectiveness in Early Learning*. London: DfES.

Pugh, G. (2005) The policy agenda for early childhood services, in G. Pugh and B. Duffy (eds) *Contemporary Issues in the Early Years*. London: Sage.

Pugh, G., De'Ath, E. and Smith, G. (1994) *Confident Parents, Confident Children: Policy and Practice in Parent Education and Support*. London: National Children's Bureau.

QCA DfES (2000) *Curriculum Guidance for the Foundation Stage*. London: QCA.

Schweinhart, L.J., Barnes, H.V. and Weikart, D.P. (1993) *Significant Benefits: The High/Scope Perry Preschool Study through Age 2–7*. Ypsilanti, MI: High/Scope Education Research Foundation.

Shonkoff, J. and Phillips, D. (eds) (2000) *From Neurons to Neighbourhoods: The Science of Early Childhood Development*. Washington: Board on Children, Youth and Families; Committee on Integrating the Science of Early Childhood Development.

Siraj-Blatchford, I., Muttock, S., Sylva, K., Gilden, R. and Bell, D. (2002) *Researching Effective Pedagogy in the Early Years*. London: Institute of Education/DfES.

Sure Start Unit (2002) *Birth-to-Three Matters: A Framework to Support Children in their Earliest Years*. London: DfES.

Sure Start Unit (2003) *Sure Start: Making Life Better for Children, Parents and Communities by Bringing Together Early Education, Childcare, Health and Family Support*. London: DfES Publications.

Sylva, K. (1994) The impact of early learning on children's later development, in C. Ball (ed.) *Start Right: The Importance of Early Learning*. London: Royal Society of Arts.

Sylva, K., Melhuish, E.C., Sammons, P., Siraj-Blatchford, I. and Taggart, B. (2004) *The Effective Provision of Pre-School Education (EPPE) Project: Technical Paper 12 – The Final Report: Effective Pre-School Education*. London: DfES/Institute of Education, University of London.

Sylva, K., Painter, M. and Roy, C. (1980) *Childwatching in Playgroup and Nursery School*. Oxford: Blackwell.

UNCRC (2006) *General Comment No. 7 (2005) Implementing Child Rights in Early Childhood*, www.uncrc (accessed 30 November 2006).

UNICEF (2006) *State of the World's Children: Excluded and Invisible*. New York: Oxford University Press.

Wood, E. and Bennett, N. (2001) Early childhood teachers' theories of progression and continuity, *International Journal of Early Years Education*, 9(3): 229–43.

SECTION ONE
A UNIQUE CHILD

Introduction to Section One

Janet Moyles

Every child is a competent learner from birth who can be resilient, capable, confident and self-assured.

(EYFS Principle 1)

Anyone who has ever really known children will acknowledge and celebrate the fact that each child is unique: no two are ever the same, even from the same family and even twins. To have the uniqueness of each child 'validated', so to speak, through the *Early Years Foundation Stage* and *Every Child Matters* is an important step forward, particularly for policy-makers. It implicitly recognizes the basic issue of 'starting from the child' (Fisher 2002) and the need for each practitioner thoroughly to understand and be in empathy with the very being of each child in her/his setting. It has immense implications both for practitioner training and for the establishment of close relationships with parents and carers: to truly acknowledge each child as unique, one needs a deep and meaningful understanding of children's overall and universal development and of the context of the individual child's life experiences.

Children appear to be growing up much more quickly these days: it seems as if this is encouraged by parents, government and society on the whole, and it's easy to think they are more knowledgeable than they are. But at age 5 years, they have only been in independent existence for 60 months! They might have been bought 'designer' clothes from babyhood and have sophisticated equipment, such as computers, DVD players, Gameboys and cameras from a very early age but, as Elkind (2001: 20) suggests, 'When young children are expected to dress, act and think as adults, they are really being asked to play act, because all of the trappings of adulthood do not in any way make them adults.' He goes on to say: 'To treat children differently from adults is not to discriminate against them but rather to recognize their special state ... to treat children as adults is really not democratic or egalitarian' (2001: 21). Sue Palmer emphasizes this further when she says, 'The quick-fire world of modern technology is in direct contrast to the slow process of dealing with biological development' (2006: 145–6). She also stresses that children's responses to everyday events are in 'slow-time', thus making a nonsense of exhortations by policy-makers to ensure children's literacy activities, for example, move at a speedy 'pace' or come 'first, fast and fore-most'. We must acknowledge that biological development is slower and more thorough than modern life.

Foremost in working with each unique child has to be ensuring they play and work in contexts which (1) make sense to them and (2) allow for natural development and, nowadays, also for our knowledge of the new brain the-ories to be put into practice (see Sunderland 2006). Whatever the external trappings of childhood, biological development and the needs of healthy brain development do not change: all children with normal development learn to walk, run, climb, skip, talk, generally in the same kind of sequence and we now know that very young brains need certain types of stimulation to grow and develop appropriate connections to ensure emotional, social and cognitive well-being. Yet each child does it at his/her own pace, stage and level, influenced by both 'nature' (the rich genomes on which they draw) and on environment (the family, settings and community of which they are an integral part) (see e.g. Greenfield 2002; Trevarthen 2003). To be a skilful communicator and a competent learner in the first five years of life requires the child to have close, warm and loving relationships with adults who model these very traits. This is particularly important in the developmental period before children have verbal language. Rod Parker-Rees shows this clearly in Chapter 2 when writing about 'primary communication' by which he means non-verbal interactions between under-3s and significant adults.

Research has suggested that many children do not necessarily have these vital experiences within the family (Compass 2006) in this work-oriented, busy twenty-first-century world, and it is beholden on practitioners in set-tings to try to redress this – a difficult but rewarding task. Empathize with the 2-year-old who arrived in a pre-school setting unable to join in with rhymes and songs and afraid to get too close to the adults in case they suddenly 'disappeared'. The same child within a very few weeks knew several nursery rhymes, was able to recite them enthusiastically and with feeling sitting close up to her key worker and eventually 'performed' songs and rhymes to the whole group (while holding the hand of a new, special friend!).

Differences in this child's early family experiences meant particular challenges and responsibilities for the practitioners handling her unique needs and a review of the kinds of pedagogical practices appropriate in dif-ferent situations. We cannot now practise as if there is one style of pedagogy which suits every child. In our progressively more diverse society, practi-tioners have increasingly to deal inclusively with children from a range of cultural and ethnic backgrounds as well as those unique individuals for whom learning or socialization, for example, present specific challenges: this means practitioners being extremely flexible in their pedagogic approaches. Theo-dora Papatheodorou outlines some of these challenges in Chapter 3.

A child's unique identity is bound up with a sense of who they are and of belonging and this includes gender, race and culture as emphasized by Naima Browne in Chapter 4. Naima discusses the issue of 'multiple gender identities' and encourages practitioners to think more broadly about the way they handle children of both sexes in the setting/classroom in inclusive and anti-discriminatory ways. For some time now it has been recognized that boys, for example, require a different kind of pedagogical approach from girls (Browne 2004), their learning being much more physically oriented and some brain-functioning being slower to develop than that of girls at quite an early age (see Stein, quoted in Scott 2002; Sunderland 2006).

Children's identities, culture and child-rearing practices all have a significant impact on different aspects of young children's learning and development, including health and physical and emotional well-being, another aspect of the unique child. It must be of concern to us as practitioners that emotional problems have apparently increased rapidly even in children as young as four years and behavioural problems, too, have escalated not only in the UK but internationally. The UK Statistics Office in 2004, for example, reported that 10% of children had some form of emotional, hyperactivity or behavioural disorder. The question has to be raised, however, as to whether our concepts of acceptable behaviour have changed or whether society itself is creating some of these problems by the very changes in the social/cultural context of child-rearing and concepts of childhood (Timimi 2006).

Enabling children to develop normally requires great effort, time and commitment on the part of all the adults with whom they come into contact. Keeping safe (not covered explicitly in this short book but well documented elsewhere, e.g. Lindon 2003), is a broad concept obviously closely associated with children's health and physical and emotional well-being. It is not simply, however, a matter of protecting children: allowing children to take risks is a known essential in early education and care. Through risk-taking children learn about their own physical and mental parameters (as well as those of others); make choices and judgements and cope with unknown situations. Protection merely makes them dependent on the protector and gives a feeling of 'helplessness' – unacceptable for the competent, resilient, capable, confident, self-assured and unique learners who are the focus of this section.

References

Browne, N. (2004) *Gender Equity in the Early Years*. Maidenhead: Open University Press.

COMPASS (2006) *The Good Society* edited by Jonathan Rutherford and Hetan Shah. London: COMPASS, in association with Lawrence and Wishart.

Elkind, D. (2001) *The Hurried Child: Growing Up Too Fast Too Soon*, 3rd edn. Cambridge, MA: Da Capo Press.

Fisher, J. (2002) *Starting from the Child: Teaching and Learning from 3–8*. Maidenhead: Open University Press.

Greenfield, S. (2002) *The Private Life of the Brain*. London: Penguin Press.

Lindon, J. (2003) *Too Safe for Their Own Good?* London: National Children's Bureau.

Palmer, S. (2006) *Toxic Childhood*. London: Orion.

Scott, W. (2002) Making meaningful connections in early learning, in J. Fisher (ed.) *The Foundations of Learning*. Buckingham: Open University Press.

Sunderland, M. (2006) *The Science of Parenting*. London: Dorling Kindersley.

Timimi, S. (2006) Paper presented at the conference Childhood, Well-being and a Therapeutic Ethos, Roehampton, 14 December.

Trevarthen, C. (2003) Infancy, mind, in R. Gregory (ed.) *Oxford Companion to the Mind*. Oxford: Oxford University Press.

2   Primary communication
What can adults learn from babies?

Rod Parker-Rees

Abstract

Babies' first experience of communication is in the context of private, intimate relationships with familiar others. This primary communication provides an important affective foundation for social interaction but it is frequently undervalued as we hurry children into more public ways of communicating. This chapter will argue that we have much to learn from the earliest forms of communication between babies and their carers, not just about how to engage with very young children but also about differences between 'communicating with' and 'talking to' in all kinds of relationships between professionals, children and parents. Long after we have learned to talk, read and write, we still depend on primary communication to develop and maintain relationships by 'reading between the lines'. A better understanding of primary communication may help early years professionals to feel confident about interpreting their practices and policies, adapting these to meet the particular needs of individual children and caregivers.

Introduction: why primary communication?

'Effective communication and engagement with children, young people, their families and carers' is the first of the areas of expertise identified in the *Common Core of Skills and Knowledge for the Children's Workforce* (DfES 2005: 6), and the Draft Standards for *Early Years Professional Status* (CWDC 2006) include sections on 'Relationships with children' and 'Communicating and working in partnership with families and carers'. Early years practitioners are frequently reminded of their responsibility to communicate sensitively and responsively with children, parents and colleagues and official documents and policies emphasize the need to use all available means of communication, but there is still a tendency to present the earliest forms of communication as necessary but temporary alternatives to spoken language. In the *Early Years Foundation Stage* consultation document (DfES 2006), 'Making relationships' is one of the subheadings in the first Area of Learning, 'Personal, Social and Emotional Development', but the area of learning entitled 'Communication, Language and Literacy' represents communication almost exclusively in terms of the development of language.

When communication is understood to be more or less synonymous with talk, it is easy to slip into an unintentionally negative view of babies, seeing them in terms of what they cannot yet do. Infants (from the Latin *in fans* meaning 'lacking speech') are 'limited' to 'pre-verbal', 'pre-symbolic' or 'unspoken' forms of communication and in our haste to remedy these childish deficiencies we can undervalue this stage of 'pre' existence. It is easy to assume that skills and attributes which are acquired early in life, easily and by almost everyone, are less important and less valuable than those acquired later, which require more effort and which are achieved only by a few people.

I prefer, therefore, to use the term 'primary communication' to describe the intimate, unmediated interactions which enable babies to forge relationships with familiar others well before they begin to adopt the public, formal structures of spoken languages. Primary communication is primary in the same sense that primary inter-subjectivity (Trevarthen 1979) and primary socialization (Berger and Luckmann 1966) are primary; not just because they come first but also because they provide essential foundations for what will come later.

In England and Wales we are now very familiar with the concept of a foundation stage of education; a stage which is even more primary than primary education (QCA/DfEE 2000; Fisher 2002). The introduction of the rather awkwardly named Early Years Foundation Stage (EYFS) (DfES 2006) has taken the foundations even deeper, redressing the indefensible implication that the laying of foundations did not begin until children reached the age of 3. Unfortunately the EYFS still looks like a curriculum in the original meaning of the word – a running-track which will contain and channel children as they race towards achieving prescribed desirable learning outcomes while their parents are pressed into proper, paid work (see also Chapter 14).

We live in a society in which our ideas, our work and the extent of our networks are valued more than our feelings, our leisure time and the depth of our relationships, even though we know that it is the quality of relationships, more than anything else, which determines how happy we are (Martin 2005; Smith 2005). By focusing attention on primary communication, I hope to show how rich forms of communication, which both require and develop a relationship between particular individuals, still have a primary function throughout our adult lives. Languages allow us to manage interactions with a wide range of people who do not know us and whom we do not know, because languages depend on relationships between symbols rather than between people. A conversation with someone who knows us and who is interested in us feels very different from a more formal exchange with someone for whom we are just one interchangeable instance of a generic type, such as 'customer', 'employee' or 'fussy parent'. Without primary communication, the exchange of linguistic symbols may contribute very little to our experience of social connectedness, our well-being and our happiness.

Reflection point

1   Think of different kinds of interactions you have experienced recently (with children, parents, colleagues) – what was the balance of primary communication (relationship maintenance) and symbol trading in each? What should the balance be?

The origins of primary communication

One of the most essential, and often most difficult, adjustments that adults must make when studying primary communication is to get away from the assumption that communication is all about the intentional exchange of snippets of information. The details of what we are talking about are often much less important than the simple fact that we are paying attention to each other. We can think of primary communication as everything other than language we use to develop and maintain relationships with other people. This includes the quality of our own movements, touch, gestures, facial expressions and eye contact, the 'musical' qualities of our speech (which can provide reliable information about our emotional state) and, most importantly, the extent to which our own behaviour is contingent on, responsive to and attuned with the behaviour of our communication partners.

The origins of primary communication can be understood both in terms of their evolution over thousands of generations and in terms of their unfolding in the life of an individual. The evolution of primary communication may be understood by reference to other species' use of touch (licking, nuzzling, grooming) to establish a close bond between mother and baby (Schanberg and Field 1987; Caulfield 2000) and to maintain relationships between adults. Corballis (2002) has argued that spoken language is more likely to have evolved from a gestural form of communication than from 'broadcast' vocalizations like the alarm, mating and territorial calls found in other species which share with language the facility to communicate widely without relying on particular relationships. Donald (2001) also concluded that the 'missing link' between other apes and modern humans was a period in which our ancestors developed a mimetic form of communication based on gesture, purposeful representation of actions and highly responsive imitative exchanges. The social, integrating power of this sort of 'primal' primary communication is clearly evidenced in the success of the 'intensive interaction' approach developed by Nind and Hewett (2005) and Tortora's (2005) 'dancing dialogue', both of which are ways of establishing relationships with people who cannot be reached through language alone.

Highly attuned, responsive action seems to be central to primary communication and vocal sounds provide a particularly flexible and expressive medium for this sort of interaction. Mithen (2005) has suggested that a form of audible gestures or wordless 'singing' allowed early humans to 'keep in touch' with larger social groups than could be maintained by the physical grooming and nit-picking which regulate other primate groups. Mithen describes this form of communication as 'Hmmmmm' (holistic, multi-modal, manipulative, musical and mimetic) and suggests that it offered a 'multi-media' package of expression, gesture, tone and vocalization similar to the musical qualities of infant-directed speech which still help mothers and infants to share and communicate their 'emotion states' (Mithen 2005: 197).

We must look for the origins of primary communication not only in the history of spoken language but also in the much longer history of our abilities to manage and maintain increasingly complex webs of relationships. We must, therefore, be cautious when we talk about the ontogeny of primary communication, its development in individuals. Narrowing our focus to changes 'within' a child can distract us from the importance of the dynamic, evolving relationships between children and their caregivers.

The first such relationship will always be between mother and baby. However much we may want to include fathers and other caregivers, we cannot escape the fact that babies begin their development inside their mother's womb. Here the growing foetus is literally immersed in the life of its mother, surrounded by her voice, her patterns of sleep and activity, and a cocktail of hormones, nutrients and toxins which pass through the umbilical cord. The foetus knows no other world than this and studies of newborn babies' sensory responses (Eliot 1999; Kellman and Arterberry 2000; Fogel 2001) show that experiences in the womb provide foundations for the baby's ability to differentiate between familiar and novel sensations from the moment of birth.

In 'minority world' societies, birth often marks a rather abrupt separation of baby from mother as the newborn is taken away to be wrapped in unfamiliar materials and put in a cot or crib to sleep. Thankfully the days of dangling the newborn by its ankles and smacking it on the bottom to promote crying are past but the transition from womb to wide world is still less gentle and gradual than it might be. In many other cultures babies may spend most of their first months held close against their mother's body, surrounded by sounds, smells and tastes which are already familiar. Aspects of this practice are being rediscovered by 'high-tec' Special Care Infant and Baby Units where the health benefits of skin to skin, 'kangaroo care' for premature babies (and their mothers) have been widely confirmed (Anderson 1999; Feldman et al. 2002). Like kangaroos, human newborn babies are still highly dependent on their parents and the relationships developed by touch, massage, feeding, conversations, singing, rocking and jiggling, provide a secure, familiar base which allows mother and baby to continue to develop the relationship which began in the womb (Standley, in Mithen 2005).

In some societies, babies have two births; a physical birth, when they emerge from their mother's womb and a 'psychological' birth, some six weeks later, when they emerge from the dream-like condition of the newborn to engage actively in interactions with others (Rochat 2001). This second birth is associated with the baby's first intentional smile and with a change in eye contact which is much more difficult to describe but which significantly alters the quality of the relationships between the baby and other people. This transition marks the beginning of primary inter-subjectivity, the baby's ability to represent its 'subjectivity' to others (Trevarthen 1979). A baby's smile offers an intense emotional reward for appropriate, attentive care and is therefore a powerful tool for training familiar communication partners to indulge in sustained periods of 'gooey' interaction, the only purpose of which is to shape and tune an affective relationship.

Even in this purest form of primary communication, much is being learned. The mother is tuning in to her baby's likes, dislikes, moods and tempo and the baby is getting to know its mother in the same way but with the added bonus that the mother stands *in loco communis* (Cheyne and Tarulli 1999), acting as an agent of her culture. Because she is steeped in a particular set of social rules and patterns of behaviour, she cannot avoid filtering her baby's actions and vocalizations when she imitates them in her responses, turning them into something more 'at home' in her culture's ways of communicating (Parker-Rees 2007). To communicate is to 'make common', to negotiate a shared, common understanding and this involves a much more subtle process than just a simple handover of knowledge from mother to child. What the mother introduces, the baby transmutes, just as the mother interprets what the baby offers, so it is the relationship between mother and baby that develops. While it can be argued that the baby is 'acquiring communication skills', this is misleading because the baby's engagement in interactions is highly context-sensitive and dependent on the familiarity of relationships with particular partners.

Gerhardt (2004: 196) has described the level of contingency in mothers' interactions with their babies (the extent to which they are influenced by, and responsive to, what their babies do) as 'the X factor, the mystery tonic that enables babies to thrive as soon as they get it' but she also points out that 'each baby needs a tailor made response, not an off-the-shelf kind, however benign' (2004: 197). Bigelow (1997) has shown that babies aged 4–5 months old discriminate between familiar and unfamiliar partners on the basis of a familiar level of contingency; strangers who are more responsive than the baby's mother appear to be just as disturbing as those who are less contingent. It is not a simple matter of 'more is better' – indeed, infants whose mothers are almost obsessively responsive to their every move are more likely to develop anxious-avoidant attachment patterns (Jaffe et al. 2001). What seems to be best for everyone is an attentive but relaxed two-way relationship, rather than one which is all about the baby.

Reflection point

2   It can be very difficult to observe this form of intimate communication, partly because adults may be self-conscious when they are being watched and partly because it is easy to miss subtle cues which may be important to participants. How can early years practitioners gain experience of primary communication between parents and babies?

Familiarity – a foundation for joint attention and playfulness

The last months of pregnancy and the first weeks after birth provide oppor-tunities for mother and child to get to know each other's bodies and phy-siological rhythms but the delightful intimacy of primary inter-subjectivity raises the dynamic development of the relationship to a new level. Frequently repeated bouts of primary communication contribute to the extension of familiarity as each partner comes to know the patterns in the other's actions and responses, learning to read affective significance into subtle variations on familiar themes:

> Repeating action patterns with minor variations are ideally suited to create expectancies, avoid habituation, maintain the infant's atten-tion, and create subtle nuances for the infant's affective experience ... The co-creation by mother and infant of relatively stable expec-tancies is a critical accomplishment of early social relatedness, cog-nition and acculturation.
>
> (Jaffe et al. 2001: 14)

Kaye (1982: 35) argued that 'a mother and child do not begin to be a social system until the infant, too, has expectations of how the mother will behave'. These expectations are not innate: 'like the expectations spiders have about the behaviour of flies', they must be 'based on experience together'. The 'relatively stable expectancies' which emerge from repeated interactions with a familiar partner provide the ideal conditions for further learning because they allow both baby and parent to focus their attention on just those aspects of a particular situation which are unexpected and therefore potentially interesting. Familiarity with each other's bodies provides the foundation for learning about emotional states which gives the baby a secure base for first-hand exploration of the world of physical objects and then for entering into 'triadic relations' (Hobson 2002) when baby and communication partner jointly pay attention to a common focus. Joint attention involves much more than merely aiming one's eyes in the same direction as someone else. What makes it so powerful as a tool for learning is that it allows us to pay attention to another person's response, yielding information about the situation but also about the person and about cultural values. Trevarthen and Hubley (1978) identify this ability to pay attention to another person's attention as the beginning of secondary inter-subjectivity. Infants now show an active interest in familiar people not just as emotional partners but as windows onto a whole world of knowledge about the cultural significance of objects and events. What makes mum smile and relax? What makes her anxious or angry? What surprises her?

It is easy to underestimate the levels of familiarity which are required to enable a child to engage in joint attention with an adult. 'Joint attention always occurs within affectively charged interpersonal relationships' (Carpendale and Lewis 2006: 105) because a 9-month-old infant needs to be able to draw on a wealth of shared experience to be able to read the cues which reveal not only what another person is interested in but also the nature of their interest. The fact that infants can engage in joint involvement episodes with their mothers does not mean that they have 'acquired' a set of skills which can be deployed in any interaction. Sroufe and Wunsch (1972) point out, for example, that actions which are most likely to make a child laugh when they are performed by a parent are also most likely to make the child cry when they are performed by a stranger. In primary communication, the meaning of an event will always depend on the nature of the relationships between the people involved.

When we communicate with strangers, we have to increase our level of contingent responsiveness, paying careful attention to how our new partner responds to our actions and trying to respond appropriately ourselves. Jaffe et al. (2001: 115) describe this 'interactive vigilance' as a way of reducing the risk of embarrassing or awkward misunderstandings and show that even 4-month-old infants demonstrate higher levels of 'coordinated interpersonal timing' when they interact with a stranger in the laboratory than when they are at home with their mother. For infants, as for all of us, the game cannot be separated from the relationship between the players, and it will only be really playful if they know each other well enough to relax their interactive vigilance.

Reflection point

3   It is relatively easy to capture the 'language' of interactions, the public and generalizable 'rules of the game' but it is much more difficult to identify the primary communication involved in negotiating the subtle details of how the game will be played with a particular partner. Try to observe different adults playing the same 'game' with different children. Can you find ways to represent what your observations show about how adults use their familiarity with children to adapt the way they play?

Primary communication beyond the family

The scale of the challenge faced by settings offering 'out of family' care for children aged under 2 years has been widely acknowledged (Goldschmied and Jackson 2004; Biddulph 2005; Barnes et al. 2006; Gerhardt 2004). However dedicated practitioners are, and even when infants have regular contact with the same key worker, there will always be a 'familiarity gap' in their relationship, making primary communication more of a challenge. Where the adults are inexperienced, overstretched and undervalued, this gap can widen to the point where children and adults seldom experience relaxed, playful interactions with a familiar partner (Rolfe et al. 2002). If adults working with young children do not recognize how much primary communication contributes to children's growing ability to make sense of other people's behaviour, this gap may feel normal; an inevitable consequence of children's inability to express themselves clearly in spoken language. Early years professionals, who are responsible for developing the quality of practice in their settings, may need to begin by raising awareness of the importance of primary communication, and by encouraging practices which support the development of close familiar relationships. It may be impossible for practitioners to offer the level of familiarity which children have been busy co-constructing with their primary caregivers from before they were born, but group settings can offer opportunities for children to practise developing new, more symmetrical kinds of familiar relationships with other children. Sensitive practitioners can nurture supportive communities by offering and maintaining a social space in which children can practise and develop their skills in primary communication as they watch each other's interactions, show interest in each other's actions and feelings, and gradually get to know each other.

Professional expertise – the generalization of familiarity

Although no amount of experience will enable early years practitioners to close the familiarity gap completely, the process of developing relationships with many different babies, infants and children can contribute to the refinement of a personal model, theory or set of expectations about how different kinds of children are likely to respond in the kinds of situations they are likely to encounter. Much as a growing knowledge of the traits and quirks of familiar caregivers allows an infant to detect any discrepancies from expected patterns, so a growing knowledge of different children can help practitioners to focus their attention on what is particularly interesting about each child. Of course, professionals don't have to reinvent this familiarity for themselves; they can access models developed and published by others but, as Engel (2005) has observed, they must appreciate the difference between what children do in the context of laboratory studies and what they are capable of in the context of joyful play with familiar partners. A great deal of research into the capabilities of babies has tended to strip away the context of familiar relationships to study responses to black and white gratings, still images and isolated sounds, smells and tastes but critical practitioners can use this outline to help them to make sense of their own experiences with real children, colouring it in and constantly adjusting it to accommodate unexpected responses. Being a professional requires an active engagement between other people's ideas and practices and one's own, with a view to challenging and improving both. When practitioners do not continue to explore and question their personal theory, it can harden into a fixed set of stereotypes and prejudices. Instead of using their expertise to enable them to develop an individual relationship with each child, these practitioners may prefer to adjust children to fit their assumptions about what children should be like.

Child-menders or rule-benders?

If our 'theory' of communication is based primarily on spoken language, it is easy to focus on what 'pre-verbal' children cannot do and this attitude can spread into other aspects of our work. Carr (2001) has shown how a 'folk model' of assessment can lead us to compare children against a checklist of expected developmental milestones in order to identify deficits or delays which we then set about 'fixing' by providing remedial activities or resources. This 'child-mending' approach prioritizes the generalized abstraction of 'normality' over the complex, messy and unpredictable individuality of each child and allows adults to engage with children *en masse* by talking not to each child but to an idea of what every child ought to be. There may be some advantages for some children in this sort of introduction to a more public form of communication but adults who work with children who are just beginning to talk should be aware of how challenging it may be for these children to manage without the support of familiar relationships and primary communication. Much as delivery from the womb to the wide world can be treated as a gradual transition rather than an abrupt entry into a new stage of life, so a child's induction into the public world beyond the family can be eased by early years practitioners who aim to develop 'bespoke' relationships with each child and caregiver. Rather than aiming to 'repair' children who do not fit a prescribed norm, sensitive and confident practitioners can find ways to ease the expectations and rules for their setting so that these can accommodate the different needs of different children and families.

Reflection point

4   Think about specific situations in which you have found yourself acting as a 'child-mender' (thinking about children in terms of what they are lacking) and situations in which you have acted as a rule-bender (adjusting normal procedures to accommodate the interests or needs of individual children or families). How might these situations affect children's or caregivers' understanding of their relationship with you?

Conclusion: Primary communication and warm professionalism

When adults acknowledge the importance of primary communication, it is not only children who benefit. Active engagement with the unique individualities of particular children and families can help to develop adults' confidence to challenge, interpret and adjust policy decisions rather than simply apply them 'across the board'.

The *Common Core of Skills and Knowledge for the Children's Workforce* (DfES 2005) includes a section on 'Sharing Information' which stipulates that practitioners should: 'Be able to use clear language to communicate information *unambiguously* to others including children, young people, their families and carers' (p. 21, my emphasis). But on the next page practitioners are also required to understand that: 'inference or interpretation can result in a difference between what is said and what is understood' (DfES 2005: 22). We cannot assume that 'what is understood' will be the same for everyone who hears 'what is said'. If we really want to communicate information unambiguously, we must make time to develop and maintain the warm relationships which allow us to make sense of the subtle cues provided by primary communication.

Points for discussion

- Try to observe a colleague communicating/interacting with a very young child in your setting – you might even video it to share later. Who takes the lead? How much does body language have a part in the interaction? What emanates from the child and what from the adults? Could this situation be enhanced?
- What do you understand as the differences between 'what is said' and 'what is understood'? Can you think of a situation you've been in where discrepancies have occurred?
- How do you and your colleagues share time to communicate with each other about children? Is this time sufficient/well used/ frustrating? What can you do about it?

References and further reading

Anderson, G.C. (1999) Kangaroo care of the premature infant, in E. Goldstein and A. Sostek (eds) *Nurturing the Premature Infant: Developmental Intervention in the Neonatal Intensive Care Nursery*. Oxford: Oxford University Press.

Berger, P. and Luckmann, T. (1966) *The Social Construction of Reality: A Treatise on the Sociology of Knowledge*. London: Penguin.

Biddulph, S. (2005) *Raising Babies: Should Under-threes Go to Nursery?* London: Harper Thorsons.

Bigelow, A.E. (1997) Infants' sensitivity to familiar imperfect contingencies in social interaction, *Infant Behavior and Development*, 21, 149–62.

Carpendale, J.I.M. and Lewis, C. (2006) *How Children Develop Social Understanding*. Oxford: Blackwell.

Carr, M. (2001) *Assessment in Early Childhood Settings: Learning Stories*. London: Paul Chapman.

Caulfield, R. (2000) Beneficial effects of tactile stimulation on early development, *Early Childhood Education Journal*, 27(4): 255–7.

Cheyne, J.A. and Tarulli, D. (1999) Dialogue, difference, and the 'third voice' in the zone of proximal development, *Theory and Psychology*, 9(1): 5–28.

Corballis, M. (2002) *From Hand to Mouth: The Origins of Language*. Princeton, NJ: Princeton University Press.

CWDC (Children's Workforce Development Council) (2006) *Draft Standards for Early Years Professional Status*. London: CWDC.

DfES (Department for Education and Skills) (2005) *Common Core of Skills and Knowledge for the Children's Workforce*. Nottingham: DfES Publications.

DfES (2006) *The Early Years Foundation Stage: Consultation on a Single Quality Framework for Services to Children from Birth to Five.* Nottingham: DfES Publications.

Donald, M. (2001) *A Mind So Rare: The Evolution of Human Consciousness.* New York: Norton.

Eliot, L. (1999) *What's Going on In There: How the Brain and Mind Develop in the First Five Years of Life.* London: Allen Lane/Penguin.

Engel, S.L. (2005) *Real Kids: Creating Meaning in Everyday Life.* Cambridge, MA: Harvard University Press.

Feldman, R., Eidelman, A.I., Sirota, L. and Weller, A. (2002) Comparison of skin-to-skin (kangaroo) and traditional care: parenting outcomes and preterm infant development, *Pediatrics*, 110(1): 16–26.

Fisher, J. (2002) *The Foundations of Learning.* Buckingham: Open University Press.

Fogel, A. (2001) *Infancy: Infant, Family, and Society*, 4th edn. Belmont, CA: Wadsworth/Thompson Learning.

Gerhardt, S. (2004) *Why Love Matters: How Affection Shapes a Baby's Brain.* London: Routledge.

Goldschmied, E. and Jackson, S. (2004) *People Under Three: Young Children in Daycare*, 2nd edn. London: Routledge.

Hobson, P. (2002) *The Cradle of Thought: Exploring the Origins of Thinking.* London: Macmillan.

Jaffe, J., Beebe, B., Feldstein, S., Crown, C.L., and Jasnow, M.D. (2001) Rhythms of dialogue in infancy. *Monographs of the Society for Research in Child Development*, 66(2), (Serial No. 265). Washington, DC: Society for Research in Child Development.

Kaye, K. (1982) *The Mental and Social Life of Babies.* Chicago: University of Chicago Press.

Kellman, P. and Arterberry, M. (2000) *The Cradle of Knowledge: Development of Perception in Infancy.* Cambridge, MA: MIT Press.

Martin, P. (2005) *Making Happy People: The Nature of Happiness and its Origins in Childhood.* London: Fourth Estate.

Mithen, S. (2005) *The Singing Neanderthals: The Origins of Music, Language, Mind and Body.* London: Weidenfeld and Nicholson.

Nind, M. and Hewett, D. (2005) *Access to Communication: Developing the Basics of Communication with People with Severe Learning Difficulties through Intensive Interaction.* London: David Fulton.

Parker-Rees, R. (2007) Liking to be liked: imitation, familiarity and pedagogy in the first years of life, *Early Years*, 27(1): 3–17.

QCA/DfEE (Qualifications and Curriculum Authority) (2000) *Curriculum Guidance for the Foundation Stage.* London: QCA.

Rochat, P. (2001) *The Infant's World.* Cambridge, MA: Harvard University Press.

Rolfe, S., Nyland, B. and Morda, R. (2002) Quality in infant care: observations on joint attention, *Australian Research in Early Childhood Education*, 9(1): 86–96.

Schanberg, S.M. and Field, T.M. (1987) Sensory deprivation stress and supplemental stimulation in the rat pup and preterm human neonate, *Child Development*, 58: 1431–47.

Smith, M.K. (2005) Happiness and education – theory, practice and possibility, the encyclopaedia of informal education. Available at: www.infed.org/biblio/ happiness_and_education.htm. (accessed 27 June 2005).

Sroufe, L.A. and Wunsch, J.P. (1972) The development of laughter in the first year of life, *Child Development*, 43(4): 1326–44.

Tortora, S. (2005) *The Dancing Dialogue: Using the Communicative Power of Movement with Young Children*. Baltimore, MD: Brookes Publishers.

Trevarthen, C. (1979) Communication and cooperation in early infancy: a description of primary intersubjectivity, in M. Bullowa (ed.) *Before Speech: The Beginning of Interpersonal Communication*. Cambridge: Cambridge University Press.

Trevarthen, C. and Hubley, P. (1978) Secondary intersubjectivity: confidence, confiding and acts of meaning in the first year, in A. Lock (ed.) *Action, Gesture and Symbol: The Emergence of Language*. London: Academic Press.

3 Difference, culture and diversity

Challenges, responsibilities and opportunities

Theodora Papatheodorou

Abstract

Increasingly early years settings present greater than ever diversity in terms of young children's linguistic, cultural, religious, social, ethnic and racial backgrounds, reflecting the diversity of the wider society. It is now estimated that the average of ethnic minorities in the UK is 13.1 per cent (in CRE 2006). At the same time, as the number of 3- and 4-year-olds in early years settings has grown and national policies and statutory requirements about inclusion have been introduced, the number of young children identified as having some form of special educational need has also increased. Advances in medical practice have made it possible to identify some difficulties much earlier.

This chapter discusses a range of issues which need to be considered by practitioners if all young children are to be treated as the unique individuals they are. These include dealing with children from different cultural backgrounds, those with special educational needs, issues of difference and diversity, inclusion policies and appropriate pedagogy.

Introduction

Despite much awareness about cultural diversity, special needs and issues of inclusion, and against the backdrop of a number of national policies, such diversity in early years care and education is not without its challenges. Indeed, Siraj-Blatchford (2006) points out that ethnic, cultural, linguistic, class, gender, ability or disability diversity often form the basis of intentional and unintentional disadvantages to young children. Practitioners clearly need to consider their roles in supporting children with diverse needs and this chapter aims to support such reflection by focusing on:

- the challenges which early years practitioners face, with particular reference to culture and special educational needs;
- the issues of difference and diversity, inclusion policy and pedagogy arising from such challenges;
- the responsibilities and opportunities deriving from current policy in addressing difference and diversity by affirming principles of early childhood pedagogy.

Each of these will be taken in turn and case studies offered to support readers' reflection and understanding.

Challenges

Culture

The following is an extract from Eva Hoffman's (1998) book, *Lost in Translation*, where she describes her experience when she and her family fled Poland and migrated to Canada in the 1960s. As an adult and accomplished writer, she gave voice to the child whose feelings, at the time, were unacknowledged and whose past was wiped out in an instant. She was able to describe how the teacher and Mr Rosenberg had made their mark in her life on that very first day in the Canadian school, despite their best intentions to make her and her sister feel welcome and take a place in the new world.

Case study 1

We've been brought to this school by Mr Rosenberg, who, two days after our arrival, tells us he'll take us to classes that are provided by the government to teach English to newcomers. This morning . . . we've acquired new names. All it takes is a brief conference between Mr Rosenberg and the teacher, a kindly looking woman who tries to give us reassuring glances, but who has seen too many people come and go to get sentimental about a name. Mine – Ewa – is easy to change into its near equivalent in English 'Eva'. My sister's name – Alina – poses more of a problem, but after a moment's thought, Mr Rosenberg and the teacher decide that 'Elaine' is close enough . . . The twist in our names takes them a tiny distance from us – but it's a gap into which the infinite hobgoblin of abstraction enters. Our Polish names didn't refer to us; they were as surely us as our eyes or hands. These new appellations, which we ourselves can't yet pronounce, are not us. They are identification tags, disembodied signs pointing to objects that happen to be my sister and myself. We walk to our seats, into a roomful of unknown faces, with names that makes us strangers to ourselves.

(Hoffman 1998: 105)

In Eva Hoffman's autobiography, the teacher's decision may be better understood in terms of the notion of assimilation which prevailed in education at the time. Assimilation required that migrants and refugees should learn the language and embrace the culture of the host country in order to function properly and acquire a place in the new world (Rutter 1994). However, assimilation failed to acknowledge, as Ewa so poignantly did, the importance of culture and identity. The new names meant nothing to Ewa and her sister and, more than anything else, alienated them from their past and their identities.

Ewa's sentiments and perceptions of the interwoven nature of culture, language and identity are now better understood in the light of socio-cultural theories which maintain that language and thinking and, therefore, understanding are inherently embedded in culture (Vygotsky 1986; Bruner 1990). The way we speak, the way we think and the way we express ourselves are deeply rooted in and influenced by our own culture (see Chapter 4). Our sense of who we are, our identity, is ingrained in our language and culture (Papatheodorou, forthcoming). As such, our identity reflects an emotional and often unconscious connection and commitment to that language and culture.

Reflection point

1   In your setting, how do you address diversity?

Cultural fluidity

Our understanding of the interconnectedness of language and culture gradually gave way to the notion of multiculturalism, where home language and culture have been acknowledged as integral parts of an individual's learning and development of thinking (Levine, in Meek 1996; Bialystok 2001). The *Curriculum Guidance for the Foundation Stage* (CGFS) (QCA/DfEE 2000) makes particular reference to children's linguistic and cultural background, pointing out that practitioners should value children's linguistic background and provide them with opportunities to develop and use their home language in their play and learning. Although English remains the language of instruction, bilingual support is recommended, too, if required.

Awareness of cultural diversity has brought about many positive practices but, if not careful and alert, such awareness may inherit the danger of making too broad cultural groupings where individuals may be assigned on assumed shared characteristics (e.g. physical appearance, accent, etc.) and lead to stereotyping and prejudice (Leyens and Codol 1988; Eiser 1990; Macrae et al. 1994). Yet, this is not always the case. In fact, individuals may be associated with, and have membership of multiple cultural and linguistic groups and their experiences may not fit neatly in any specific group only.

Perhaps, thinking and acknowledging *cultural fluidity* is more important than thinking in terms of cultural separateness and distinctiveness. Ang (2006), in her critique of the CGFS, notes that conceptualization of cultural and linguistic diversity as discrete categories that deserve special attention, fails to acknowledge the complex relationships and membership of some children and their families and may lead to stereotyping. Siraj-Blatchford (2006: 13) points out that early years practitioners 'should be critically aware of the danger of stereotyping and should always focus upon individuals and individual needs'. The mother's testimony in Case study 2 provides a striking illustration of such situation.

Case study 2

Today, when I went to pick up my son from the nursery school, the nursery teacher was pleased to tell me how well he is doing. He is happy, confident and playing well with the other children. He is very talkative and communicates well with both adults and children; he speaks English very well. The nursery teacher asked me whether we speak English, at home.

I am of Thai origin and my husband is from China. English is my first language and my husband speaks English, too; he has been living in England since he was 2 years old. We are both British citizens and we speak English as our first language.

The nursery teacher assumed ... perhaps from our names, striking oriental features, accent? – I don't know ... that English is not my son's first language. She was surprised when I told her that we speak English at home.

(A parent's testimony)

Whatever clues the teacher might have used, she had categorized and stereotyped the child as belonging to a specific group whose language was assumed not to be English.

Reflection point

2   Think of three ways in which your understanding of cultural fluidity may change your current practice.

According to Daniels (2006), when needs are complex and confusing, professionals usually apply a category to solve their confusion rather than meeting the needs of the child. They use categorization to cope with the demands of their job and the distribution of resources, but such categorization may assume simplistic protocols and magic answers and have consequences for the identity formation of young people (for example in Eva's case) (Hjörne and Säljö, in Daniels 2006).

Categorization, by overestimating and exaggerating differences between groups and underestimating differences within groups (Taylor 1981; Calhoun and Acocella 1990), can lead to paying attention to 'difference of a kind' rather than to 'difference of a degree' or vice versa (O'Brien 2005). For example, in Case study 3, knowing that George's home language is different from that of his peer group, the teacher was able to understand his difficulty in terms of this information which represents difference of a kind (language) between groups (George's family and the school). As a result, the teacher failed to pay due attention to George's different level and degree of achievement across all areas of learning and seek alternative explanations.

Case study 3

At parents' evening, last December, I talked to Mrs Capps, George's mother. I told her that George is doing very well. He has settled well to the new class; he is well behaved, very thoughtful and attentive. He loves playing with other children and he has his own group of friends with whom he plays during free time. He is doing well in following instructions, reasoning, maths, reading and writing. He takes, however, some time to respond to questions.

I've told his mum that this is understandable given that English is not his first language. Mrs Capps told me that, actually, George has a slight hearing impairment in his right ear. His late response to questions is because he does a lot of lip-reading. She told me that the school had had this information since George was in the nursery class.

Mrs Capps was obviously upset when she realized that, despite the reassurance given to her by the school, the information had not been passed on to me. This incident made me think that the school's inclusion policy might not work as well as we think. On reflection, I think that more personal and proactive actions may have avoided such oversight.

(Year 1 teacher)

Reflection point

3   Do you have any examples where difference of a kind or of a degree may have taken precedence over the other? Why has this happened?

Special educational needs and inclusion

Although categorization and the use of readily available information may have contributed to the teacher's failure to suspect or detect George's hearing impairment, her/his expectations about the school's inclusion policy may have also been a contributory factor. Being aware of the school's policy, the teacher expected that the information held by the school about George would have been communicated to her/him. The teacher's reflection on the failure of the school's policy echoes some of the concerns expressed by researchers and writers who have argued that inclusion has mostly focused upon national policy and strategic direction. Statutory guidance, too, has largely taken an administrative approach by focusing on the structures and procedures for the management of inclusion (DfES 2004). As a result, the inclusion debate has placed much emphasis on where the child is educated rather than how, that is, the pedagogy behind inclusion (Aubrey 1994; Garner, in Farell 2003).

However, despite the criticisms which inclusion may have received, the positive impact of its structural and procedural approaches are well documented in Case study 4.

Case study 4

Today, we went out to the playground. We all lined up. I was first in the line, sitting in my wheelchair. Amir and Tina were holding on to my wheelchair with one hand, each. They had their other arm open like this (shows how by extending his arm sideways). I, too, opened my arms wide open like wings.

We paused for a minute. Then, with all our strength we pushed the wheelchair out of the door, over the ramp and ... oops ... there we went ... into the playground.

We played football. Amir and Tina were in my team. I was very fast. I reached the football and chased it to the goal post. Tina held on to my wheelchair and we ran as fast as we could. We reached the goal post and then we scored ... My wheelchair nearly turned upside down.

Everyone was cheering ... Tina was jumping up and down ... I swung my wheelchair to the left and made three big circles, shouting and waving my hands in the air ... Tina told me "You are a good footballer ... I nearly toppled you upside down ... Sorry!" she said, and laughed. "Sometimes I forget you are in a wheelchair."

Tina forgets that I am in a wheelchair ... All children forget ... Everyone wants me to be in their football team.

(Tony, Year R experience)

Tony's experience clearly demonstrates that when people are assigned equal status and are facilitated to co-operate and create interpersonal relationships through personal contact, inter-group relations, understanding, attitudes and possible prejudices change (Allport 1954; Bailey 1998; Booth and Ainscow 1998). Attending the local school with his friends and having easy access to all areas, Tony is able to join his peers and participate in all curricula and play activities and experience enjoyment, sense of achievement, peer acceptance and belongingness. For his schoolmates, Tony is a worthy member of their team and his contribution is acknowledged.

Reflection point

4 How typical is Tony's story? How can policies and structures promote such positive experiences?

Issues

Difference and diversity

The four case studies have illustrated some of the challenges and issues raised in early years settings by making particular reference to assumed or evidenced cultural and special educational needs diversity. The cameos have also demonstrated that the picture is not clear-cut and diversity does not fall into neat categories of culture, language, special educational needs. Instead, diversity is constantly evident in individual variation in terms of, for instance, ethnicity, language, culture, age, sex, life style, and so on.

In education, however, when we speak about diversity, and especially cultural diversity, we do not refer to individual differences, but only to those individual differences which confront and challenge the expected norms or models which we have in mind for our group of pupils, their learning and behaviour (InterGuide, undated). In this sense, individual linguistic, cultural, ability and disability differences may become points of reference to define and identify diversity in groups which otherwise would have been considered homogenous.

The identification and acknowledgement of difference in education can have a powerful and incisive function; it can be emancipatory or discriminatory (O'Brien 2005). On the one hand, it prevents us from making too broad categories and groupings (for example, English as an additional language or special educational needs), where inclusiveness is not warranted, and it also enables us to unpack, analyse and interrogate the cohesiveness of such groupings (Case studies 2 and 3) (Gordon 2005). On the other hand, it may lead to the identification of explicit and rigid sub-categories where the complexity of individuals' real-life situations is underestimated (Case studies 2 and 3). In addition, if these sub-categories become the point of reference for action, then there is a danger that more people may find themselves as being, or being judged, as outsiders or marginal (Case study 1) (Irwin 2005).

The functions of the acknowledgement of difference may also be understood at different and multiple levels, that is, at ideological and political, institutional, structural and sub-cultural levels. At the ideological and political level, difference is defended in international and national policies which, for example, deal with the rights of the child, antiracism, multi-culturalism and inclusion. At this level, acknowledgement of difference is justified in the name of ideals of equitable treatment and social justice for all. At the institutional level, difference is promoted by sanctioning and diffusing norms and policies that reflect these ideals. At the structural and procedural level, difference is acknowledged by setting out structures and procedures which identify and challenge power relationships. At the sub-cultural level, difference is used to identify and challenge broad and cohesive social systems which undermine equality of treatment and opportunity for all (Troyna and Hatcher 1992; Gordon 2005; Irwin 2005).

In this context, it is not surprising that the phrase 'celebrating diversity' has now become the new mantra which implies equitable education for all pupils, regardless of their background and experience. However, what this may mean in practice for practitioners who have no personal experience of diversity and little understanding of inequity is rather unclear (King 2004). As Giroux (1991: 72) has argued, there is a 'danger of affirming difference simply as an end in itself without acknowledging how difference is formed, erased, and resuscitated'. Borrowing from Gidden's dual structure of inequality (cited in Siraj-Blatchford 2006), it can be argued here that the identification and acknowledgement of difference can have a dual function, that is, to be a medium for, and the outcome of social practices. For this and drawing on Rawls (1999), it can also be argued that the acknowledgement of difference and diversity can be justified and seen as just only when it is used for the distribution of resources to increase the advantages of the least favoured groups in society.

Reflection point

5   How do you define diversity? What is the role of difference in such definition?

Inclusion policy

Rawls's (1999) powerful statement and defence of the difference and diversity discourse have been better embodied in the inclusion policies and debates that have been introduced into education and care settings during the past 15 years. Inclusion policies encourage and require schools and settings to change their structures, pedagogical approaches, assessment practices and learning environments to meet the diverse needs of all pupils and ensure their effective participation in the learning process (Wade 1999; Farell 2003). It means that all pupils, regardless of their special educational needs, should be educated in the local context rather than in a special school (DfEE 1997) and have access to and participate in the same curricula activities. In terms of inclusion, the range of pupils' abilities and interests is seen as enrichment for the school and the community (Booth and Ainscow 1998).

Although, initially, inclusion in schools was introduced as an alternative to integration for children with special educational needs, it is now seen as having a broader remit and focus. According to OfSTED (2000), inclusion not only concerns groups of pupils with special educational needs and/or those pupils who face exclusion from school, but refers to equality of opportunity for all pupils regardless of their ethnicity, culture, language, ability, attainment, age or gender. Inclusion is a struggle against deficit models and social injustice associated with any one of these groups. It is a political and ideological struggle against exclusive attitudes, systems, structures and approaches (Barton 1995; Ballard 1995; Slee, in Farell 2003). It is a right based on equitable treatment and social justice for all (Evans 2000). As such, the focus of inclusion has largely been on how school management structures and procedures produce inclusive policies, and create inclusive cultures and practices to enable pupils with a wide range of needs and abilities to participate in the education process (Booth et al. 2000).

The limitation and, more importantly, the reduction of inclusion policies to bureaucratic and paperwork exercises have been explicitly acknowledged in the document *Removing Barriers to Achievement* (DfES 2004), where a firm commitment has been made to counteract this situation. The document, too, acknowledges the need for improving classroom practice. Yet, much of its recommendations are regarding the rhetoric of skills and competencies improvement and strong leadership (at headteachers, SENCOs and other skilled professionals' level).

Reflection point

6   Do you agree with the view that inclusion policies have become too bureaucratic? How might this situation be counterbalanced?

Pedagogy

When policy-informed teaching takes the place of pedagogy and categorization determines action, there is a danger of practitioners reacting to situations rather than dealing proactively with complex and diverse needs. Had the teacher first of all not categorized and seen George's variable achievement in terms of his linguistic background and, second, assumed/expected that the school's inclusion policy would have been effectively implemented, he or she might have sought alternative explanations. It can be argued here that the emphasis placed on difference, .as an action category, and the managerial implementation of inclusion have led practitioners to seek, and adopt, tips for teaching rather than engaging with pedagogy (Epstein 1993).

Pedagogy is often defined as, or considered synonymous with, teaching. This, however, is a narrow definition (Levine, in Meek 1996). Teaching is the act and performance of presenting curricula subjects, while pedagogy is both act and discourse (Alexander 2000). Pedagogy involves both teaching and the thinking behind teaching and practitioners' actions (Lewis and Norwich 2005). According to Alexander:

> Pedagogy encompasses the performance of teaching together with the theories, beliefs, policies and controversies that inform and shape it ... Pedagogy connects the apparently self-contained act of teaching with culture, structure and mechanisms of social control.
>
> (2000: 540)

With its emphasis on performance, policy-driven teaching has, in turn, become policy- and curriculum-driven and centred. Pedagogy, on the other hand, by focusing on the being and experience of those involved in the learning process (both pupil and teacher), takes an ontological dimension and becomes *person-centred*. It acknowledges, considers and critiques extant knowledge (subject and learning specific theories); reflects on experience and folk- or common-sense theories; invests in the dialectical relationships between learner and teacher and acknowledges the particular cultural, social and structural context where such relationships develop. Ultimately, pedagogy encapsulates unacknowledged concepts of what teaching is about (Levine, in Meek 1996).

Early childhood pedagogy has some distinct principles which are reflected in the discourse of, and debate about, early years professionalism. These include inclusivity, reflexivity, responsivity and affectivity; over-consciousness, empathetic engagement and personal involvement with children, their families and communities; and strong beliefs, feelings and commitment about the protection and support of children. Early childhood pedagogy is underpinned by passionate commitment (Osgood 2006).

However, the emotionality of early childhood pedagogy is seen as the professional limitation of early years practitioners (Moyles 2001). This limitation can be negatively counteracted by top-down, prescriptive and policy informed practice, where outcomes and outputs count (Ball, in Osgood 2006). Indeed, although overwhelmingly committed to this pedagogy, when it comes to practice, early years practitioners resort to didactic and teacher-centred approaches following national guidance (e.g. see Chapter 17) and beliefs that such approaches will satisfy inspectors (BERA: Early Years Special Interest Group 2003).

Early years professionals then face the challenge of reclaiming and affirming early childhood pedagogy that is based on accumulated extant knowledge of many disciplines and their professional wisdom.

Reflection point

7   What do you understand by the term 'pedagogy' and what are its implications for your everyday practices?

Towards a dialectical relationship between policy and pedagogy

The introduction of standards and prescriptive statutory guidance has directly influenced and often determined classroom practice. However, this is a rather limited and narrow top-down approach which may reflect and seek to impose the values and ideals of the majority (and dominant sections?) of society. A dialectical and dynamic relationship between (1) policy, and statutory requirements and guidance; (2) structures, procedures and processes; and (3) classroom practice, mediated by pedagogy, would afford greater contextual coherence and cohesiveness in educational praxis (Figure 3.1). Pedagogy offers the lenses and filters through which policy, statutory regulation and guidance, and practice may be critically examined, critiqued, questioned and appropriated to meet the needs of all and every individual child. At the same time, pedagogy, too, is informed and shaped by this dialectical relationship.

Borrowing from Bronfenbrenner (1999), pedagogical principles assumed in guidance for good practice (e.g. *Key Elements for Effective Practice* (DfES 2005a) and *The Common Core Skills and Knowledge* (DfES 2005b) may be seen as being:

- *person-centred*, that is, based on knowledge about the child, his/her family, the early years practitioner and other professionals;
- *process-centred*, that is, based on knowledge about relationships, communication and processes of engagement and collaboration with all persons involved in educational practice;
- *context-specific*, that is, based on knowledge about the broader context of international and national policy; statutory and non-statutory regulations and guidance; the immediate early years setting policy, environment and practice;
- *time-subject*, that is, based on the acknowledgement that persons, processes and context are not static, but ever evolving on the basis of experience, advances in extant knowledge and policies introduced.

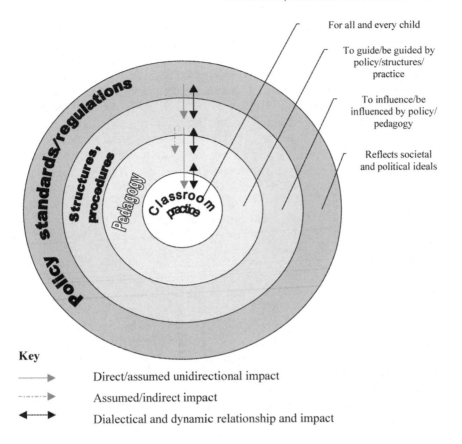

For all and every child

To guide/be guided by policy/structures/practice

To influence/be influenced by policy/pedagogy

Reflects societal and political ideals

Key

→   Direct/assumed unidirectional impact

⇢   Assumed/indirect impact

◄──►   Dialectical and dynamic relationship and impact

Figure 3.1 The dialectical and dynamic relationship between policy, practice and pedagogy

---

Reflection point

8   Can you identify the pedagogical principles which underpin the skills and competencies identified in key documents such as *Key Elements of Effective Practice* and *The Common Core*?

Responsibilities and opportunities

Once again, the responsibilities and opportunities for early years professionals to implement inclusive practice and address difference and diversity come from national policies that have taken precedence during the last few years, that is, the *Every Child Matters* Green Paper (HMSO 2003). Under the mandate of this framework, disparate children's services (e.g. education, health, social and other services) came under one Children's Service, placing responsibility on local authorities to safeguard and promote children's welfare and rights. At the same time, the five intended outcomes for children and the emphasis of the framework on prevention rather than intervention make great demands upon, and place great responsibility for, early years practitioners' understanding of difference and diversity and its implications for early intervention.

Until now statutory requirements focused on children with complex and severe needs and, almost two-thirds of resources available were spent on services for these children (DfES 2004). *Every Child Matters* has shifted attention to those children who receive universal services and whose needs, if identified early, may call for additional targeted support. The focus of the *Common Assessment Framework* (CAF) in *Every Child Matters* is on the threshold between universal and targeted services (see Figure 3.2).

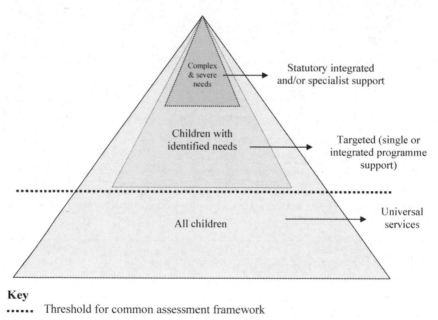

Key
••••• Threshold for common assessment framework

Figure 3.2 Provision and support for children in early years settings

The threshold between universal and targeted support is less obvious and clear than the cut-off point for severe and complex needs, as it depends on subtle and, often, unnoticed differences. In the case of young children, it is also difficult to make judgements whether such subtle cues and signs of difference reflect developmental milestones or needs that deserve attention for additional support. In addition, the situation is further complicated by the fact that false identification of special and/or additional needs may lead to stigmatization.

Awareness and explicit acknowledgement in *Every Child Matters* that neglect of early identification of children's needs may contribute to their exaggeration and children's prolonged and long-term disadvantage cannot afford complacency. Consequently, early years practitioners are assumed and assigned the responsibility to demonstrate understanding and appreciation of concepts and notions of difference and diversity so as to make informed decisions for individual children.

Although statutory and non-statutory guidelines are helpful tools, it is pedagogical principles applied to individual children that will allow early years practitioners to notice, interrogate and negotiate subtle cues of difference and, consequently, make judgements about children's needs that may require targeted additional and/or special support. It is the application of pedagogical principles that may accord notions of difference and diversity either emancipatory or discriminatory powers.

To recall and paraphrase Freire (1998), it is the human capacity to compare, judge and decide to intervene or not, that gives or takes away opportunities for equality for all; not practice that is conditioned by policy and statutory requirements. We may also like to remind ourselves that

> the curriculum content and the way in which teachers are trained and selected are important factors on the development of the educational process. But education is not a technical matter, nor an 'experts' issue, but a human process in which teachers are core agents, and they have much to say and to do.
>
> (InterGuide undated: 106)

Reflection point

9   Has *Every Child Matters* changed your ways of working with children? If it has, in what ways? What prompted these changes?

Conclusion

The four case studies in this chapter have demonstrated some of the challenges and issues which early years practitioners experience in their direct work with young children. Culture is one issue that we are gradually becoming more aware of than ever before. Yet, culture is not an all-embracing concept; indeed, there is much more cultural fluidity than cultural distinctiveness. A range of multiple policies have brought awareness about special educational needs and inclusion issues. But, despite their positive impact, such policies have also been flawed by their managerial focus and detrimental effects on pedagogy. However, it is again recently introduced policy that provides the responsibilities and opportunities for early years professionals to examine their understanding of difference and diversity and affirm their pedagogical principles for early identification of children's needs that may require targeted additional and/or special support.

Points for discussion

- Discuss your understanding of ethnicity, race and culture and any differences and similarities between them.
- Consider the spectrum of needs (from mild to severe) which exist in your setting and discuss which ones you serve best and why.
- Record all changes which took place in your setting as a response to *Every Child Matters*. Discuss their positive aspects and any limitations with particular focus on your underpinning pedagogical principles. Bring together your findings and decide on *three* changes you would like to bring about in your setting: identify their practical implications and set out a clear timescale.

References and further reading

Alexander, R. (2000) *Culture and Pedagogy: International Comparisons in Primary Education*. Maiden, MA: Blackwell.

Allport, G.W. (1954) *The Nature of Prejudice*. Reading, MA: Addison-Wesley.

Ang, L. (2006) Critical perspectives on culture, diversity and the early childhood curriculum, with reference to the foundation stage curriculum in England, paper presented at the 16th EECERA Conference in Reykjavik, Iceland.

Aubrey, C. (1994) A testing time for psychologists, in S. Sandow (ed.) *Whose Special Need?* London: Paul Chapman.

Bailey, J. (1998) Australia: inclusion through categorization, in T. Booth and M. Ainscow (eds) *From Them to Us: An International Study of Inclusion in Education*. London: Routledge.

Ballard, K. (1995) Inclusion, paradigms, power and participation, in C. Clarke, A. Dyson and A. Millward (eds) *Towards Inclusive Schools?* London: David Fulton.

Barton, L. (1995) The politics of education for all, *Support for Learning*, 10(4): 156–60.

BERA (British Educational Research Association) Early Years Special Interest Group (2003) *Early Years Research: Pedagogy, Curriculum and Adult Roles, Training and Professionalism*. Notts, UK: BERA.

Bialystok, E. (2001) *Bilingualism in Development: Language, Literacy and Cognition.* Cambridge: Cambridge University Press.

Booth, T. and Ainscow, M. (1998) *From Them to Us: An International Study of Inclusion in Education.* London: Routledge.

Booth, T., Ainscow, M., Black-Hawkins, K., Vaughn, M. and Shaw, L. (2000) *Index for Inclusion: Developing Learning and Participation in Schools.* Bristol: Centre for Studies in Inclusive Education.

Bronfenbrenner, U. (1999) *Growing Chaos in the Lives of Children, Youth and Families: How Can We Turn It Around?* Proceedings of the conference 'Parenthood in America', held in Madison, Wisconsin, 19–21 April 1998. Available at: http://parenthood.library.wisc.edu/Bronfenbrenner/Bronfen brenner.html (accessed 31 December 2006).

Bruner, J. (1990) *Acts of Meaning.* Cambridge, MA: Harvard University Press.

Calhoun, J.F. and Acocella, J.R. (1990) *Psychology of Adjustment and Human Relationships.* New York: McGraw-Hill.

CRE (Centre for Racial Equality) (2006) *Diversity and Integration.* Available at: http://www.cre.gov.uk/diversity/map.html (accessed 27 December 2006).

Daniels, H. (2006) The dangers of corruption in special needs education, *British Journal of Special Education*, 33(1): 4–9.

DfEE (Department for Education and Employment) (1997) *Excellence for All Children: Meeting Special Educational Needs.* London: The Stationery Office.

DfES (Department for Education and Skills) (2001a) *Inclusive Schooling: Children with Special Educational Needs.* Nottingham: DfES Publications.

DfES (2001b) *Special Educational Needs Code of Practice.* Nottingham: DfES Publications.

DfES (2004) *Removing Barriers to Achievement: The Government's Strategy for SEN.* Nottingham: DfES Publications.

DfES (2005a) *Key Elements of Effective Practice.* Nottingham: DfES Publications.

DfES (2005b) *Common Core of Skills and Knowledge for the Children's Workforce.* Nottingham: DfES Publications.

Eiser, J.R. (1990) *Social Judgement.* Milton Keynes: Open University Press.

Epstein, D. (1993) *Changing Classroom Cultures.* Stoke-on-Trent: Trentham.

Evans, P. (2000) Including students with disabilities in mainstream schools, in H. Savolainen, H. Kokkala and H. Alasuutari (eds) *Meeting Special and Diverse Educational Needs: Making Inclusive Education a Reality.* Helsinki: Ministry for Foreign Affairs of Finland.

Farell, M (2003) *Understanding Special Educational Needs.* London: Routledge.

Freire, P. (1998) *Pedagogy of the Oppressed*, new revised 20th anniversary edition. New York: Continuum Publishing Co.

Giroux, H.A. (1991) Postmodernism and the discourse of educational criticism, in S. Aronowitz and H.A. Giroux (eds) *Postmodern Education: Politics, Culture, and Social Criticism.* Minneapolis and Oxford: University of Minnesota Press.

Gordon, M.M. ([1947] 2005) The concept of the subculture and its application, in K. Gelder (ed.) *The Subcultures Reader*. London and New York: Routledge.

HMSO (2003) *Every Child Matters*. Norwich: The Stationery Office.

Hoffman, E. (1998) *Lost in Translation*. London: Vintage.

InterGuide (undated) *A Practical Guide to Implement Intercultural Education at Schools*. Sócrates Comenius 2.1 INTER Project, no. 106223-CP-1-2002-1-COMENIUS-C21. Available at: http://inter.up.pt/inter.php?item=inter_guide (accessed 27 December 2006).

Irwin, J. ([1970] 2005) Notes on the status of the concept subculture, in K. Gelder (ed.) *The Subcultures Reader*. London and New York: Routledge.

King, J.E. (2004) Dysconscious racism: ideology, identity, and the miseducation of teachers, in G. Ladson-Billings and D. Gillborn (eds) *Multicultural Education*. London: Routledge.

Lewis, A. and Norwich, B. (eds) (2005) *Special Teaching for Special Children?* Maidenhead: Open University Press.

Leyens, J.P. and Codol, J.P. (1988) Social cognition, in M. Hewstone, W. Stroebe, J.P. Codol and G.M. Stevenson (eds) *Introduction to Social Psychology*. Oxford: Basil Blackwell.

Macrae, C.N., Milne, A.B. and Bodenhausen, G.V. (1994) Stereotypes as energy-saving devices: a peek inside the cognitive toolbox, *Journal of Personality and Social Psychology*, 66(1): 37–47.

Meek, M. (1996) *Developing Pedagogies in the Multilingual Classroom: The Writings of Josie Levine*. Stoke-on-Trent: Trentham Books.

Moyles, J. (2001) Passion, paradox and professionalism in early years education, *Early Years: An International Journal of Research and Development*, 21(2): 81–95.

O'Brien, T. (2005) Social, emotional and behavioural difficulties, in A. Lewis and B. Norwich (eds) *Special Teaching for Special Children?* Maidenhead: Open University Press.

OfSTED (Office for Standards in Education) (2000) *Evaluating Educational Inclusion: Guidance for Inspectors and Schools*. London: OfSTED.

Osgood, J. (2006) Professionalism and performativity: the feminist challenge facing early years practitioners, *Early Years: An International Journal of Research and Development*, 26(2): 187–99.

Papatheodorou, T. (forthcoming) *Supporting the Mother Tongue: Pedagogical Approaches* (submitted).

QCA/DfEE (Qualifications and Curriculum Authority) (2000) *Curriculum Guidance for the Foundation Stage*. London: QCA/DfES Publications.

Rawls, J. (1999) *A Theory of Justice* (revised edition). Oxford: Oxford University Press.

Rutter, J. (1994) *Refugee Children in the Classroom*. Stoke-on-Trent: Trentham Books.

Siraj-Blatchford, I. (2006) Educational disadvantage in the early years:

how do we overcome it? Some lessons from research, *European Early Childhood Education Research Journal*, **12(2): 5–20.**

Taylor, S.E. (1981) A categorisation approach to stereotyping, in D.L. Hamilton (ed.) *Cognitive Processes in Stereotyping and Intergroup Behavior*. Hillsdale, NJ: Lawrence Erlbaum.

Troyna, B. and Hatcher, R. (1992) *Racism in Children's Lives: A Study of Mainly White Primary Schools*. London: Routledge.

Vygotsky, L.S. (1986) *Thought and Language*, 3rd edn. Cambridge, MA: The MIT Press.

Wade, J. (1999) Including all learners: QCA's approach, *British Journal of Special Education*, 26(2): 80–2.

4 Identity and children as learners

Naima Browne

Abstract

When thinking about supporting young children's learning and development, it is vital that practitioners consider the issue of children's identities. How children position themselves has far-reaching implications for them as learners. This chapter explores the role that different discourses play in shaping children's emerging identities. The issues and challenges related to how children draw on different masculinities and femininities in developing their identities is examined. Emphasis is placed on the need for practitioners to acknowledge the multi-faceted, fluid nature of identity and to ensure that children are provided with access to a wide range of discourses and 'ways of being'.

Introduction

This chapter begins by exploring the concept of identity as this is the key to understanding children as learners. There are so many facets to identity that it helps to focus on one, and this chapter focuses on gender, but issues of 'race' and social class will also be considered. The chapter looks at the ways in which children's sense of who they are, and in particular their gender identities, develop within a social context. Drawing on my extensive discussions with young children and early years practitioners, the chapter explores and illustrates how young children begin to develop their gendered identities. The relationship between children's growing identities, their emotional well-being and the possible consequences for children's approaches to learning is also considered.

A child's identity and sense of self: what is it?

In normal conversation, we tend to use the term 'identity' in a generalized way to mean 'who someone is'. When we talk about having a sense of identity or sense of self we mean 'knowing who you are'. How do children come to know who they are?

Dorais (1995) has argued that identity is about being aware of the specific group of whom one is part in terms of beliefs, values, language and practices. It would seem, therefore, that children's identity develops as they interact with others during the course of their lives. This is not to suggest that babies do not have an identity but rather that as children grow and develop, so too does their understanding of who they are. It is our life experiences that help shape our view of ourselves and our identities shift and are reconstructed over time. Our sense of self, therefore, is not fixed or stable but changes with experience.

Furthermore, our understanding of who we are, our 'identity', is composed of a variety of 'selves'. We have multiple identities that do not arise and develop spontaneously (Davies 1989a; Dowling 2000; Mac Naughton 2000): they come to know who they are and how they can position themselves as a result of learning to make sense of their social interactions and experiences. This multiplicity of identities enables children to adopt a variety of positions and roles in the various social contexts in which they find themselves.

That we have a range of identities is evident in the way we all adopt a variety of roles in the different social contexts we operate within during the course of a day. This means that a young child may know that she is a 'really good author' when people enjoy her stories at school, that she is mummy's and daddy's 'lovely little girl', her baby brother's 'kind older sister' or her older sister's 'annoying baby sister' when she wants to join in her games.

Children do not just passively absorb their identities; instead they are active agents in creating them. Children's identities emerge through their engagement in a range of discourses: not all of these discourses will provide the same world-view and some of the discourses will conflict with each other.

Discourse theory

The term 'discourse' can be used to describe: 'A body of ideas, concepts and beliefs which become established as knowledge or an accepted worldview. These ideas become a powerful framework for understanding and action in social life' (Bilton et al. 1996: 657). The term 'discourse' has also been used to refer to 'the emotional, social and institutional frameworks and practices through which we make meaning in our lives' (Mac Naughton 2000: 50).

Discourses are very powerful as they produce or create a 'reality'. The emphasis on the importance of the mother–child dyad for young children's development and the notion of the naturally developing child are just two examples of dominant discourses currently influencing early years practice and provision (Browne 2004). One way in which dominant discourses can be seen to be powerful is that they may inhibit examination and exploration of alternative discourses by determining what is seen to be 'true' or 'the right thing to do'. It is possible to think of discourses as lenses that can determine what you see and what you do not see. Discourses, therefore, can also distort what you see.

Discourses create a 'reality' by providing words and conceptual frameworks for determining what can be said, written and possibly even thought about:

> each society has its regime of truth ... that is the types of discourses which it accepts and makes function as true, the mechanisms and instances which enable one to distinguish true and false statements, the means by which each is sanctioned; the techniques and procedures accorded value in the acquisition of truth; the status of those charged with saying what counts as true.
>
> (Foucault 1980: 131, cited in Dahlberg et al. 1999: 30)

In the early years field, for example, the dominant discourses in society and the field of education create 'truths' about young children and their needs (e.g. the naturally developing child moves through a series of universal developmental stages). These 'truths' are evident in official policy documents (e.g. *Birth to Three Matters*, the *Curriculum Guidance for the Foundation Stage*, *Key Elements of Effective Practice*) and the criteria used for assessing and evaluating the quality of provision (e.g. OfSTED inspections). The 'truths' also emerge in early years practice (such as resourcing, staffing, planning).

Foucault's ideas about the relationship between knowledge, power and discourse are stimulating in that he argued that dominant discursive regimes (i.e. those discourses that have a significant effect on shaping specific practice) are powerful because in identifying what is 'true' and 'right' they influence practice, as no practitioner would want to do what is generally regarded as 'wrong'. We need to be aware that diverse and dissenting views are silenced by the dominant discourses and Foucault's ideas about 'regimes of truth' invite us to imagine the unimaginable and look at fundamental issues in new ways.

As early years practitioners we need to develop the habit of reflecting critically on the dominant discourses influencing and shaping our work with children and develop a willingness to consider alternative discourses.

Reflection points

1   How are children influenced by parents/society from an early age in relation to their sex?

2   How far do you treat children as 'boys' and 'girls'? What consequences does this have in your practice?

3   What do you consider when you are selecting materials for use by children in your setting? How far is gender an issue?

Discourses and the development of identity

Considering alternative discourses is important when thinking about the process through which children develop their sense of self. In this society, for example, knowing whether you are a girl or a boy is deemed to be important. Sometimes even before a child is born, the mother is asked whether baby is a girl or boy. From the moment the child is born, adults will label the child as a girl or boy: 'Who's a beautiful girl then?' or 'You're a tired boy.' Young children are expected to learn whether they themselves are a girl or a boy and also accurately to assign others to one of two categories: male or female. Young children growing up in Western societies are introduced to the dominant gender discourse that maintains that there are only two options: female or male. Furthermore, female and male are considered to be mutually exclusive categories: you are either one or the other – you cannot be both.

   Davies (1989a) has argued that the language we use perpetuates social structures and embedded within the English language is the 'fact' that people are either female or male. This is important when considering how children come to develop their identities because the categories female and male are not natural; they are socially constructed. This means that children will not 'naturally' behave like a girl or a boy: instead they have to learn how to relate to others and perform in 'gender-appropriate' ways.

   Hegemonic masculinity is the term used to describe the dominant or culturally accepted form of masculinity within a society (Connell 1987, 1995, 2000). This delineates what it means to be a 'real' boy or man. In Western society, hegemonic masculinity emphasizes physical strength, rationality and men's superiority over women. Furthermore, hegemonic masculinity is complemented by 'emphasized femininity' which stresses empathy, conformity and caring (Connell 1987).

   Although a child can be said to be socially constructed in that his/her identities do not develop in a social vacuum, children also have a degree of control over how they construct themselves. Children are constrained by the range of experiences they have and their access to alternative discourses which would provide them with further options but 'she none-the-less exists as a thinking, feeling, subject and social agent capable of resistance and innovations produced out of the clash between contradictory subject positions and practices' (Weedon 1987: 125).

An individual's personal and social identity is created through a process which involves her being made a subject or subjected to other people's readings of her and her positioning within society while she, simultaneously, makes highly personal decisions about the satisfaction she gains from the various ways in which she is able to position herself. This means that each child is a 'co-constructor of knowledge, identity and culture' (Dahlberg et al. 1999: 48) rather than a 'passive' recipient or 'culture reproducer' (1999: 44). If children are 'co-constructors', we have to consider the role that children themselves play in shaping their culture and identities. Many experienced early years practitioners and parents have learnt that attempts on the part of the adult to enable a child to broaden ideas of what it means to be a girl or boy, or to explore another way of being, are doomed to failure unless the child is willing to engage in the venture.

One gender identity or multiple gender identities?

From a very early age children are exposed to a range of discourse about what it means to be a 'normal' girl or boy. It is by deciding how to position themselves in different contexts and in relation to the various discourses that children begin to develop their sense of self or subjectivity (Rowan et al. 2002). Increasingly, when discussing identity, the term subjectivity has been used because it highlights the process by which our multi-faceted identities develop and also recognizes that all of us have more than one possible self (Davies 1989a; McNaughton 2000; Rowan et al. 2002). It is possible to continue to use the more familiar terms 'sense of identity' and 'sense of self' provided we are conscious of the process by which we create our identities, are aware that we have multiple identities and that our concepts of who we are or of 'self' are unstable and fluid, changing with context and over time.

When we observe young children and listen to what they have to say about themselves and others, we are witnessing a small part of the on-going process by which the children are developing ideas about who they are, rather than observing a 'finished product'. Listening to children highlights the discourses the children appear to have access to, helps identify which discourses appear to provide the children with positive emotional feedback and also may indicate how children position themselves. Gaining an understanding of the signs and symbols that produce the social representations of gender that the children are exploring or aligning themselves with helps educators better comprehend the reasons and motives for children's behaviours, attitudes, concerns and interests. It also helps educators to understand the discourses of gender with which the children are engaging. Unless we know where children are coming from and what it is that appeals to them on a deep emotional level, we cannot hope to effect change or develop our practice to suit children's needs.

While young children are active agents in constructing their identities, they are still influenced by the opinions and views of others and will be particularly sensitive to the views and opinions of people to whom they are close, e.g. parents, carers, teachers, friends, siblings, and such like.

Operating effectively within the dominant gender discourse means that a child can relate unproblematically and unambiguously, in gender terms, with others. It also tends to attract a positive response from those around the child ('He's a real boy isn't he?' or 'You're such a good girl; so kind'). This means that for some children 'correctly' positioning themselves within a dominant gender discourse brings about positive emotional feedback. As Paley has noted: 'Kindergarten is a triumph of sexual self-stereotyping. No amount of adult subterfuge or propaganda deflects the five-year-olds' passion for segregation by sex' (1984: ix). When I have talked to young children about what girls and boys like to play with, the majority of them declared that girls liked to play with Barbie dolls and play mummies and daddies while boys liked to play with cars and superhero play and fighting (Browne 2004). These activities are good examples of emphasized femininity and hegemonic masculinity. Many girls are equally clear about the position they adopt, a position described by Davies (1989a: 121) as 'home corner girls'. These girls talked enthusiastically about playing mummies and daddies and 'playing houses' (Browne 2004: 73).

Other children may choose to adopt a different position. Five-year-old Helen talked in a disparaging tone about 'girly girls' and said 'Girly girls like playing with Barbies, but I don't. I like playing with the dolls house.' (Browne 2004: 75) This would suggest that Helen was aware that there were different ways of being a girl and at that moment she was not opting to be a 'girly girl'. Similarly, Stephen, aged 4, chatted cheerfully about his enjoyment of jigsaw puzzles, tennis, superhero play as well as the games he enjoyed playing with the girls in the home corner (Browne 2004). Stephen appears to be a good example of a young child who feels that being a boy does not require total adherence to a hegemonic style of masculinity.

It is important to acknowledge that other styles of masculinity and femininity exist alongside these dominant forms because the dominant discourses are construed as providing us with taken-for-granted 'truths'. We need to remember that:

> 'being a boy' relates not only to experiences of a male body, but also
> to factors associated with race, ethnicity, economic status, physical

ability, sexuality, religion, first language, physical appearance and so on. In other words, many factors combine to determine the ways in which an individual boy will be ranked within a particular gender hierarchy.

(Rowan et al. 2002: 43)

Although Rowan et al. are focusing on boys, the same is true for girls. 'Race', social class and sexuality overlay all styles and hierarchies of masculinity and femininity. Those who have access to discourses of power because of their social class or 'race' have the opportunity to adopt styles of femininity and masculinity that position them as having power over other girls or boys. The high status versions of femininity and masculinity are those that do not challenge the notion of the binary gender divide or the power relations between men and women (Davies 1989a; Rowan et al. 2002).

There are, however, hierarchies even within the high status styles ways of being: 'Rough, tough princesses and sirens are higher status than "home corner" girls ... All are nonetheless unequivocally "feminine"' (Davies 1989a: 127). Children who are developing their sense of self need support to explore and possibly appropriate other ways of being a girl or a boy. Practitioners who have attempted to broaden children's play preferences or choice of friends may have found that this is easier said than done.

Kohlberg's cognitive-developmental theory seems to provide an explanation for young children's rigid views about gender-appropriate behaviour and interests. According to Kohlberg, children are able to identify themselves as girls or boys by the age of 3 but the concept of gender constancy is not established until around the age of 5 or 6. Furthermore, it is not until children are aged approximately 10 that they understand that gender roles are not 'natural' or biologically determined but are social constructs. Kohlberg's theory sits uneasily with theories of multiple femininities and masculinities and also does not explain why some older children and adolescents may hold very rigid views about gender-appropriate behaviour. The theory also fails to take account of the range of styles of masculinity and femininity a child may adopt and the power of different discourses in helping a child decide what is 'gender-appropriate' and 'gender-inappropriate'. It is also possible to argue that young children's rigid views about gender are not so much related to a search for a stable personal identity as manifestation of participation in a joint endeavour with others in society that aims to maintain socially constructed gender categories (Browne 2004).

Reflection points

4   How can talking to children about gender provide us with insight into their developing understandings of gender?

5   How can we broaden children's play preferences in relation to gender, or choice of friends?

Category maintenance work and identity

Maintaining the binary gender divide and perpetuating the dominant gender discourses and dominant styles of masculinity and femininity require category maintenance work (Davies 1989a). This is relevant when considering children's developing identities because children who deviate from the gender norm are likely to experience disapproval from other children and adults. Young children will engage in category maintenance work (Davies 1989b; Browne 1999). A 6-year-old girl told me that she thought girls liked to play with Barbie and Polly Pocket and boys preferred KNex and then went on to say that 'If they [boys] like Barbie they must be gay' (Browne 2004: 73). Although this child may not have fully understood the meaning of the word 'gay', she knew the word could be used as an insult. Furthermore, her message was quite clear – any boy who failed to live up to the standards of hegemonic heterosexual masculinity and who was more feminine was not socially acceptable and should be rejected.

Practitioners may also engage in category maintenance work, possibly without being aware of it. In one nursery where I was interviewing adults and children, two girls showed me two pieces of wood they had nailed together to form a cross and proudly informed me that this was a sword. The nursery assistant looked quizzically at the two girls before saying, 'I don't think so. I thought it was an aeroplane' (Browne 2004: 74). The girls said nothing more about their 'sword'. Observing this interchange, it appeared to me that the girls were being told that playing with weapons was not something they should be doing and that the girls had not 'correctly' positioned themselves.

Many children may find that adopting alternative styles of femininity and masculinity are dissatisfying, partly because of the negative feedback from peers and significant adults. Children such as Stephen who was referred to earlier, may manage to adopt a multiple of positionings. Stephen engaged in activities associated with hegemonic masculinity (e.g. superhero play) and having thus assured his status as a 'real boy', he was able to explore less 'masculine' ways of being without censure.

Practitioners' roles in broadening children's choices

Not all educationalists agree on how best to support children's developing gender identities. Paley has argued that we ought to 'let the boys be robbers, then, or tough guys in space. It is the natural, universal, and essential play of little boys. Everything is make-believe except the obvious feelings of well-being that emerge from fantasy play' (1984: 116).

In contrast, Davies argues that:

> Children need to be given access to a discourse which frees them from the burden of the liberalist humanist obligations of coming to know a fixed reality in which they have a unified and rationally coherent identity separate and distinct from the social world ... They need to have access to imaginary worlds in which new metaphors, new forms of social relations and new patterns of power and desire are explored ... They need the freedom to position themselves in multiple ways.
>
> (Davies 1989a: 141)

Constructions of gender and emotional development and behaviour

The dominant gender discourses have an impact on a range of aspects of young children's learning and development including emotional development and behaviour.

Emotional development

When researching young children's play preferences, a significant issue to emerge was the difference between girls' and boys' dramatic role play themes (Browne 1999, 2004). Girls took on a wide range of roles in their role play including highly feminized characters such as princesses. In the case of boys, superhero play predominated (Browne 1999: 2004). These differences are important when we consider children's identity and their emotional development.

As a result of her extensive observations of children, Paley has concluded that there are few taboos in girls' play in terms of exploring emotions and relationships. With boys, the picture is somewhat different: 'When something makes a boy sad, he simply becomes a powerful superhero. He is not compelled to act out confusing events face-to-face, as are the girls' (Paley 1984: 111). In documenting her young grandson's play, Pidgeon (1993) felt that his superhero play did not develop the affective side of his understanding.

One view is that boys seek to overcome their feelings of anxiety and vulnerability through identification with superheroes. The question we need to ask ourselves is whether we want to encourage boys to feel that anxiety and vulnerability are not 'masculine' characteristics and that the best way of dealing with these feelings is to adopt identities that conform to hegemonic styles of masculinity.

Mac Naughton has argued that practitioners must:

> work hard to provide boys with understandings of masculinity in which dominance is not always seen as positive. They will also need to work equally hard to provide girls with understandings of femininity that enable them to assert their rights.

> (2000: 125–6)

By adopting a *laissez-faire* attitude towards children's dramatic role play, we are in danger of short-changing the children in our care as we are not enabling girls and boys to explore other ways of being through introducing children to alternative discourses they may choose to draw on in developing their identities. We need to provide children with the opportunity to make a range of choices and in so doing they may come to realize that although they may have a favourite dramatic play script or favourite story, there are a range of possible fantasies and roles that are satisfying in different ways and which can be turned to and enjoyed when they find that a different side of themselves is looking for fulfilment.

Behaviour issues

When children move from being cared for at home to attending an early years setting or school, they have to add another facet to their identities: that of the nursery child or school child. This identity is connected with gender because in learning how to position themselves as 'a pupil', children will be drawing on the familiar gender discourses they were introduced to at home or in their previous setting. The DfES has recognized that during transitions practitioners need to 'consider issues of identity' (DfES 2005: 17).

It has been argued that before children start in their new setting or school they have understandings about how they, as girls or boys, are supposed to behave and react:

> much of girls' social learning has introduced her to performances of submission, passivity and courtesy, much of boys' learning has been different. His learning is more likely to have introduced him to performances of activity and maverick individualism.

> (Gilbert and Gilbert 1998)

Research has certainly suggested that many children are introduced to dominant gender discourses very early in life. Parents, for example, tend to play more roughly with boys than with girls and offer them 'sex-typed' toys which serve to maintain 'sex-appropriate' play themes (Leaper and Gleason 1996).

If this is children's experience, then developing an identity of the 'good pupil' may prove more problematic for many boys. When a group of practitioners were asked to consider challenging behaviour and define what made an 'ideal' pupil, the response was:

> Ideal or well-adjusted children listened to and followed instructions, worked through tasks set, learned school routines and followed them, were anxious to please, sociable (but not too talkative) and possessed a suitable degree of independence. In contrast, children who were less confident or outgoing, wanted adult support or attention, did not pay attention to adults or the rules for classroom behaviour, did not want to do the work given and preferred to make their own choices were thought of as posing difficulties, for teachers and for themselves.
>
> (Stephen and Cope 2003b: 268)

Primary teachers in Stephen and Cope's survey (2003a) noted that children who were 'cheeky', who challenged rules or complained about rules and routines were less likely to establish positive relationships with the adults in the setting.

Recent research into challenging behaviour suggests that gender is a significant influencing factor in terms of children's behaviour and how they are labelled. The OfSTED Report, *Managing Challenging Behaviour* (2005) noted that in some early years settings up to 40% of the children have challenging behaviour. Furthermore, it was noted that:

> boys are more likely than girls to be defiant and both physically and verbally abusive ... Loud raucous behaviour by boys is often the focus of teachers' attention, while inappropriate behaviour by girls is sometimes unnoticed or ignored ... A significant proportion of pupils with challenging behaviour have poor language and social skills and limited concentration spans. This association is evident in all the early years settings and in three-quarters of the primary schools.
>
> (OfSTED 2005: 8–9)

Some early years practitioners were recently interviewed about their perceptions of children in general and, more specifically, how they perceived girls and boys (Browne 2004: 99–100). Only three out of the 75 interviewed felt that there were no discernible behavioural differences in the early years. The remainder made comments such as:

> Boys are more boisterous and interested in being noisy and running around. Girls are more able to sit and concentrate.
>
> (Nursery assistant)

> Generalizing, the 'rough' children in the classroom tend to be boys. Boys generally seem to be more energetic and less likely to start an activity.
>
> (Student teacher)

> Boys generally are more physical when they interact with their peers. Girls generally are more sensible and organized, enjoying reading, writing and drawing, organizing activities and mothering younger peers.
>
> (Childminder)

> Boys are more competitive, aggressive and confrontational. Boys are more interested in competition, mathematical and logical activities. Girls are more interested in interpersonal communication and aesthetics.
>
> (Student)

The ways in which we interpret children's behaviour clearly have an impact on how the children see themselves and play a part in determining the desirability of different positionings.

Reflection points

As practitioners we need to ask ourselves what styles of femininity and masculinity we are enabling children to explore. We also need to reflect on the consequences of positioning girls and boys in different ways.

6   Are we positioning boys as lively, noisy, messy, confrontational, aggressive, while simultaneously positioning those who conform to this form of masculinity as disruptive and challenging?

7   In so doing are we enabling or even encouraging boys to behave in challenging ways?
      The OfSTED report *Managing Challenging Behaviour* (2005) notes that the most common form of poor behaviour is what is regarded as 'low level disruption' that is perpetrated more often by boys than by girls. This low level disruption consists of 'talking out of turn ... hindering the work of others, being rowdy and making inappropriate remarks' (OfSTED 2005: 5).

8   Do we discourage girls from being assertive, lively and physical by positioning 'good' girls as helpful, thoughtful and quiet?

Harrison's (2004) study is thought-provoking in that it provides insights into how young children experience gender stereotyping from a very young age in school. The children's perceptions were compared with their teachers' assessments of each child's competencies (e.g. good peer social skills, ability to concentrate on and complete tasks and the ability to work without adult support) and school-related challenging behaviour (e.g. aggression and dis-ruptiveness, withdrawal and timidity, lack of motivation, difficulty in fol-lowing instructions, etc.). Among other things, the study revealed that boys who said they liked playing at school were viewed as confident and task-orientated, while girls who enjoyed playing were described as lacking con-fidence and having poorer task-orientated skills.

Harrison has suggested that the teachers were stereotyping the girls in that they positioned girls who are school-work orientated as girls who were behaving 'properly', and therefore described them in positive terms. Girls who are more interested in playing are seen to be not behaving as girls should and are therefore positioned and described in negative ways. It would appear that the practitioners were engaged in a degree of category maintenance work in that girls who had not positioned themselves 'correctly' and conformed to gender-appropriate behaviour were criticized.

Practitioners need to consider how their practice and provision are shaped by discourses that impact on expectations about children's behaviour and adults' responses to children. Reflecting on how dominant discourses within the setting can result in challenging behaviour and why certain groups of children may seem to be 'challenging', helps to move the 'problem' away from the child and to provide alternative ways of looking to deal with young children's challenging behaviour.

Conclusion

If we want to ensure that our settings and schools enable all children to learn and grow in supportive environments, we need to be aware of the central role 'identity' plays in children's learning and development. In this chapter, we have looked at the issues and challenges related to how children draw on different masculinities and femininities in developing their identities. Early years and primary settings need to ensure that children gain emotional satisfaction from the positions they adopt. The challenge for the practitioner lies in providing opportunities for children to explore diverse forms of fem-ininity and masculinity. In practice, this means, for example, that both girls and boys need to have opportunities to be caring, assertive, sensitive, reflec-tive, adventurous, daring, willing to take risks and to talk about or express their feelings in a range of ways.

Self-identity and self-esteem are closely linked. When children are developing their identity, they are learning to see themselves as others see them. Self-esteem is the value placed on one's own identity. Just as self-identities are shifting and changing, so too does someone's self-esteem. A child may feel very valued in one context but less so in another. These changes in self-esteem will be related to how others respond to the child. If a child feels that important adults in their lives care about them, value them and accept them as they are, the child is likely to have a high level of self-esteem. In order to support children as they develop their sense of self and ensure their self-esteem remains high, practitioners need to be aware of and be sensitive to the discourses children have access to in order to better understand the ways children are choosing to position themselves or are being positioned by others. Practitioners also need to bear in mind the multi-faceted, fluid nature of identity and work to provide children with access to a wide range of discourses and 'ways of being'.

Points for further discussion

- What strategies could you implement to find out more about how young children position themselves and about the range of identities they are developing?
- What strategies do you have in place to help you discover more about the diverse range of discourses to which children in your setting have access?
- In what ways can early years practitioners enable children to explore and develop their sense of self by encouraging children to investigate different 'ways of being'?

References and further reading

Bilton, T., Bonnett, K. and Jones, P. (1996) *Introductory Sociology*. London: Macmillan.

Browne, N. (1999) *Young Children's Literacy Development and the Role of Televisual Texts*. London: Falmer Press.

Browne, N. (2004) *Gender Equity in the Early Years*. Maidenhead: Open University Press.

Connell, R.W. (1987) *Gender and Power*. Stanford, CA: Stanford University Press.

Connell, R.W. (1995) *Masculinities*. Berkeley, CA: University of California Press.

Connell, R.W. (2000) *The Men and the Boys*. St Leonards, NSW: Allen and Unwin.

Cowie, H., Boardman, C., Dawkins, J. and Jennifer, D. (2004) *Emotional Health and Well-Being: A Practical Guide for Schools*. London: Paul Chapman.

Dahlberg, G., Moss, P. and Pence, A. (1999) *Beyond Quality in Early Childhood Education and Care: Postmodern Perspectives*. London: Falmer Press.

Davies, B. (1989a) The discursive production of the male/female dualism in school settings, *Oxford Review of Education*, 15(3): 229–41.

Davies, B. (1989b) *Frogs and Snails and Feminist Tales: Pre-school Children and Gender*. Sydney: Allen and Unwin.

DfES (Department for Education and Skills) (2005) *The Common Core of Skills and Knowledge for the Children's Workforce*. London: DfES.

Dorais, L-J. (1995) Language, culture and identity: some Inuit examples, *The Canadian Journal of Native Studies*, 15: 293–308.

Dowling, M. (2000) *Young Children's Personal, Social and Emotional Development*. London: Paul Chapman.

Foucault, M. (1980) *Power/Knowledge: Selected Interviews and Other Writings, 1972–1977*. London: Harvester Wheatsheaf.

Gilbert, R. and Gilbert, P. (1998) *Masculinity Goes to School*. St Leonards, NSW: Allen and Unwin.

Harrison, L.J. (2004) Do children's perceptions of themselves, their teachers, and school accord with their teachers' ratings of their adjustment to school? Paper presented to the Australian Association for Research in Education National Conference. Melbourne, 29 Nov.–2 Dec, 2004. Available at: www.aare.edu.au/04pap/har04829.pdf (accessed 31 October 2006).

Leaper, C. and Gleason, J.B. (1996) The relationship of play activity and gender to parent and child sex-typed communication, *International Journal of Behavioural Development*, 19: 689–703.

Mac Naughton, G. (2000) *Rethinking Gender in Early Childhood Education*. London: Paul Chapman Publishing.

OfSTED (2005) *Managing Challenging Behaviour*. London: OfSTED.

Paley, V.G. (1984) *Boys and Girls: Superheroes in the Doll Corner*. Chicago: University of Chicago Press.

Pidgeon, S. (1993) Superhero or prince, in M. Barrs and S. Pidgeon (eds) *Reading the Difference: Gender and Reading in the Primary School*. London: Centre for Language in Primary Education.

Rowan, L., Knobel, M., Bigum, C. and Lankshear, C. (2002) *Boys, Literacies and Schooling: The Dangerous Territories of Gender-based Literacy Reform*. Buckingham: Open University Press.

Stephen, C. and Cope, P. (2003a) *Moving on to Primary 1: An Exploratory Study of the Experience of Transition from Pre-School to Primary*, Insight 3. Edinburgh: Scottish Executive Education Department.

Stephen, C. and Cope, P. (2003b) An inclusive perspective on transition to primary school, *European Educational Research Journal*, 2(2): 263–76.

Sure Start/DfES (2002) *Birth-to-Three Matters Framework*. London: Sure Start/DfES.

Sure Start/DfES (2005) *Introduction to the Framework (Birth-to-Three)*. London: Sure Start/DfES.

Weedon, C. (1987) *Feminist Practice and Post-Structuralist Theory*. Oxford: Basil Blackwell.

SECTION TWO
POSITIVE RELATIONSHIPS

Introduction to Section Two

Janet Moyles

Children learn to be strong and independent from a base of loving and secure relationships with parents and/or a key person.

(EYFS Principle 2)

Relationships are at the heart of effective education and care and nowhere more so than for babies and young children who, for the most part, are totally dependent on adults for their nurture and well-being. To 'empower' relationships means to do everything one can to ensure that communication, interaction and rapport are effective and successful for all those involved in education and care both within and outside the setting and across the wider 'educare' community (see e.g. Chandler 2006; Hawker 2006). It is perhaps not surprising that early years student teachers have always found the sheer numbers of people potentially involved in the early years, and the range of backgrounds and disciplines from which they come, as difficult to conceptualize.

Relationships between involved adults depend on trust, effective communication and a shared understanding of how we believe our youngest children should experience their highly formative years (Selleck et al. 2003). If we believe that children's lives should be fun, cognitively and physically challenging and full of love, for example, then we will all work to provide an environment which fulfils this ambition. Interpretation of such documents as the *Early Years Foundation Stage* and *Every Child Matters* is not just a matter of reading the words but agreeing on what they mean to all those involved in a particular setting and planning accordingly. Concordance demands time, effort, give-and-take, good humour, knowledge, a willingness to learn from others and strong leadership in the setting to keep it all together (Moyles 2006), to name but a few issues.

To promote and enhance young children's development and learning alongside parents, practitioners must understand, respect and manage a broader range of cultural and ethnic backgrounds than ever before (Siraj-Blatchford and Clarke 2000; Wolpert 2005). Interactions with parents and children must be positive – leave the 'blame culture' behind: trust is only achieved through honesty, genuine communication and sincere respect. As the document *Key Elements of Effective Practice* (DfES 2005: 5) stresses, 'Effective practitioners use their own learning to improve their work with young children and their families in ways which are sensitive, positive and non-judgemental.'

Listening skills are paramount for everyone, especially listening to children (Clark and Moss 2001), one major source of assessment information. Effective teaching requires practitioners to reflect conscientiously and carefully upon their own roles, especially the impact of their interactions with children, parents and colleagues (see e.g. Atkinson and Claxton 2000; Moyles et al. 2002; Ghaye and Ghaye 2004; Adams 2006). Interactions with children are known to be supported by 'shared sustained thinking', the phrase adopted by policy-makers from the *Effective Pre-School Provision* project (DfES 2004).

Relationships are inevitably fluid and flexible and will not always go smoothly, however hard we try! Children, practitioners and parents need to learn that it is acceptable to make mistakes, that these are an integral and genuine part of overall learning. Making mistakes together ensures that both see the learning potential in this situation and the deliberate opportunities playful approaches provide for everyone in retaining self-esteem. The fine line between interacting, intervening and interfering are also worth some discussion if harmony is to prevail: everyone has a different way of approaching their roles and tasks and no one way is ever going to suit all children and all situations.

In this section there are five chapters exploring just some of the issues embedded within the heading 'Positive Relationships'. In Chapter 5, Pat Broadhead uses some of her research to explore the importance of practitioners talking, working and planning together to support children's progress in learning through play. The need for practitioners to review and evaluate practice jointly, ensuring particular support for children with emotional and developmental needs is highlighted. Parent views and partnerships are the focus of Emmie Short's chapter. In Chapter 6, Emmie writes of her concerns about current early years provision and the urgent need to review our understanding of children and childhoods in the twenty-first century. As she says, 'Our children cannot choose the kind of world into which they are born, but depend on adults to make the right decisions for them.' She urges everyone involved in children's education and care to evaluate and, where relevant, challenge current policies on behalf of young children.

The challenge in Chapter 6 is a huge and distressing one: Rose Griffiths writes about the influences on children of a bereavement or other kind of loss in families and the vital role of significant others in the lives of children so affected. The death of a close relative is not something that occurs with regularity for young children, thank goodness, but from Rose's research it would seem that up to 8% of children under 8 years may experience bereavement through the death of a parent or sibling. It is clear that children can also suffer similar trauma when, for example, families split up or children are taken into care and a loved parent or sibling may no longer be regularly available. The importance of secure attachments and shared care is emphasized and clearly perceptive communication between all those involved can help alleviate some of the child's pain.

In Chapter 8, the role of mentor teachers in early years settings is outlined and analysed by Jackie Eyles, a mentor teacher herself. Her vital role, as she sees it, is to encourage and promote self-evaluation and critical reflection among practitioners and to offer help with planning, assessment and personal action planning in support of children's learning and development, in this way empowering practitioners and raising their self-esteem.

In the final chapter in this section, Tricia David considers how early years education and care have changed in the past few years and how, in particular, practitioners' roles have become increasingly more complex. She emphasizes the skilled nature of caring for and educating under-3s in particular and how competence in the practitioner role depends not only on responsiveness and instinct but also on training and qualifications.

Professional relationships and respect for others feature prominently in this section. There is so much more that could be said about empowerment and high quality interactions and we touch on these again in the third part of the book.

References

Adams, S. (2006) Practitioners and play: reflecting in a different way, in J. Moyles (ed.) *The Excellence of Play*, 2nd edn. Maidenhead: Open University Press.

Atkinson, T. and Claxton, G. (eds) (2000) *The Intuitive Practitioner*. Buckingham: Open University Press.

Chandler, T. (2006) Working in multi-disciplinary teams, in G. Pugh and B. Duffy (eds) *Contemporary Issues in the Early Years*, 4th edn. London: Paul Chapman.

Clark, A. and Moss, P. (2001) *Listening to Young Children: The Mosaic Approach*. London: National Children's Bureau.

DfES (2004) *The Effective Provision of Pre-School Education Project: Findings from Pre-School to End of Key Stage 1. Final Report*. London: DfES/SureStart.

DfES (2005) *KEEP: Key Elements of Effective Practice*. London: DfES/SureStart.

Ghaye, A. and Ghaye, K. (2004) *Teaching and Learning Through Critical Reflective Practice*, 2nd edn. London: David Fulton.

Hawker, D. (2006) Joined-up working in the development of children's services, in G. Pugh and B. Duffy (eds) *Contemporary Issues in the Early Years*, 4th edn. London: Paul Chapman.

Moyles, J. (2006) *Effective Leadership and Management in the Early Years*. Maidenhead: Open University Press.

Moyles, J. and Adams, S. (2001) *StEPs: Statements of Entitlement to Play*. Buckingham: Open University Press.

Moyles, J., Adams, S. and Musgrove, A. (2002) *SPEEL: Study of Pedagogical Effectiveness in Early Learning*. Report No. 363. London: DfES.

Pugh, G. and Duffy, B. (eds) (2006) *Contemporary Issues in the Early Years*, 4th edn. London: Paul Chapman.

Selleck, D., Goldschmeid, E. and Elfer, P. (eds) (2003) *Key Persons in the Nursery: Building Relationships for Quality Provision*. London: David Fulton.

Siraj-Blatchford, I. and Clarke, P. (2000) *Supporting Identity, Diversity and Language in the Early Years*. Buckingham: Open University Press.

Wolpert, E. (2005) *Start Seeing Diversity: The Basic Guide to an Anti-Bias Classroom*. St Paul, MN; Redleaf Press.

5   Working together to support playful learning and transition

Pat Broadhead

Abstract

This chapter focuses on practitioner research into playful learning in two schools: in nursery, Year R and Year 1. The chapter examines how a culture of collegiate co-operation might be engendered to create and sustain playful learning environments for children while also supporting the development of a deep understanding of how children's play progresses in educational contexts as they become older and more experienced players and learners.

Introduction

The 1990s brought about a gradual but relentless diminishing of the status of play both within Year R and Key Stage 1 classrooms and, in parallel, within the curricula of early years teacher education courses around the country. This was due, in part, to the increasingly teacher-directed approaches to teaching and learning arising from the implementation of the National Curriculum and the associated rise of subject-specific learning. This accelerated as Standard Assessment Tasks – as first named, prior to being re-labelled 'Tests' – also came on stream. Readers may recall that when first proposed, it was envisaged that SATs would 'task/test' every subject of the curriculum. As we know, some rapid slimming down was undertaken but the era of accountability through testing children was taking hold. The culture in a majority of infant and primary schools changed to accommodate this new climate and in this competitive era of league tables, teacher-directed learning began to dominate as an ethos of play and child-directed investigation diminished (David 1999).

The diminishing of play was also accelerated by the demands to implement the never-statutory literacy and numeracy strategies. As with the pressure to prepare children for SATs at age 6/7, so too, the pressures to 'do the hour' was manifest in a majority of reception classrooms. In many cases, this was because the local authority teams implementing the strategies were separate from the early years' teams and were largely unfamiliar with the culture and ethos of the reception classroom as a site for learning through play.

This diminishing was further exacerbated by the introduction of Baseline Assessment for reception classes. In its first manifestation it took place within 14 weeks of the 4-year-olds' entry into reception; it breathed the air of accountability and it was within this context that reception teachers were trained for implementation. While Baseline Assessment was to be substantially reviewed and changed, being subsequently located at the end of the reception year, this was one more nail in the coffin of play-based learning. The 4-year-olds in reception classrooms have hovered between the culture of nursery education and that of formal schooling but during this era, they were scooped into the formal schooling pool despite studies showing the detrimental impact (Bennett and Kell 1989; Cleave and Brown 1991) of 'too formal too soon' (Sylva 1991).

The school day became crowded with subjects (the National Curriculum was revised three times to address this but never quite made it) and alongside this, the punitive OfSTED regime was impacting on the curriculum in schools as well as the curriculum in teacher education (Jeffery and Woods 1998). Where play survived during these years – and it did survive – it did so because strong-minded individuals fought a rearguard action to keep it alive in their research as academics and as educators in the classroom, because well-informed head teachers promoted play and because local authority staff kept the debates open with colleagues and simultaneously nurtured good examples in local nurseries and schools. Professional development opportunities during these years rarely focused on the theory and pedagogy of learning through play where we know teachers need support (Wood and Bennett 2000; Moyles et al. 2002). This reception teacher involved in research in the late 1990s commented:

> I feel I am being pushed in many ways by target setting, of getting the children to a certain standard, ready to access National Curriculum at level 1. I feel I am being pushed by the government in one way – you must get children doing this – but feel that little children shouldn't be doing this until they are ready. I do feel that we push children into formal work far too early and I hope that a review of the learning goals will bring more flexibility for reception teachers to interpret the curriculum a way that suits the needs of children.

Reflection point

1   Does this statement have resonance for you? Does this account of the diminishing of play hold true?

She was reflecting at a time when we were awaiting the curriculum to replace the *Desirable Outcomes for Children's Learning* (DfEE 1998). However, the *Curriculum Guidance for the Foundation Stage* (QCA/DfEE 2000) had little to say about play. There was a brief mention in the principles:

> There should be opportunities for children to engage in activities planned by adults and also those that they plan or initiate themselves. Children do not make a distinction between 'play' and 'work' and neither should practitioners. Children need time to become engrossed, work in depth and complete activities.
>
> (2000: 11)

Following on was a brief section on p. 25 in which the authors elaborated with exemplars within the Areas of Learning. However, it has been recognized that the prevailing climate of measurement and accountability within which this curriculum was delivered steered early years practitioners towards the *Stepping Stones* – the early learning goals – rather than towards the exemplars for practice. Ultimately, the document represented a narrow depiction of young children's capacities and capabilities (Broadhead 2006).

The emerging curriculum for birth–5, the *Early Years Foundation Stage* (EYFS) (DfES 2006) is seeking to embrace play, exploration and problem-solving in an integrated way recognizing it as the basis for learning. *The Childcare Bill* (HL Bill 85 2006) enshrines the importance of care and learning in the early years within legislation for the first time in this country and, along with the agenda emerging from *Every Child Matters* Green Paper (DfES 2003), a new spirit of 'child-focus' and 'the rights of the child' is gaining sway. EYFS is substantially influenced by *Birth-to-Three Matters* (Sure Start 2002) with its emphasis on conceiving the learning environment as meeting the child's potential and entitlement as an initiator of learning.

The debates on EYFS are on-going. Many would like to see a higher profile for play; some would like a stronger acknowledgement of the pedagogical challenges in creating a co-constructed curriculum with play at its heart. Many feel that insufficient attention has been given to the varying cultural experiences of young children that they bring into their early years settings. They ask whether this new curriculum is doing enough to demonstrate the need for educators to actively engage with every child's cultural and ethnic heritage through curricular provision.

Reflection points

2   How far do you think teachers and other educators have been able to develop their approaches to learning through play?

3   How far do you feel children's ethnic and cultural heritage is reflected in the play-based learning in your school?
4   If play is valued in your school, where is it valued? Can this be extended and how do you think the children would benefit?

Playful learning and transition

It is within these contexts and against this background that I have been engaging with early years educators in educational settings to research children's learning through play both prior to and throughout this period of change in policy and practice, a period that many believe has seen a detrimental impact on the learning environment for young children. In the remainder of this chapter, the aim is to focus on more recent work in two schools to explore aspects of working together to bring about playful learning.

In one school – pseudonym Purple School – the research has been undertaken in the nursery and Year R classes and has seen new approaches to classroom-based provision and to supporting transition emerge for a teacher from Year R and a nursery nurse from the nursery. In the second school – Blue School – the research has been undertaken in the nursery, Year R and Year 1 and has also seen new approaches to provision and debates about supporting children's transitions. These approaches are reflected both in changes in practice and as reflective conversations leading to changes in understanding about the nature of learning through play. The two schools are in different parts of England; each is a 3–11 primary school and both serve communities with high levels of economic deprivation.

The on-going research, within which these two schools are participating, dates back over 20 years (Broadhead 1986, 1997, 2001, 2004, 2006). It has sought to illuminate children's learning through play with peers in classroom settings. From earlier phases of the research an observational tool emerged: the Social Play Continuum (SPC).[1] This describes children's action and language in four progressive domains of sociability:

- Associative Domain
- Social Domain
- Highly Social Domain
- Co-operative Domain.

The Co-operative Domain is characterized by high levels of cognitive activity such as problem-setting and solving, a shared understanding of goals and sustained dialogue supporting the development of play themes, plus other characteristics. The SPC was used to support all observations of children's play across the age ranges of the two schools and thus brings some degree of comparability to the data. Use of the SPC underpins judgements about the domains in which the observed play is located and supports reflections by observers on the pedagogical steps to promote play in the Co-operative Domain. Observations do not categorize individual children but do reveal which children are skilful at introducing and developing play themes to create momentum and high levels of reciprocity among interacting peers to take the play into the Co-operative Domain. The research watches children playing with peers, and its interpretation and reflection on the observations stimulate insights for pedagogy; this has always been the key thrust of the research.

Researching with practitioners in Purple School

Joint observations using the SPC were undertaken in Purple School in the nursery with Diane and in the reception class with Jenny. I had become involved with the school because they had been looking for someone with whom to work in relation to concerns about the increasing levels of conflict among pupils, across the school. In discussions with the head and senior staff, it appeared there was something I could offer in the early years around play-based learning. A meeting with the nursery nurse leading in the nursery and the Year R teacher revealed their interest. I secured a small grant from a funding body[2] and we began paired observations. We based observations on the five areas wherein the research has always focused:

- large construction;
- small construction and small world;
- sand play;
- water play;
- role play.

These are areas of provision that have potential for bringing interacting peers together in traditionally resourced early years settings. The nursery was resourced with this play provision but the reception class lacked almost all of it – a legacy of the prevailing culture. The reception teacher borrowed materials from the nursery. She also brought small world materials from home where she had daughters. This skewed the gendered nature of the resources; however, she supplemented where she could and observations began.

One of our earliest findings was to note that the levels of play in the *Highly Social* and *Co-operative Domains* were higher in the nursery setting than in Year R – these domains, it should be recalled, have higher levels of cognitive challenge for interacting peers. In effect, the nursery children were more expert players, quite possibly because they had had constant and extended access to the full range of play materials being observed; the nursery children were more likely to engage at a higher intellectual level in their play, their use of language and their capacities for problem-setting and solving were all greater than that being exhibited by the reception children. Therefore, we could not claim that it was the children's social background and home experiences holding them back. Nor could we claim that a level of chronological maturity was necessary to engender play in these cognitively challenging domains.

As the research progressed, the nursery nurse and the Year R teacher took time to observe in each other's classrooms. The Year R teacher confirmed that what she was seeing was a more challenging and engaged level of play in the nursery than observed in Year R; she also gained insights into resourcing areas of play provision. The nursery nurse, with great sensitivity, commented that she felt that the reception children who had been in nursery the previous year appeared to be losing their ability to engage in extended play activities. We reflected together on the long-standing impact of the policy imperatives in previous years and explored their potentially detrimental impact on how practice had been shaping in the reception classroom. The Year R teacher recalled her own initial teacher training and the emphasis on play and how she had felt unable to sustain such a learning environment in more recent years. Her own day at this time was peppered with the literacy and numeracy requirements; she also shared her own deep concerns about the many behavioural difficulties that children were exhibiting in their formal learning environment, echoing comments from the teacher quoted above. Many of the children had considerable difficulties within their home environments, reflecting their families' low incomes, poverty and associated circumstances but it also became apparent that despite these factors, the nursery children were playing at a higher level of cognitive challenge, of engagement and of purposefulness.

At this time in the research, I introduced Diane and Jenny to the 'whatever you want it to be place'. This is an open-ended approach to role play provision that grew out of an extended research period with Year R teachers in York schools (Broadhead 2004). The underpinning rationale is that if non-themed and flexible resources are provided for children, they draw on their own ideas and experiences; this is more likely to sustain the growth of momentum and reciprocity. Earlier research had shown that children draw these themes from a wide range of inputs, from their curricular experiences in school, from the media, from experiences at home and with parents and carers outside the home and from their local community experiences. The York research had shown a potential for open-ended play provision (named as 'the whatever you want it to be place' by one 5-year-old – 'Because it can be whatever you want') to stimulate play in the *Co-operative Domain*. However, it has many pedagogical challenges for practitioners who are more familiar with the provision of themed play areas, such as the home corner, the hospital, the café, the travel agent, etc. However, I am not claiming that themed forms of provision are redundant.

Both Diane and Jenny established the area. Diane established it in the nursery with cardboard boxes and pieces of fabric and other resources and we began to see its positive impact on children's play. Interestingly, we did not see the same impact when the resources were taken outside during the long summer of 2006. In our joint research, we noted that once outside, the resources were scattered. This started us reflecting on the extent to which it was the *collective* impact of the open-ended resources that prompted co-operation. At the same time, Jenny in Year R began working with her newly appointed colleague in reception, Abbey. Abbey had taken an interest in the on-going research as she came into post and thought that 'the whatever you want it to be place' was 'a great idea'. Jenny and Abbey began developing it within an extended corridor alongside the two reception bases. I worked with them to think about the organization of access to the area for the children in each of the two bases. The continuing research fed into their reflections about how to sustain and develop the area and about how to justify and explain its purpose and potential to parents and colleagues in school; something that they felt was extremely important as this extended area looked very unlike anything else in school. During this period of development, they engaged in opportunistic discussion with Diane in nursery and gradually, it emerged that they were seeking a seamless development of play provision for children from nursery into reception; to ensure that reception was not just replicating nursery but was offering a greater challenge to these older and more experienced players.

Alongside this, as Abbey and Jenny re-conceptualized the learning spaces in reception, with play at the forefront, so Diane began to re-conceptualize the spaces she had access to and the associated routines she had maintained for the children over a number of years in nursery. The on-going research and the associated reflective conversations with the researcher and with her colleagues were beginning to stimulate new kinds of thinking and understanding about children's learning through play, and, in parallel to this, re-conceptualizations of the nursery learning spaces.

The nursery was located in two good-sized rooms. Diane had, for a long time, conceived of one room as a space for adult-initiated activity with small groups alongside some self-selected activity. This was mainly but not solely table-based. The second room was where solely child-initiated play was supported, a space that had remained looking much the same in design terms for an extended period. Children's access to these spaces was determined by well-established daily routines. After seeing the impact of 'the whatever you want it to be place' on the quality and purposefulness of children's play and after watching and discussing with Abbey and Jenny their own re-designing of the learning spaces, Diane began to think differently, to conceive of a new approach to pedagogy, born of her own growing understanding of learning through play. She began to think about what she had learned about children's engagements with each other and with their environment in 'the whatever you want it to be place' might help her to achieve two goals:

1   To turn the whole of one of the play spaces into a 'whatever you want it to be place', building on what she had learned about the positive impact of flexible resources. The notion of a 'whatever you want it to be room' was an exciting development for the research overall moving it beyond the idea of an 'area of provision'.

2   The second goal concerned a more fundamental re-structuring of the daily routines, to resonate with what Diane had learned about the children's abilities to self-direct, self-select and focus in a more open-ended learning environment. Diane was looking to restructure the whole experience for children and to allow greater opportunities for adults and children to together construct the curricular experiences in a more integrated and self-directed rather than teacher-directed way.

In both the nursery and the reception classes, new approaches to learning through play emerged; together, the respective educators were thinking about what this would mean in terms of building on the achievements of children in the nursery setting as they progressed into reception. Their structuring of the learning through children's play experiences was inter-connecting through the adults' shared experiences and reflections as practitioner-researchers.

Researching with practitioners in Blue School

Blue School had supported play-based learning for children throughout the long days of its disappearance nationally. Some of the early stages of my own research had been conducted in the nursery there many years previously. An opportunity presented itself to work with them once again, introducing some of the more recent developments arising from the research, including the 'whatever you want it to be place'. I visited the school and spoke to the head about the development of the work from those early days and she asked the nursery, Year R and Year 1 teachers if they were interested in getting involved. They all agreed. The two Year 1 teachers felt that the research would be a challenge for them as they felt they had little experience of offering a curriculum that placed substantial value on playful learning; they were more familiar with a teacher-directed day. However, the positive ethos of the school towards play was sufficient to encourage them to grasp the nettle.

The 'whatever you want it to be place' had little impact in the nursery. In effect, what the nursery staff had already achieved was that which Diane above was in the process of implementing – the whole nursery in Blue School was a 'whatever you want it to be place' where the interconnections between children's play and learning were well understood and continually applied.

The Year 1 teachers established the 'whatever you want it to be place' in an enclosed outdoor area and observations began. One essential element of this concept is the opportunity for children to create enclosed spaces or dens which become the sites of their play themes; the same enclosure can progress from being a home, to a shop, to a hospital as the play themes and associated ideas emerge and either take root and begin to build momentum or move on to reflect new ideas. When the momentum begins to build, the progression towards the Highly Social and Co-operative Domains also becomes manifest, otherwise the play may remain in the Social Domain, as it changes but does not necessarily develop. These enclosures might come through cardboard boxes or frames that support fabric to makes tents or dens. The Year 1 children had access to long, foam tubes which when curved and placed in empty milk crates could support pieces of fabric; many of the original resources in the early stages of our joint research provided for the Year 1 children came from the nursery where the staff had had long experience of open-ended provision; they were pleased to be able to share this expertise with colleagues to support the transition of play into this older age range.

The Year 1 teachers found the observations surprising and enlightening and began to understand the potential of the space in relation to learning through play. They began to see evidence of children's problem-solving in how they were using these materials and began also to reflect on the impact of the children's earlier nursery experiences in the development of these skills – which previously, they would not have had a chance to extend in the Year 1 classroom. The two teachers decided to take the space indoors for the new school year and also began thinking about ways to introduce other learning through play activities into the classrooms and simultaneously, to think about re-structuring the school day to accommodate these activities alongside their teacher-directed activities.

As a new school year began, the experienced nursery teacher was to take her knowledge of learning through play into the reception classroom, a large base with two teachers and support staff. She introduced 'the whatever you want it to be place' into the classroom, talked about the idea of a space where the children's ideas were important and invited them to think of a name for it. At circle time, they discussed the space, what they would need and what might go into it. As they began to understand the concept, one child said:

'We could put chairs to watch' (something children often do, almost as if watching a performance) and when talking about what was needed, another child said 'Things to make a tent'. The discussion had continued with another child saying they 'must take off shoes or we'll get hurt' and when prompted to think of a name for it the conversation had involved across several children:

- Imagine ... like on CBBC;
- the imagination space;
- the magical circle;
- a princess corner;
- the other room;
- the magical thinking area.

It was finally called The Magical Area and located in one of the bases, where interestingly, it was played in mainly by boys. When the staff re-located it to see the effects of a new location, it was mainly girls that were using it. Interestingly, Diane had noticed something similar in her re-location of 'the whatever you want it to be place' in Purple Nursery. When indoors and sited near the brick area, the boys had been more inclined to play in the area. When located outside and in close proximity to home play resources, the girls had played there more frequently. Throughout the research, there have been many interesting aspects of gender to explore and reflect upon, including the adult's role in encouraging mixed gender play.

The focus on learning through play built around 'the whatever you want it to be place' is on-going in both schools. Quite recently, I undertook observations in Blue School, Year R. One of the activities observed was the use of large bricks to create a platform by two girls. They, and later two others, used the platform as a site for writing and talking over a half-hour period. This included occasionally re-designing the bricks and settling down again to more writing and talking. At another point, two children entered the area, one of whom began 'reading' a story to another child, clearly a familiar book. I commented to Angie, the teacher: 'It was lovely to watch; it made me think that now they have the literacy day rather than the literacy hour.' She gave a rueful smile and went on to tell me that the school had become involved in the rolling out of synthetic phonics. One of the trainers had visited the reception classroom to talk about the work. Angie felt that, overall, the comments he was making suggested to her that he thought that this was not a classroom in which children were currently learning to read. It made us both reflect on how secure the learning through play environment might be in our early years settings.

Providing for learning through play in early years settings

In bringing back play into their early years settings, these educators have benefited from a collegiate approach based on the observation of play and the development of a reflective culture – watching play, interpreting and reflecting on children's engagement and considering how the play provision might be developed. They have started to understand play as an integral part of the classroom and learning experience for children and not as something offered as a reward or a time filler when 'work is done'. They have seen previously unacknowledged skills and knowledge used by children cooperatively and creatively and they have gained insights into the children's cultural heritage and interests, as expressed through their play.

Reflection points

5   How often do you observe the children's play and reflect on children's interests and knowledge?

6   How often do you talk with colleagues about how the play provision on offer might be developed, based on those observations?

7   Are there ways in which the school might support joint observations of play to assist reflective, collegiate dialogues on learning though play alongside the implication for transition?

In each of the classrooms, the development of an open-ended role play area assisted insights for educators into learning through play. They used cardboard boxes, sturdy wooden clothes-horses and long foam tubes with large pieces of fabric to allow children to build dens and enclosures. They provided many types of fabric to allow children to create characters in their play; they provided literacy materials to allow children to write, make posters, make books, etc. as an integral part of their play. They discussed the play themes that emerged and reflected on the implications for curriculum development by integrating these themes. For example, if a hospital theme emerged in the play, they talked to the children about what other resources might be useful for them; they located related books around the area and read with the children.

Reflection points

8   Do you know which of the play areas you provide have greatest potential for promoting co-operative play among peers?

9   What kinds of things do children learn from one another when they co-operate in their play?

---

10   How often do you review or develop the play areas based on your knowledge of the children's interests or do play areas emerge largely from your own decisions about themed areas?

In engaging with debates about play, based on their own research and observations, these teachers and nursery nurses also began to think about the meaning of a co-constructed curriculum and began to see the classroom as a place where the adults' responsibility to teach can sit alongside the child's ability to bring their own world into the classroom through play. They began to re-conceive play as something that belongs to the children rather than something that is provided by adults and also began to think of ways of engaging with children in designing the learning environment – re-call the children's naming of the open-ended play space in Blue School's reception classroom as 'The Magical Area'.

Points to consider

- Think about establishing an open-ended role play area; perhaps do as Blue School did and develop it in nursery, Year R and Year 1. Share ideas about what to use; share insights into how children use the space; discuss the organizational challenges it presents or perhaps any responses from parents or colleagues.
- Examine your own feelings about apparent untidiness or 'noise'. Children come to understand that resources warrant respect and that responsibility for tidying is theirs – however young they are – if adults give consistent and illustrative guidance: share ideas on achieving this. Often, on closer scrutiny, 'noise' reveals itself as integral to the play and it's only deemed noise by adults.
- Think creatively and laterally about perceived difficulties and discuss them with colleagues to support a resolution to the implementation of a new idea that suits both you and the children.

Notes

1   The Social Play Continuum (SPC) is available online at http://www.routledge.com/textbooks/0415303397/resources/.
2   Thanks and appreciation to the Vicky Hurst Trust for two grants to support this on-going work in these two schools.

References and further reading

Bennett, N. and Kell, J. (1989) *A Good Start? Four Year Olds in School*. Oxford: Blackwell.

Broadhead, P. (1986) *A Continuum of Social Play in the Early Years*. Sheffield Educational Research Current Highlights 8: October.

Broadhead, P. (1997) Promoting sociability and co-operation in nursery settings, *British Educational Research Journal*, 23(4): 513–31.

Broadhead, P. (2001) Investigating sociability and cooperation in four and five year olds in reception class settings, *International Journal of Early Years Education*, 9(1): 23–35.

Broadhead, P. (2004) *Early Years Play and Learning: Developing Social Skills and Cooperation*. London: Routledge/Falmer.

Broadhead, P. (2006) Developing an understanding of young children's learning through play: the place of observation, interaction and reflection, *British Educational Research Journal*, 32(2): 191–207.

Cleave, S. and Brown, S. (1991) *Early to School: Four Year Olds in Infant Classes*. Windsor: NFER-Nelson.

David, T. (ed.) (1999) *Young Children Learning*. London: Paul Chapman Publishing.

DfEE (Department for Education and Employment) (1998) *Desirable Outcomes for Children's Learning*. London: HMSO.

DfES (Department for Education and Skills) (2003) *Every Child Matters* (Green Paper). London: HMSO.

DfES (2006) *The Early Years Foundation Stage: Consultation on a Single Quality Framework for Services to Children from Birth to Five*. Nottingham: DfES Publications.

HL Bill 85 (2006) *The Childcare Bill*. London: The Stationery Office.

Jeffery, B. and Woods, P. (1998) *Testing Teachers*. London: Falmer Press.

Moyles, J., Adams, S. and Musgrove, A. (2002) *SPEEL: Study of Pedagogical Effectiveness in Early Learning*. Report No. 363. London: DfES.

Qualifications and Curriculum Authority (QCA)/Department for Education and Employment (DfEE) (2000) *Curriculum Guidance for the Foundation Stage*. London: QCA/DfEE.

Sure Start Unit (2002) *Birth-to-Three Matters: A Framework to Support Children in their Earliest Years*. London: DfES.

Sylva, K. (1991) Educational aspects of daycare in England and Wales, in P. Moss and E. Melhuish (eds) *Current Issues in Daycare for Young Children*. London: HMSO.

Wood, E. and Bennett, N. (2000) Changing theories; changing practice: exploring early childhood teachers' professional learning, *Teaching and Teacher Education*, 16: 635–47.

6   Somebody else's business
A parent's view of childhood

Emmie Short

Abstract

This chapter, written by a parent and childminder, explores the current situation in the UK regarding how, as a society, we view children and childhood and whether we should be doing things differently for the current generation. The present political and social context of today's childhood is critiqued and found to be wanting in many regards. The focus specifically is placed on social attitudes to children and childhood, commercial issues in modern life and the effects of a testing-led educational regime which has evolved in England. These aspects are analysed and evaluated using a range of up-to-date, accessible resources.

Introduction

On 12 September 2006 over 100 well-established academics, children's authors and other specialists in childhood matters wrote to the *Daily Telegraph* to raise their concerns about what has been called 'toxic childhood' (Palmer 2006). The signatories were from a wide variety of professional backgrounds, each with their own observations and knowledge of childhood in the twenty-first century but all coming to the same conclusion: that adults are doing something to children which, despite all our best intentions, is not working: children are now leading more stressful lives, their waking moments rigidly timetabled, monitored and measured, and that from a very tender age we are exposing children to influences and experiences which may well be harming them. This is how I also feel as a parent and a childminder. This chapter, therefore, will seek to outline the various aspects of children's lives as I see it, in the way that it directly affects our children.

The good life?

Children appear safer than ever before and yet our feelings of anxiety about them, as parents and as a society, are increasing rather than diminishing. We have access to the best diet that has ever been available to ordinary people, we have powerful technology to help with healthcare, education and work, and economically the country is stable; there are high levels of employment, low inflation, a buoyant housing market, and so on. And yet, a third of the current generation of children is obese – it has been suggested that some children could die before their parents as a result of diet-related health problems (Meikle 2004). Levels of childhood depression and other psychiatric illness are at the highest levels since records began (*Medical News Today* 2004) and the UK's children and teenagers have gained a reputation for displaying the worst behaviours and some of the highest levels of teenage pregnancy and drink-related problems in Europe (Margot and Dixon 2006). It seems the more we achieve socially and economically, the more elusive happiness, health, satisfaction and personal achievement become.

Yet we have so much for which to be grateful: despite having the benefit of many social and economic advances, we seem to be making our children more unhappy and unhealthy rather than less. A York University study, using World Health Organisation data, has rated Britain 21 out of 25 European Union countries in measures of children's well-being (Bradshaw et al. 2006).

My three main concerns centre on:

1   social attitudes to children and childhood – who we think children 'belong' to and who is responsible for their welfare and well-being;
2   the commercial issues in modern life and how they are affecting children more directly and more deeply than ever before;
3   the effects of the testing-led educational regime which has evolved in England in a fairly short space of time and which seems to be a response to our economic values rather than a tool which genuinely helps children and practitioners.

These concerns are mainly focused on British systems and UK children but there are similar concerns in many other parts of the 'developed' world.

Reflection point

1   What is your view – as parent or practitioner – of 'modern childhood' and society's attitudes to children? How is it different/similar from when you were a child? What are the challenges and issues in thinking about childhood as YOU see them now?

Social attitudes to children and childhood

Parenthood has changed my point of view on many things and, to me, the roots of the problems already outlined stem from society's deeply ambivalent attitudes towards children (Palmer 2006). It appears that children are not seen as intrinsically important, or their care and welfare relevant to the general well-being of all unless there is a direct financial benefit, for example, paying for childcare to free parents for work (Anning et al. 2004). This is a stated aim of recent initiatives from the British government and something it has tried to engineer through the working tax credit scheme, childcare vouchers and the Sure Start programme. These have all been interesting ideas and not without merit but before they can succeed, something much more fundamental needs to be addressed, namely, why we as a society do not put greater value on the care and development of children.

The idea, for example, that there is a social benefit in supporting parents because, among other reasons, one day their offspring might look after their parents' generation (even the childless ones) or that it might sometimes be appropriate for parents to put their children's welfare before the demands of the workplace, still seems absurd. Yet in Scandinavian countries they would be astonished at this attitude. Similarly, the notion that we all have a vested interest in the nurture and education of children (even if only because everyone pays a price when things go wrong) still appears to be regarded as unreasonable.

Where this outlook originated is unclear but partly as a result of attitudes like this, where individuals look out for themselves (so-called 'narcissism' – Lowen 2004), we have not noticed how children have been adversely affected by the development of the economy and the pressures that it has introduced into all their lives. Margaret Thatcher allegedly once said 'There is no such thing as society.' Whether or not she said this doesn't matter – the philosophy is the same: individuals should take responsibility for themselves and not rely on the state. In return, taxation could be lowered and people enabled to choose for themselves such things as how they used healthcare, education and transport. However, this way of thinking lies behind a consistent failure by the UK government to support families and probably contributes significantly to the high rates of relationship failure and family breakdown we experience. In my view, we need to radically change the way we view children and parents, both when they are in work and when they are not, since the motivation behind virtually all public transactions, business and legislation in the UK is the market economy. In the past few years there has been an improvement in the leave available to the parents of young children which has brought us further in line with more enlightened European countries, but it still appears 'normal' for employers to complain about the burden this places on business. Perhaps we need to help businesses to understand the long-term benefits that such leave can provide – and have a government prepared to give small businesses meaningful financial support to make it possible.

Britain has lower birth rates than many of our most closely comparable European partners and this may be one reason why, as parents, we quite rightly regard our smaller families as very precious. We have high expectations about the care they should receive and their education, and the government has done a lot to raise these expectations but it still seems as if no-one wants to pay the real cost. In a newspaper debate, Purnima Tanuku, Chief Executive of the National Day Nurseries Association, said: 'when we look at Scandinavia there are no such discussions [as to the value of funding childcare] as childcare is properly funded by the government and is of a very high standard' (2006: 15).

Norman Glass, one of the architects of the government's early years childcare programme Sure Start, said, 'On childcare we are in danger of heading towards a very British compromise – Scandinavian ambitions and British funding levels' (2005). He was referring to the fact that since its inception, the funding for the scheme, which was originally ring-fenced, has been diluted as the programme was rolled out. Despite some early signs of success, many people, both within and outside government have begun to doubt the long-term commitment to the whole scheme which was to have helped the most needy families. At its inception, Sure Start was one of the most credible proposals to come from New Labour's idea of 'joined-up' government, but we need a change of attitude to the care of all children everywhere, no matter what their social class, ethnicity or economic situation (Brooker 2002). Unfortunately, despite great improvements in the standard of living for the economically better off, the gap between the poorest and richest in English society is widening every year. This is the single most significant factor in a country's overall health, educational, economic and social outcomes.

Reflection points

2   Do you agree that our British society shows ambivalence towards children? If so, in what ways?

3   Have you noted any increase among the children you know in their social abilities and social adjustment? To what do you attribute any changes?

Commercial issues in modern life

As a childminder, my experiences confirm my belief that our current commitment to children's early years care adds up to lots of talk but not much substance. For example, in the north of England hourly rates for childminding are £3.00 per hour (the national minimum wage is currently £5.35 an hour for those aged 22 years and older), but for a cleaner it is £6 an hour. The BBC's *Lifestyle and Parenting* website (http://www.bbc.co.uk/parenting/childcare/paying_index.shtml) advises parents that they can expect to pay an *average* hourly rate in England and Wales of £2.40 (rising to a maximum of £6.00). In the UK, we are asking people who care for our children (*in loco parentis*) – *and* deliver a form of national curriculum – to accept half, or less, of the hourly rate of a domestic help. Frean (2006) gave an average cost for a full-time childminding place outside London as £130.00 per week, and £142.00 for a full-time nursery place for a child under 2 years. These are small amounts once you take into account expenditure on food, nappies, toys, play materials, outings, insurance, and such like, plus the expense of staffing and training. But for many families the costs are still a large proportion of their total income and although there are a number of rather complex mechanisms to help claim back some of the costs, clearly many parents still struggle. Christine Walton, Chief Executive of the Daycare Trust, has commented, 'We urgently need a review of the funding system for childcare to ensure that all children have access to good quality services, regardless of their family income' (Frean 2006). The consistent under-funding of all forms of childcare is one area in which I feel the UK is also letting its children down. I think this is important because it sets the tone for the way children are treated subsequently.

In pre-schools, playgroups and nursery settings, rates of pay and conditions of service are generally better than for childminders, although there is no uniformity and some playgroups are still staffed with unqualified workers. Realistically most people need the incentive of a dignified and competitive rate of pay which reflects the skills and responsibilities required of them before they are prepared to change their working practices to meet the demands made by parents and by OfSTED, the body which assesses and registers them. Children also deserve the best possible carers and educators.

In England, we employ low-skilled workers to look after children but require them to begin implementing a form of education or curriculum as soon as children enter their care, which may be as young as 6 weeks. The academic results of our children at the end of their school careers speak for themselves by comparison. Instead of stimulating children and providing them with proper educational opportunities, we are over-prescribing formal activities which do nothing to raise the overall standards. In short, by not allowing children time and opportunity to play, we are burning children out with too much, too soon (see e.g. Elkind 1988; Postman 1994).

Most of the workers in early years childcare settings, are, like most childminders, decent, caring and dedicated people, but as with childminding, provision is not consistent throughout the country. Availability and standards of provision vary despite the OfSTED regulation. Parents who rely on such services so that they can keeping working, often find employers unsympathetic when work hours don't match available childcare. Again, work is being done to improve the situation with the introduction of wrap-around care in many schools but employers still lag behind in their levels of co-operation and willingness to support parents. We seem to have made work and economic activity the be-all and end-all of our lives. Many of our European counterparts manage to be just as, or more, successful than us by working shorter hours and having more holidays. When research on the problems that children are experiencing is published, it provokes anguished debate in the press but I don't feel that any of it is very surprising: as a nation, we have allowed the demands of work and business to dominate life and have relegated the needs of children and the arrangements for their care to the margins, while at the same time, being happy to target them directly as putative or mini-consumers (see e.g. Compass Report 2006).

Much research has been done which shows that children have a hard time discriminating between unbiased information and 'facts' in advertisements (American Psychological Association 2004; Gunter et al. 2005). With a large proportion of children having access to unsupervised television and the internet, often in their bedrooms, we should be considering how children may be adversely affected by media which can be very positive, but can also have bleaker effects (Large 2003). Instead of developing good social skills and emotional maturity, computer games and internet access can cause us to disassociate ourselves from others, reduce our capacity for imaginative thought and encourage our natural narcissism and love of passive and sedentary entertainment and occupation (Healy 2004).

In my view, parents need to protect children from the 'grown-up' world. It has suited advertisers and powerful commercial lobby groups to blur the distinction between childhood and adulthood, and the modern concept of 'choice' has worked to the benefit of the market. Children have been co-opted by the commercial world and given a great deal of power, not necessarily all of it in their best interests. In an effort to make sure that children's voices are better heard, adults have often confused giving children the freedom to voice their feelings and preferences, with allowing them to make choices about everything they do without adult guidance. The ethos of 'choice' has, sadly, worked its magic. Even very young children are targeted by advertising on television (Large 2003). My quite militant approach is to say 'No!' to any product which the children have seen on the television. I am prepared to be unpopular with my children and regarded as eccentric by other parents but I don't want my children to suffer because of my choices. Even though I try to explain to the children why I don't like the advertisements and how they influence thinking often adversely, the children just don't understand and I know they are not unusual.

Modern technology, far from making children more discriminating, seems to be making them more vulnerable. Over the past 20 or so years the ideology of choice and free enterprise has become so deeply embedded in our political and cultural life that politicians generally seem to accept it as an unquestionably 'good thing'. Yet we know that children are not just smaller adults with an innate understanding of everything: they are intellectually immature until fairly late on in their teens and still very impulsive. Some adults have become very muddled about who has the right to make choices that involve or affect a child and that we, as parents, are often anxious about seeming strict or old-fashioned. It isn't complete freedom and lack of boundaries which make a child thrive: they grow up most securely where there are recognizable routines, boundaries and where they can feel secure that adults are 'in charge' and can take responsibility for their care. And of course, most importantly of all, children thrive when they feel loved, valued and wanted. Do we do anything like enough in UK society to make children feel welcome or wanted?

In 2006, the Think Tank, Compass, described how advertisements and marketing 'are shaping the way children see themselves and the world and are impacting on their values, aspirations, health as well as the way they feel about themselves' (Compass 2006: 4). The report suggested that the results of the pressure included stress, depression and low self-esteem and said that the marketing industry had come up with ever more ingenious ways of infiltrating children's worlds. In an article about the report, Ward (2006) suggests that 'children are being forced to grow up too soon' with products aimed at them which were unsuitable for pre-teens and sexualize the play of pre-pubescents. Brooks (2006) suggests:

> consumer culture offers children access to areas of adult life from which they have traditionally been excluded. But the desire to get older younger is not a new one. Adulthood has always meant freedom to the child who feels restricted. What is new is that the template of adulthood presented to them is one of conspicuous consumption. It is, surely, adulthood that has been most grossly distorted by consumer culture, and reflected back to children as a venal, vapid, selfish place. Perhaps it's adulthood rather than childhood that's in crisis.

This is echoed by the writer Anne Karpf (2006):

What's wrong with modern childhood is part of what's wrong with modern adulthood. The lack of time for children to be aimless exactly matches that suffered by their parents. The encouragement of a precocious, clothes-and-make-up-driven sexuality mirrors the same experienced at the other end of the ageing spectrum.

Every experience has become commodified and commercialized and the incredible pressure to get ahead, to be economically successful and to stay ahead starts the minute a child is conceived. A baby can become a consumer even before birth and there is a lucrative market for products like those which play the stimulating music of Mozart to a baby *in utero*. Once a child arrives in the world, its parents have thousands of toys to choose from, including the sort that use pseudo-scientific hype ('improves hand–eye co-ordination') to lend a bogus validity. The mother and baby catalogues are crammed with hundreds of unnecessary gadgets which the inexperienced and anxious parent can easily be persuaded to buy because everyone wants to give their child the best start in life. It's the way we live now and it plays to all our psychological weaknesses as parents and as human beings. I think it's also part of a more pernicious phenomenon, that in order for our market economy to remain stable and to grow, which apparently is essential if we all want to maintain and aspire to improve our standard of living, then our children must in their turn be taught how to become consumers. Children not only form a very important market in their own right worth millions of pounds but are increasingly recognized for the power they have acquired in the household, determining what purchases their parents make over items as significant as computers and cars. It's all part of a full-on, non-stop, lights constantly blazing, 24/7 world which is driving us all mad. Life has become focused on the constant need to generate income from economic activity and our ideas about children, childcare and education have to a very great extent been geared to this end.

Reflection points

4   What could practitioners in early childhood care and education do to enhance their roles and their value to society?

5   What impact do you see in the children with whom you work and play in relation to television advertisements and programmes?

The effects of the testing-led educational regime

John Crace, science correspondent of *The Guardian*, reported earlier this year on new research funded by the Economic and Social Research Council (ESRC) and carried out by Michael Shayer (with results that had been replicated in Australia, Greece and Pakistan) showing that 11- and 12-year-olds are 'now on average between two and three years behind where they were 15 years ago', in their cognitive and conceptual development. Shayer comments:

> It's a staggering result . . . before the project started, I rather expected to find that children had improved developmentally. This would have been in line with the Flynn effect on intelligence tests, which shows that children's IQ levels improve at such a steady rate that the norm of 100 has to be recalibrated every 15 years or so. But the figures just don't lie. We had a sample of over 10,000 children and the results have been checked, rechecked and peer reviewed . . . I would suggest that the most likely reasons are the lack of experiential play in primary schools, and the growth of a video-game, TV culture. Both take away the kind of hands-on play that allows kids to experience how the world works in practice and to make informed judgments about abstract concepts.
>
> (Crace 2006)

The education process has unfortunately become part of the problem. Commercial pressures filter down into the curriculum because of the demands for workers with particular skills, and businesses are able to exert much influence on government policy because of their financial power and, for example, private finance initiatives in academies. Childhood is not valued for its own sake: we impose on children the continuum of the world of work and the kinds of management regimes, monitoring and auditing experienced by adults. We are projecting on to children the anxiety we feel about achieving social and academic advantages or being 'losers'. A system has been put in place to monitor and observe everything children do throughout their educational careers, yet we are still not achieving the desired results.

In his article, John Crace also quotes Paul Black (Chair of the 1988 National Curriculum Task Group on Assessment and Testing), who said of Shayer's findings:

> Research from around the world shows that, when the stakes are high, teachers teach to the tests . . . This produces a short-term, three-year uplift in results before they plateau. We also get to see some artificial results, such as in the US, where every state is above the

national average in its test scores. In the UK, the National Audit Office has questioned the validity of some SATs scores ... We also need to ask what the tests test. Do they measure what's important or what doesn't matter?

Ten years separate my son and the first of his three sisters and in that time the education system really changed. The National Curriculum was introduced while my son was at primary school and was just bedding in, but my daughters really felt the full-on shock of its force. This was something I couldn't easily protect them from: suddenly they were not wholly within my control or shelter. After the preliminary reception year experiences, which both older girls enjoyed, they moved on to a world of school which seemed to have become a microcosm of the world of work. The girls complained of school being tiring and that they wanted more time for 'choosing' or free play. In their reception classrooms there was no home or dressing-up areas because there just wasn't time to play with those things. The school was oversubscribed in an area with a lot of new housing and not enough school places, and every class was the maximum size. SAT results for the school seemed to be a constant pressure even in non-SAT years, and the children were very aware of them and of the need 'to do well'. I felt that the staff, although extremely dedicated, were often tired and over-burdened with the quantity of work to get through each term, and dispirited that suddenly their own experience and judgement seemed to count for very little. Times that I had loved at school on projects like The Romans or Transport, had evaporated. The pace was accelerated and there wasn't enough time in the curriculum to go back on areas the children had not quite grasped or to dwell on things that caught their imaginations. It felt as though everyone was on a treadmill and there was no joy about school.

I was extremely fortunate in being able to move my children to a small school just outside the town. Their lives were transformed. The head had taken a decision that SATs would take a back seat: his primary concern was that children should develop optimally in confidence and social skills. He felt that education and learning were more than mere curriculum content and skills: it was about children who enjoyed what they were engaged in and who wanted and were ready to go to school each morning. At least now my children were not trapped in a dreadful experiment gone wrong!

I began to feel that although there was a lot that was laudable in the National Curriculum, with its drive to raise and maintain high educational standards, the big picture had been lost and a kind of general panic had set in about what children and teachers should be doing, completing, capable of and striving for, and that failure was unacceptable (while actually inevitable). This NC process would eventually result in naming and shaming and even a withholding or reduction of funding. A system that was designed to give children confidence, skills and independence was really infantilizing those responsible for implementing it with a rigid application of its principles and a fixation on targets and goals. It is a system that, to me, distrusts teachers' judgement and abilities. During a discussion about education on *You and Yours* on BBC Radio 4 (2006), the SATs system was compared to the FTSE index, with the implication that it had become a very blunt and crude method of assessing schools' performance and that too much of what really mattered in schools had been forgotten. Libby Brooks (2006) wrote 'children will continue to be over-tested at school for as long as we support an education policy that views them as units of future human capital'.

Once my daughters moved school, the transformation in them was huge. After a couple of weeks at the new school, my eldest daughter came home and said, 'It's like a wonderful holiday. I never want to have a day off.' The school does simple things like letting the children stay outside all day, (even the day before SATs!), and finds more time for art and creative activities, but these things make such an enormous difference to a child. They have retained a proper kitchen and lunches are cooked on the premises with an interesting, balanced and varied menu. The children sit together, help serve the food and have made the midday meal a part of the whole educational experience, developing important social skills and learning to appreciate good food (see Chapter 13). Despite the approach to the curriculum being more relaxed, my children are actually doing better than before as they don't feel so anxious and the staff slow down and move forward at the children's pace rather than teach to targets or tests.

Reflection points

6   How far does the Early Years Profile influence learning and teaching in your setting?

7   Do you feel that children in your setting have sufficient quality time to play and have choice? How is this achieved/not achieved?

Conclusion

Our children cannot choose the kind of world into which they are born but depend on adults to make the right decisions for them. As a parent, I want to put the brakes on what we call 'progress' as outlined above, to protect children and allow them the space to be children, free of inappropriate influences and experiences. I want to ensure that this generation of children can cope as they grow up in a world with some new and very difficult challenges. We must be honest about what we are doing to them and the results we are seeing, both negative and positive. I feel we should be doing far more to shield them from the voracious demands of a consumerist society and the ubiquitious images of sexuality that are available in an extremely permissive culture. We also need to back off in terms of constant monitoring and testing. We need to understand better what the real dangers are for our children and what is only our imagined fear. We also need to understand when to leave our children alone and let them be.

Points for discussion

- What role should government play in protecting children and young people from commercial pressures?
- Why have we tended to believe that national and prescriptive testing will tell us accurately what is going on in schools, classrooms, and for individual children? What are the best ways of monitoring and evaluating performance and achievement?
- How could we 'let go' more and make the educational experience more relaxed so that formal academic work starts later as in the Scandinavian countries? Is it really the case that those models would not work in Britain or are we just locked into an out-dated system?

References and further reading

American Psychological Association (APA) (2004) *Report of the APA Taskforce on Advertising and Children*. Washington, DC: APA.

Anning, A., Cullen, J. and Fleer, M. (eds) (2004) *Early Childhood Education, Society and Culture*. London: Sage.

BBC (2006) *Lifestyle and Parenting*. Help with three- and four-year-olds. Available at: http://www.bbc.co.uk/parenting/childcare/paying_index.shtml (accessed 19 December 2006).

Bradshaw, J., Hoelscherand, P. and Richardson, D. (2006) An index of child well-being in the European Union, Social Indicators Research Online. (1573–0921). Available at: http://www.york.ac.uk/inst/cdw/ (accessed 19 December 2006).

Brooker, L. (2002) *Starting School: Young Children Learning Cultures*. Buckingham: Open University Press.

Brooks, L. (2006) So you want them to be happy? *The Guardian*, 16 September. Available at: http://education.guardian.co.uk/schools/story/0,,1873604,00.html (accessed 21 December 2006).

Claxton, G. (1997) *Hare Brain, Tortoise Mind*. London: Fourth Estate.

Compass (2006) *The Commercialisation of Childhood*. Available at:

http://www.compassonline.org.uk/campaigns.asp (accessed 20 December 2006).

Crace, J. (2006) Children are less able than they used to be. *The Guardian*, 28 January. Available at: http://education.guardian.co.uk/egweekly/story/0,,1692952,00.html (accessed 20 December 2006).

Elkind, D. (1988) *The Hurried Child*. Reading, MA: Addison-Wesley.

Frean, A. (2006) Child minders charge £500-a-week to look after your little treasures, *The Times*, 8 February. Available at: http://www.timesonline.co.uk/article/0,,2–2029981,00.html (accessed 23 January 2007).

Glass, N. (2005) Surely some mistake? *The Guardian*, 5 January. Available at: http://education.guardian.co.uk/earlyyears/story/0,,1383617,00.htm (accessed 23 January 2007).

Gunter, B., Oates, C. and Blades, M. (2005) *Advertising to Children on TV: Context, Impact, and Regulation*. Mahwah, NJ: Lawrence Erlbaum Associates.

Healy, J. (2004) *Your Child's Growing Mind: Brain Development and Learning from Birth to Adolescence*. Louisville, KY: Broadway Publishers.

Karpf, A. (2006) *The Human Voice: The Story of a Remarkable Talent*. London: Bloomsbury Publishing.

Large, M. (2003) *Set Free Childhood: Parents' Survival Guide to Coping with Computers and TV*. Stroud: Hawthorne Press.

Lowen, A. (2004) *Narcissism: Denial of the True Self*. Hamilton Hill, Australia: Simon and Schuster Ltd.

Margo, J. and Dixon, M. with Pearce, N. and Reed, H. (2006) *Freedom's Orphans: Raising Youth in a Changing World*. London: Institute of Public Policy Research.

Medical News Today (2004) Tens of thousands of obese kids may die before their parents in the UK. Available at: http://www.medicalnewstoday.com/medicalnews.php?newsid=7011 (accessed 23 January 2007).

Meikle, J. (2004) Children will die before their parents, *The Guardian*, 27 May. Available at: http://www.guardian.co.uk/food/Story/0,,1225643,00.html (accessed 23 January 2007).

Palmer, S. (2006) *Toxic Childhood: How the Modern World Is Damaging Our Children and What We Can Do about It*. London: Orion.

Postman, N. (1994) *The Disappearance of Childhood*. Vancouver: Vintage Books.

Tanuku, P. (2006) Too early, too much, too long? *The Guardian* Family Forum. 25 February. Available at: http://www.guardian.co.uk/family/story/0,,1716960,00.html (accessed 23 January 2007).

Ward, L. (2006) Ads blamed for childhood stress, *The Guardian*, 12 December. Available at: http://www.guardian.co.uk/uk_news/story/0,,1969866,00.html (accessed 20 December 2006).

7   Coping with bereavement

Rose Griffiths

Abstract

This chapter tackles the difficult topic of death. It examines the ways in which babies and young children are affected by bereavement, and considers how a young child's understanding of death may differ from that of an older child or an adult. Case studies are used to discuss ways in which all the adults who know bereaved children can help them and their families and friends cope with this life-changing transition, both immediately after the death and in the months and years to come.

Introduction

Many practitioners have experienced the heart-stopping moment when they hear that a child's mother or father (perhaps a person they knew well themselves) has died, or that a brother or sister has died. In this situation, every adult who comes into contact with a young bereaved child can be a source of comfort and support, but many under-5s practitioners feel uncertain about the best things to say or do to help. The death of a parent or child is often an unexpected event, so it may be something that an early years setting has not discussed or prepared for in advance. Even with planning, it can be a difficult area of work, and may be especially distressing for any staff who were bereaved themselves as children.

It is difficult to estimate how many children will lose a parent, main carer or sibling through death. The number of children affected is likely to be greater in areas of high social and economic deprivation, since death rates are higher in deprived localities (Shaw et al. 1999). A report on young people, bereavement and loss estimated for those under 16 years of age that

> the death of a parent before age 16 is not as uncommon as might be supposed. Figures range from 3.9 per cent (Sweeting *and others*. 1998) to 7.4 per cent (Wadsworth 1991). Figures for the death of a sibling are harder to establish, but seem to be similar to (or perhaps slightly

lower than) figures for death of a parent (Harrison and Harrington 2001). The majority of sibling deaths will concern the death of an infant.

(Ribbens et al. 2005: 3)

This suggests that between 8–15 per cent of children will have experienced the death of a parent or sibling by the age of 16; perhaps between 4–7 per cent by the age of 8.

Young children who are bereaved may be affected not only by the loss of the person who has died, but also because the adults who are closest to them are themselves grieving, and feel less able to help. Sometimes, children who are friends of a bereaved child will need support. The idea that a mother, father or child can die is a shocking revelation, and a young child's reaction to this may surprise the adults around them.

Bereavement can precipitate a chain of personal, social and economic changes in a child's life, and it is important that those working with families consider how they can make use of inter-professional links to support a bereaved family. The timing of support is also relevant. Sometimes the need for help is urgent and immediate; some help is better offered at a later stage.

The professional skills which practitioners can use to help with bereavement are considerable, and are ones which can be put to good use in other situations of loss, such as when a child's parents separate or divorce, or when a child is taken into care. Supporting transitions is a significant area of expertise (see *The Common Core*, DfES 2005) and a focus on bereavement can help develop sensitive and effective practice across a broad front.

Experiences of bereavement

If you have been bereaved, you will know that you experience a wide range of emotions after the death of someone close to you. You may feel numb, angry, sad, relieved, guilty, afraid, anxious, tired and unable to see how you could ever recover.

For a large part of the twentieth century, a prevailing view in Western society was that mourning a death was a process of disengaging from the person who had died (Freud 1957), and might be seen as going through a succession of fixed stages of bereavement (Pollock 1961; Kubler-Ross 1982). More recently, there has been a growing understanding of mourning as a process where bereaved people come to terms with accepting the death, remembering the person who has died, and finding a way of forming continuing bonds with them (Klass et al. 1996). This view of mourning has long historical links, and is familiar to many cultures across the world.

Some people have found it helpful to think of the mourning process as a series of tasks, which a bereaved person will revisit over time. Worden outlines four tasks:

1 To accept the reality of the loss.
2 To experience the pain of the loss.
3 To adjust to an environment in which the deceased is missing.
4 To relocate the dead person within one's life.

Worden says:

> one never forgets a significant relationship. The task facing the bereaved is not to give up the relationship with the deceased, but to find a new and appropriate place for the dead in their emotional lives – one that enables them to go on living effectively in the world.
>
> (1996: 15)

Adult experiences of bereavement have common features but will also vary for each individual, depending on the closeness of the relationship with the deceased, the circumstances of the death, the support available, the personal resilience of the bereaved person, and many other aspects. There are several ways in which the experience of a bereaved child will be similar to that of an adult but there will be some distinctive features, too.

Reflection points

1 What do we know about how young children are affected by death?
2 What is different about a young child's experience of bereavement?

NB One source of information is to talk to adults who had this experience as a child.

Young children and bereavement

As part of a two-year project to write support materials for parents and other adults caring for young bereaved children, I was able to interview or correspond with nine adults who had been bereaved themselves as young children asking them about what they remembered. Holland (2001) outlines an interesting larger-scale project, *Project Iceberg*, in which researchers questioned adults about their childhood experiences of a parent dying. Five of his 70 volunteers were under 5 when their parent died.

Our project (*Not Too Young to Grieve* 2006) also ran focus group meetings and correspondence over a period of a year with early years practitioners from health, childcare, education and social care backgrounds, through which we collected many examples of children's, families' and staff responses to bereavement. Some of those examples are used in this chapter, with names and some circumstances changed to preserve anonymity.

It is tempting to hope that babies and very young children will be relatively unaffected by a death and that young children will recover quickly from a bereavement. One young nursery nurse, caring for a 4-year-old whose mother had died, had said to the child: 'We don't have any sad faces here', and expressed her view that the best approach was to distract the child and help him to forget what had happened. This denial of the child's sadness perhaps arose both from the desire for the child to be happy, and because a less-experienced member of staff was afraid to tackle difficult feelings.

An understanding of the attachment process (Bowlby 1969; Rutter 1995) and its importance to a child's well-being indicates that a baby or child is very likely to be distressed by the permanent disappearance of a main carer. As Judd says, in a useful pamphlet about bereavement:

> For very young children, who are unable to speak, death might be described as an unnameable fear or dread. You know how inconsolably a baby or young child can cry if they feel unsafe, or if a parent goes out of the room or leaves them for longer than they can bear. If the loved one does not return, young children can be left with fears for their own survival.
>
> (Judd 2001)

Kroen comments on the resulting anxiety that many children feel: 'Separation anxiety is a common reaction to traumatic loss among children this age. Subconsciously, they worry that other loved ones will leave them, too. They wonder what will happen to them and how they will survive' (1996: 41).

Several of our respondents reported children crying when they were taken to playgroup or nursery, and wanting to be told over and over again about how soon their adult would be back. One mother left her front door keys with the person who was minding her daughter while she went shopping, to reassure her 3-year-old daughter that she would not go home without her. Just as when any child is first left at nursery or with a childminder, the aim of the adult concerned was to reduce the feelings of stress that the child felt, until they were better able to cope. Many respondents indicated that they left their children for shorter periods of time for a while.

The father of 4-year-old Kadie, whose mother had died, said:

> Kadie asked me who would look after her if I died. I wanted to say I wasn't going to die, but I thought that wasn't much of an answer, because she knows that mums and dads can die; it's already happened to her. So I said, well, your nanny and granddad would look

after you, or your Uncle Jamie. Then she wanted to know what would happen if they all died. So I said it wasn't very likely, but if they did there were lots of kind people who would help. I said there were special people called Social Workers whose job was to help children who haven't got a mummy or daddy who could look after them, to help decide where was the best place for them to live. We talked some more and I realized she was worrying about things like she couldn't open the front door by herself, and she couldn't wash clothes. It seems extraordinary to a grown up but she seemed to think she would have to survive by herself.

Cleaver et al. in their report on children affected by a range of parental difficulties, comment on the issue of children who are not yet talking at all, or as fluently as older children:

> Pre-school children may be more at risk of emotional disturbance than older more articulate children because they are less able to express their distress verbally ... Moreover, the extent of their distress can be missed because young children's observable reaction may not tally with their emotional state.
>
> (1999: 65)

The development of language is one of four aspects of a young child's cognitive, social and emotional development that are especially relevant when we consider the ways in which bereavement will affect under-5s:

1 Talking and listening.
2 Understanding what 'dead' means.
3 Young children's concept of time.
4 Understanding cause and effect.

1 Talking and listening

Young children who do not talk cannot explain their feelings or fears, even to themselves. Some adults who were bereaved at the age of 1 or 2 have described feeling angry, frightened and unhappy for some time in their childhood, but beginning to feel calmer as they got older, when they and the adults around them were able to talk about their parents' deaths. One woman told me:

> I was 2 when our father died, and my brother was 7. I always thought that the death should have affected my brother more than me, because he knew our dad better, and people seemed to expect me to

have forgotten him. Seeing Dad's photo made me feel panicky and upset as a child. I wonder now whether I found it more difficult to cope because I wasn't able to put it into words – Mum says she thought I was fine, but I don't remember feeling fine.

Adults will sometimes assume that a child who does not yet talk will not understand what the adults are saying, and children may consequently overhear things that puzzle or scare them. Conversely, adults will sometimes assume that children do understand what is being said to them, but a child may have only a partial understanding of what they mean. Plain speaking is very important, avoiding euphemisms such as 'We have lost our baby' (which a child may take literally, and want to search for the baby) in favour of clearer statements: 'Our baby has died.'

Reflection points

3   Do you have a child in your setting who has experienced the death of someone close to them?

4   How did that child respond to the experience? Were they, for example, able to talk about it?

5   How did you and the other practitioners respond to the child's experience?

---

2 Understanding what 'dead' means

Death is a difficult idea for an adult to come to terms with, and can seem a daunting prospect to explain to a young child. It is not like sleeping; a dead creature or person cannot eat, breathe or feel anything, and they will not wake up. For many children, seeing a dead pet, or just a dead insect, will give them a clearer picture of what 'dead' means than any amount of description or explanation. It is a difficult concept, but it is an important one for all children.

Viewing the body of someone who has died is part of many people's religious, cultural or family tradition, and taking part in the rituals surrounding death can be an important part of coming to terms with a death. In the two-year Harvard Child Bereavement Study of 70 families with children aged 6 to 17 years where a parent had died, 78% of the children had been able to see the deceased parent's body, and 95% attended the funeral (Worden 1996). In Holland's interviews of adults who had been bereaved as children, only 20% reported seeing the body, and slightly under 50% had attended the funeral. Holland reports that: 'Over three-quarters of those volunteers who did not go to the funeral of their parent wished that they had so attended' (2001: 88). No-one wished they had not attended their parent's funeral.

A childminder told me about three children aged 2, 3 and 4 years playing in her garden after they had found a dead frog. It was a few weeks after the oldest child's pet rabbit had died, and her family had had a funeral for their pet. The children asked for a trowel and a piece of kitchen towel (to wrap the frog). The childminder sat nearby in the garden and listened as the two older children explained to the younger child what they were doing: 'You make a hole and put the dead thing in. Then you say nice things about it. Then you cover it up and put some flowers on top. Then you sit quietly and feel sad. Then you think about all the good things about today.'

Sometimes bereaved children will use toys or a home corner to play at funerals. Adults can find this disconcerting, but it seems to help children come to terms with what has happened, and to understand death a bit better.

3 Young children's concept of time

Anyone who has had a young child ask them 'Is it tomorrow now?' will know that the concept of time passing, the words we use for time, and an appreciation of lengths of time, are all ideas that take several years for a child to understand. For a child aged 2 or 3 years, five minutes can seem an interminably long time, and the child will have no concept of the length of a year. Partly, of course, this is simply a function of the child's own lack of experience of time passing. At age 50, the concept of a year is naturally easier to understand than at age 2.

An understanding of past, present and future requires a longer life span than age 5. The idea of the permanence of death is therefore very difficult to comprehend, as one grandparent describes:

> We told our granddaughter (aged 3) that her mummy had died, and we were very, very sad. She asked us a few days afterwards whether mummy was coming back today, and we explained that mummy had died, and she was never coming back. Then a few weeks later we realized that our granddaughter was running to the front window every time she heard a bus pull up at the bus stop near our house, in case her mum was on the bus. 'Never' is a hard idea to explain. I think it is going to take a long time.

4 Understanding cause and effect

Young children are constantly learning about cause and effect, but will sometimes be uncertain about what *they* have caused, particularly because they may overestimate the importance of their own actions. It is a common reaction for adults to feel guilty after someone has died, and sometimes to blame themselves (perhaps particularly after the suicide of someone they were close to). Children may also feel worried that they have harmed someone who died. Jane spoke of her worries when she was 5:

> My dad had cancer. He was at home for quite a while, in bed, and my mum would tell me to be quiet because daddy was poorly and needed his sleep to help him get better. When he died, I was sure it was my fault, for being too noisy.

Children may be muddled by statements such as 'Granddad died because he was ill', and worry that when they or someone else in their family are ill, that means they will die too. Kroen suggests using 'very, very, very' with children, as a way of clarifying the link between cause and effect here:

> [You can say] ... 'Sometimes people die when they get very, very, very, very sick.' This is especially important for children who have had colds, earaches or the 'flu, or those who have seen their parents or siblings come down with similar mild illnesses.

> (1996: 15)

As children grow older, they become better able to understand aspects of the death. They will benefit from hearing the stories surrounding their bereavement again, and being given more detailed information appropriate to their age.

Responding to bereaved children's needs

Parents, carers and practitioners will need to take account of a child's individual circumstances when thinking about the kinds of things they could do to support a child in the first few months after a death, and over the next few years. However, the following ten 'bereavement needs of grieving children', compiled by Worden, provide a checklist to help decide where intervention may be helpful. All are given briefly here, but are described in more detail elsewhere (Worden 1996: 140–7).

Children need:

1 *Adequate information* given in clear and age-appropriate language.
2 *Their fears and anxieties addressed* with reassurance and truthfulness.
3 *Reassurance they are not to blame* (see Figure 7.1).
4 *Careful listening and watching*, as they may express their feelings and questions through play, and through their behaviour.
5 *The validation of their feelings*: children need to express their feelings in their own way; there is not one way to grieve.

6   *Help with overwhelming feelings*: a death can elicit very strong and scary feelings, including anger and fear (see Figure 7.2).

7   *Involvement and inclusion*: for example, young children may contribute to a funeral or commemoration, by choosing flowers or drawing a picture.

8   *Continued routine activities* because they are calming and familiar, when so much else has changed.

9   *Modelled grief behaviours*: children need to be with people who can help them talk about the person who has died, and who will share their sadness.

10   *Opportunities to remember* the person who has died, over the years to come.

Children need reassurance that they are not to blame.

Robert

Figure 7.1   Children need reassurance that they are not to blame

Source: *Not Too Young to Grieve* training materials © 2006. www.childhoodbereavementnetwork.org.uk

Many of the needs described above would also apply to bereaved adults. Some are most appropriately met within the family, and others can be met jointly by the family and any friends or practitioners who know the child.

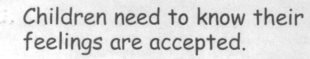

Jacob

Figure 7.2 Children need to know their feelings are accepted

Source: *Not Too Young to Grieve* training materials © 2006. www.childhoodbereavementnetwork.org.uk

Children who are friends of a bereaved child may also support them, but adults should be aware that young children will not always have the sympathy for a bereaved child which an adult expects. Some children are so shocked by the idea, for example, that a mummy or daddy can die, that they will react by rejecting the bereaved child:

> One of the children in our nursery has been shouting 'Go away' at Jade, whose mother has recently died. He won't sit near her. We've been trying to help him by talking to him quietly, and he is gradually becoming calmer. We've talked to his mum about it and said we think he's doing it because he is frightened, so he needs reassuring. We've given her a story book to read to him about a cat who dies.

Sometimes children will demonstrate a level of self-centredness that can take an adult by surprise. Joe, aged 4 years, is a friend of Millie, whose mother died four months ago. His auntie reported this conversation:

> Which is worse, if your mummy dies or your hamster dies?
> Oh, definitely, if your mummy dies, that's worse.
> But what if it's your hamster, and someone else's mummy?

But sometimes young children will impress you with their ability to think about other people's feelings. Nicola told us about her 4-year-old son's comments, when they walked through the churchyard:

> Jake was asking me about the gravestones and I said that they showed where people were buried, a long time ago. Then he ran ahead a bit, and he shouted that he'd found a baby gravestone. It was actually an adult's grave, but the stone was quite small, so he was insistent it must be a baby. He stood very still, and then he said, 'If my baby died, I'd go like this' (and he puffed up his chest) 'and then I'd go green like the Hulk, and I'd make this noise.' And then he roared, really loud, like the Incredible Hulk does on the telly. He looked so angry and sad, it made tears come to my eyes.

Children gain from the opportunity to help others, and young children can be an enormous source of comfort to each other – perhaps partly because of their lack of knowledge about social conventions that inhibit some adults. Sometimes a child will make a better decision about what to do than an adult:

> I was a parent helper one morning in playgroup, and one of the adults was supervising a table of children making Father's Day cards. A little boy came up to join the table, and the adult sent him away, saying 'No, you don't need to make a card, you can go and do something else.' The child came back a few moments later with his friend, who said very firmly to the grown-up: 'He can make a card 'cos he has got a dad, it's just that he's dead.'

It is obviously easier for people to work in a co-ordinated, sensitive and effective way with bereaved children if they have had a chance to discuss some of the issues that may arise, before they are faced with them.

Reflection point

6   What are the most important things to do, when you learn that a child's mother, father, main carer or a sibling has died?

Planning for bereavement in an early years setting

There is no one way to respond to a child's bereavement, since individual families will be in different circumstances, but here are some initial suggested guidelines.

Acknowledge the death to the child

When a child returns after a death, it can be tempting to say nothing, for fear of making the child cry. Some children will want to tell you themselves; others will be anxious because they are not certain you know what has happened. We usually share all sorts of news with the children in our care – for example, we would comment on new shoes, or a haircut – so it is important to acknowledge such a frightening and life-changing event to the child concerned. 'I am very sorry to hear that your mummy has died. All the grown-ups here know about it, and we are very sad for you' will help children feel more comfortable.

A card or a note to the child's carer will be welcome, and gives you the opportunity to offer help if appropriate.

Provide continuity of care

If a child has one particular member of staff whom they are close to, you may be able to make sure that she or he is available to spend time with the child. This is especially important when the child first comes into nursery each day, as parting from their parent or carer can be difficult for bereaved children. A key member of staff is more likely to understand what a child wants, at a time when the child may not be able to express themselves as well as usual.

Maintain familiar routines

Familiar surroundings, routines and expectations can be very comforting when so much else has changed in your life. At the same time, many of us feel less capable when we have been bereaved, and children will often seem to regress, perhaps finding it more difficult than usual to fit in with others, or to do things independently. It is important to recognize this, and to find ways of making the child's daily routine less stressful, as though they were younger:

> The mother of two of our pupils, aged 4 and 7, died after a very short illness. We were not sure the boys could cope with the ordinary routine straight away, so their teachers talked with them about what they would find most comforting. The boys wanted to stay together,

so we agreed that the older brother would come and 'help' in the nursery every morning that week, and they would have lunch with the nursery teacher, then go to visit the older boy's classroom for a while in the afternoon. The children in Year 2 were glad to sit and play with the younger brother, and the older one could be with his friends and his own teacher.

Some children's behaviour will be unexpectedly naughty after a bereavement. It is important to keep consistent boundaries, but also to acknowledge the child's feelings. It will also help if you can find activities that help a child let off steam, or become more relaxed. 'I know you are feeling very angry, but you must not kick people. Let's go outside and run round 'til you feel a bit better.'

Playing with water or dough can be very soothing. Snuggling up for a story, listening to music, rocking and dancing all may help.

Watch and listen carefully

Babies and young children may not talk yet, but they will still let you know how they are feeling. An older child's drawing, painting, and play in the home corner may all reflect the changes in their life. It is normal to draw coffins or play at funerals. It is also normal for a child to seem completely unaffected by a death at times, and to play happily.

Be aware that other children in a setting that includes a bereaved child may feel confused, frightened and upset by a death – or jealous of a child who seems to be getting more attention. It is usually appropriate to let other parents know what has happened, so they can talk to their children. Talk about feeling sad when you miss someone, and how we can look after each other and show that we care when someone is sad. Make sure children realize that sometimes people who are very sad just want to be left on their own for a while.

Consider whether you can help the family access other services

One Children's Centre gave the following examples:

> Sadly, we have had several families in the last few years, coping with bereavement – and refugee families who do not know what has happened to family members they have left behind. Local doctors and health visitors have been very helpful; some parents are in such a state of shock that it doesn't even occur to them that the doctor might be able to help them.
>
> Some people have family and friends who can help, and some have

religious beliefs and a network of people to support them. However, we always make a point of saying, 'You are bound to feel shocked at the moment, and it might feel hard to sort things out – do tell us if there is anything you are worrying about, and we will see if we can help.' We have helped look up the names of undertakers in the phone book; we've contacted the Housing Department about benefits advice; we've talked to our local beat policeman about finding a way to contact one man's sister, who was away on holiday abroad and didn't know her sister-in-law had died. Most of these things only take us a few minutes, because we know who to call on for help, but they can save the family an enormous amount of worry.

Help staff support each other

A child in distress makes us all feel very low. Staff who have been bereaved themselves, especially if it was when they were very young, may find their own feelings are overwhelming at times, and may appreciate support from others. However, talking about your own experience of loss in age-appropriate language can be helpful to a child, and make them feel less alone. 'I remember how I felt when my mummy died. I was very sad. Sometimes I felt better, and I tried to think about some of the nice things we did together. I still think about her a lot.'

You do not have to be an expert in childhood bereavement to make a difference for a bereaved child. However, there are many expert sources of help available to parents, carers and professionals living and working with bereaved children. You may already know of organizations close to you who could help – or you could contact those listed below.

Points for discussion

- Are there any children or staff in your setting who have experienced a significant bereavement? What was their experience, and how could you support them?
- Does your setting have guidelines in place to use in the event of a bereavement? What do you feel any guidelines should include?
- What local services could you liaise with, to offer additional support to a bereaved family?
- What are the professional development needs for your staff in this area of work?

Further information

Not Too Young to Grieve (2006), funded by the Parenting Fund, is a pack of professional development materials to raise awareness of the issues surrounding young children and bereavement. You can download the materials free from the Childhood Bereavement Network website (see below).

The professional development materials accompany a 14-minute animated DVD, *Not Too Young to Grieve*, which tells the stories of ten bereaved children under 5, and shows how the adults around them were able to help. You may be able to borrow it through your local library. You can purchase it from Leeds Animation Workshop, 45 Bayswater Row, Leeds, LS8 5LF; www.leedsanimation.org.uk

The Childhood Bereavement Network is a national co-ordinating organization that can help you find out more about support and training available in the United Kingdom. 8 Wakley Street, London, EC1V 7QE; www.childhood bereavementnetwork.org.uk

References and further reading

Bowlby, J. (1969) *Attachment and Loss*, Vol. 1. London: Hogarth Press.

Cleaver, H., Unell, I. and Aldgate, J. (1999) *Children's Needs: Parenting Capacity*. London: Department for Health/The Stationery Office.

Department for Education and Skills (2005) *Common Core of Skills and Knowledge for the Children's Workforce*. London: DfES Publications.

Freud, S. (1957) Mourning and melancholia, in J. Strachey (ed. and trans.) *Standard Edition of the Complete Psychological Works of Sigmund Freud*, vol. 14. London: Hogarth Press. (Original work published 1917.)

Holland, J. (2001) *Understanding Children's Experiences of Parental Bereavement*. London: Jessica Kingsley.

Judd, D. (2001) *Bereavement: Helping Parents and Children Cope when Someone Close to Them Dies*. London: The Child Psychotherapy Trust.

Klass, D., Silverman, P. and Nickman, S. (eds) (1996) *Continuing Bonds: New Understandings of Grief*. Washington, DC: Taylor and Francis.

Kroen, W. (1996) *Helping Children Cope with the Loss of a Loved One*. Minneapolis: Free Spirit Publishing.

Kubler-Ross, E. (1982) *On Death and Dying*. London: Tavistock.

Pollock, G. (1961) Mourning and adaptation, *International Journal of Psychoanalysis*, 42: 341–61.

Ribbens McCarthy, J. and Jessop, J. (2005) *Young People, Bereavement and Loss: Disruptive Transitions?* London: National Children's Bureau.

Rutter, M. (1995) Clinical implications of Attachment Concepts: retrospect and prospect, *Journal of Child Psychology and Psychiatry*, 36(4): 549–71.

Shaw, M. et al. (1999) *The Widening Gap: Health Inequalities and Poverty in Britain.* Bristol: Polity Press.

Worden, W. (1996) *Children and Grief: When a Parent Dies*. New York: Guilford Press.

8 Vision, mission, method

Challenges and issues in developing the role of the early years mentor teacher

Jackie Eyles

Abstract

This chapter will explore issues and challenges surrounding the role of the mentor teacher. It is concerned with good practice, raising standards and quality control. The collaborative/co-operative role with practitioners will be discussed and the elements of experience and expertise will be explored. The essential aspects of the mentor role as identified by different participants in one particular scheme will be examined and the kinds of success criteria identified for the role are outlined, including relationships, practicalities, specific qualities and personality.

> Those who talk about vision as essential for the future of enterprise are right, but it has to be the sort of vision that others can relate to.
>
> (Charles Handy 1994: 264–5)

Introduction

The Rumbold Report, *Starting with Quality* (DES 1990) set in motion a train of events that led to government-based initiatives to raise standards in the early years. Local authority *Early Years Development Plans* (EYDPs) instigated strategic planning that focused on the 'quality' of early years provision. The levels of 'quality' of settings with children aged 3 and 4 years funded by the government were identified by OfSTED inspections and that was used as the basis of provision of support for improving the quality of every setting through the local plan.

The Worcestershire arrangement provided a network of qualified and experienced early years teachers to provide support for clusters of settings to improve the quality of provision. Those experienced educators, called *mentor teachers*, provided support on a half-day a term basis that had some flexibility in time and context. Liaison with the inspectorate and advisory team, Family Information Services (FIS) and others gave the process a multi-professional dimension.

The key perspective of the Worcestershire strategy has been professional self-development, with and of the practitioners in the settings central to that development. The framework developed by Pascal et al. (1996) has underpinned the strategy for improving and maintaining quality. The *Key Elements of Effective Practice* document (DfES 2006) supports the role of the mentor teacher in early years settings.

The key features of the Worcestershire approach through its mentoring scheme are to provide:

- inspection support;
- opportunities for self-evaluation and improvement within settings;
- multi-professional support and advice;
- training and training guidance;
- guidance on the implementation of an appropriate play-based curriculum;
- consistency in delivering the early years curriculum;
- the appropriate implementation of the *Early Years Foundation Stage* strategy for children under 5;
- ways of using the *Birth-to-Three Matters/Every Child Matters* documents.

The advice provided by mentor teachers was central to the potential success of the strategy. Three key aspects of the role were identified:

1 It must be supportive.
2 It must include training.
3 It should include an assessor/professional evaluator role.

The challenge came in ensuring that the strategies for improvement and effectiveness were firmly rooted in a professional development model with both mentor teachers and early years practitioners reflecting continually upon their own practices. Practice based on reflection has great potential for professional improvement (Moyles and Adams 2001). The professional development model was also dependent upon an insider/outsider perspective: the practitioners 'within' the settings working in partnership with mentor teachers and local authority and Family Information Service staff – the 'outsiders'. The issue of profitable collaboration between the practitioners and mentor teachers was the main focus for delivering the strategy and reflected the four stages of development outlined in the Effective Early

Learning (EEL) project (Pascal et al. 1997): *evaluation, action planning, development* and *reflection*.

The successful implementation of the mentor programme has been based on discussion, observation, documentary evidence and evaluation of practice – and a lot of hard work by everyone! The aim was to promote the conditions necessary to improve the quality of provision for children in the early years and the challenge was to generate more effective practices on the premise that education and care are the right of all young children and families (UNICEF 1991: Article 27). It is the foundation of all future learning, achievement and quality of life.

This chapter outlines the issues and challenges surrounding the mentor teacher programme from the perspectives of those key to its development and draws some conclusions to encourage others who wish to undertake such a programme.

Reflection points

1   What do you understand by the role of mentor? Have you ever mentored anyone or been mentored yourself?
2   What purposes did the mentoring fulfil for you whether as mentor or the one mentored?

The role of the mentor teacher

Handy's (1994) reference at the start of the chapter to 'enterprise' and 'vision' encapsulated the promise of the Worcestershire programme: a vision of quality of provision in the early years grounded in good practice and raised standards through mutual professional support (Robins 2006). The commitment and enthusiasm of both mentor teachers and practitioners were the main objective of the endeavour. Such clarity of purpose and understanding of the aims of the programme were explored in a research investigation (Eyles 2002). The research revealed the complex nature of the initiative and the initial challenges experienced by all participants in formulating roles and responsibilities, and issues around participant involvement and the role of the mentor teacher in supporting early years settings, which resulted in some tensions and difficulties.

The role of the mentor teacher – practitioners' perspectives

Practitioners in early years settings believed that the mentor teacher programme was primarily concerned with mentors advising on and supporting the development of good practice in two ways: (1) they would provide guidance by sharing ideas; and (2) they would be the professional link between the mentor teachers, practitioners in other settings and the wider multi-professional community.

The programme was concerned with the notion of change involving new initiatives particularly in the areas of curriculum development and planning. The focus was the need to raise quality and standards. Central to that was the improvement of existing practices, monitoring standards and, most importantly, ensuring consistency and equality across all the county's early years settings. The mentors would oversee everyday practice to ensure it was sound and that the environments and experiences met the learning and development needs of young children. Analysing and evaluating the quality of existing provision were seen as central to that objective in support of pre- and post-OfSTED inspection arrangements.

Practitioners were clear that mentors would be the source of information concerning new government initiatives and local implementation. They would provide consistent information that was 'accurate' and 'up-to-date'. Local issues included partnership arrangements, local authority grants, funding and the development of the early years curriculum – *Birth-to-Three Matters* (Sure Start 2002) and the *Curriculum Guidance for the Foundation Stage* (QCA/DfEE 2000). The 'expert support' provided by mentor teachers was possible because of their early years qualifications and considerable expertise and experience in the field. The links with early years partnership groups placed an emphasis on ensuring consistency of information across the county, and provided a forum for exploring issues of improving practice and extending knowledge and understanding of aspects of provision. Practitioners considered that it was vital that the voice of early years was heard and that the mentor teachers would be a point of reference – almost a mediating role.

Initially, then, six main areas of involvement for the mentor teachers were identified by practitioners:

1 support for the development of the curriculum;
2 raising standards through the development of good practice;
3 inspection and the links with OfSTED;
4 involvement in the local Early Years Development and Childcare Partnerships (DfEE 1998);
5 general support from expert and experienced early years experts;
6 to be the voice of early years.

Additionally, the development of good relationships and issues of quality control were seen as vital elements in the equation. It was clear that practitioners recognized the importance of the mentoring role and felt that they needed mentors to do the following:

> give advice and new ideas and to help group(s) implement these changes by their experience and training.
>
> (Playgroup supervisor)

> help the setting progress/improve in the best possible way.
>
> (Year R teacher)

> ensure all in early years settings have consistent standards.
>
> (Pre-school supervisor)

> answer questions that have arisen, and offer advice on solving the difficulties.
>
> (Playgroup supervisor)

> sympathize and empathize with my role – to be a friendly face.
>
> (Year R teacher)

The mentor was felt also to have a significant role in the development of the settings' programme: 'to advise me on my teaching and my classroom environment in order to provide the best education possible during the Foundation Stage' (Year R teacher).

The main roles clearly identified by practitioners for the mentor teachers were those requiring skills, expertise, experience, personality and confidence to carry out the tasks involved in developing high quality provision in early years settings. The key features were identified as follows.

Raising standards

- support and help – staff, children, special educational needs;
- offering professional advice;
- solving problems;
- support with training initiatives;
- monitoring, help evaluate work of the settings;
- having an overview of the setting;
- a place in the hierarchy of decision-making.

Good practice

- sharing expertise and ideas;
- practical suggestions;
- inter-setting links and visiting other settings;
- exemplar teaching and sharing good practice;
- supporting children directly in the settings.

Outside partnerships

- liaison with outside agencies/local authority;
- liaison with local partnership groups/Family Information Service (FIS).

Curriculum development

- in-depth knowledge of national strategies: *Birth-to-Three Matters/Early Years Foundation Stage* guidance (EYFS)/*Every Child Matters/Ten Year Strategy*, etc. Information about changes;
- guidance on curriculum planning;
- advice on children's needs, including special needs;
- development of assessment and reporting procedures.

Quality control

- pre- and post-OfSTED support;
- help with developing quality control procedures;
- evaluating settings' development and appraisal processes;
- celebrating successes.

Relationships

- positive personality traits;
- positive working relationships;
- a critical friend/listening ear;
- a channel for communication/two-way exchanges;
- someone who can develop mutual respect;
- a morale booster/inspiration.

Mentor teacher skills

- knowledge and experience;
- early years expertise;

- giver of objective advice;
- skilled communicator.

Practitioners were very well aware of the complexities of the mentoring role and of the fluidity and uniqueness of the programme in the interaction between mentor teacher and setting – development and change would continue to be the key feature of mentor teacher involvement.

Reflection point

3   Do you agree with the contents of these lists? What would you add to or subtract from these attributes and skills in relation to your own knowledge, practice and identified needs?

The mentor teacher role – local authority perspective

The key features of the mentor teacher role identified by local authority personnel are shown in the following:

Raising standards

- support and help – staff, children, special education needs;
- offer professional advice;
- solving problems;
- support with training initiatives;
- monitoring, help evaluate work of the settings;
- having an overview of the setting as a whole;
- assuming a place in the hierarchy of decision-making.

Good practice

- sharing expertise and ideas;
- practical suggestions;
- inter-setting links and visiting other settings;
- exemplar teaching and sharing good practice;
- supporting children directly in the settings.

Outside partnerships

- liaison with outside agencies/local authority;
- liaison with local partnership groups/Family Information Service (FIS) (formerly Children's Information Service).

Curriculum development

- in-depth knowledge of national strategies: *Birth-to-Three Matters/Early Years Foundation Stage* guidance (EYFS)/*Every Child Matters/Ten Year Strategy*, etc. and information about changes;
- guidance on curriculum planning;
- advice on children's needs, including SEN and inclusive practices;
- development of assessment, monitoring and reporting procedures.

Quality control

- pre- and post-OfSTED inspection support;
- help with developing quality control procedures;
- evaluating settings' on-going development and appraisal processes;
- celebrating successes.

Interpersonal relationships

- positive personality traits;
- the ability to develop positive working relationships;
- the empathy to act as a critical friend/listening ear;
- provision of a channel for two-way exchanges/communication;
- mutual respect;
- positive attitudes to act as a morale booster/inspiration.

Mentor teacher professional knowledge, skills and understanding

- knowledge and experience;
- early years expertise;
- ability to offer objective advice;
- communication skills.

Clearly, expectations were high, but it is evident that there was considerable overlap between the views of local authority personnel and the practitioners.

The role of the mentor teacher – mentor teachers' perspectives

The importance of shared 'vision' was the key challenge in the mentors' views of their role. They understood the complexities of developing a framework for improving practice and raising standards. The mentors realized that they needed to rise above the difficulties of the minutiae of the day-to-day experiences and practicalities of involvement, to a more global understanding of the place of the early years programme in improving practice and raising standards for all. As Handy (1994) suggested, the ability to relate to the 'vision' is dependent upon an understanding of that vision in reference to 'idealization' – the stage that can be described as the pursuit of an ideal or a cause which is more than oneself (1994: 263). That provides the role of mentor teacher with a different perspective: not only must the mentor's involvement focus on shared initiatives but more importantly, on the need to lead and drive the programme so as to attain idealization.

The crucial difference between the mentors' and the practitioners' views of the role – the direct involvement with practitioners and children – was the more global understanding and long-term effect of engagement in mentoring. Stating aims, reaching goals, ensuring improvement and raising standards needed to be seen in the county/country context. There was a realization that the need for personal professional development would add to the expertise armoury of mentor teachers. There was, however, a strong emphasis at the grass roots level on sharing knowledge, experience and expertise. Such support provided opportunities for raising standards and improving the quality of early years provision. The willingness to collaborate with colleagues in other early years settings was tempered with the desire to develop personally and professionally. Personal and professional development could lead to new directions and have an impact on future career moves.

All involvement between mentor teachers and practitioners was challenging and stimulating. According to the mentor teachers, their role demanded 'enthusiasm', 'challenge' and 'confidence'. One mentor said:

> I relished the opportunity the post offered, the range of experiences on offer and the ability to share good practice among equally interested and enthusiastic colleagues. I recognized the personal development area and the experiences that would hopefully help me to fulfil my own future potential.
>
> (Mentor A)

This enthusiasm to be involved and the challenge of what was, initially, the unknown was a key aspect of the mentoring process. Mentor teachers were confident to support practitioners in those challenges but it was tempered by the realization that there would be gaps in their own knowledge, expertise and experience (Daloz 1999). Throughout the development of the mentor teacher programme they were both confident to engage with practitioners and in their own abilities – the qualifications, expertise and experiences they brought to the role – but because of the diversity within the settings, they needed to engage in their own training, acquisition of knowledge and additional experiences to fill the gaps. Training, professional development and peer support increased confidence as did the establishment of a job description.

The make-up of the role was mirrored by the practitioners' perceptions reported above. Key features of their own role were identified by mentor teachers as:

Raising standards

- support and advice;
- instilling confidence/sense of achievement;
- training support;
- new initiative information;
- own development/training/courses.

Outside partnerships

- develop Partnership groups;
- liaison with outside agencies/Family Information Services (FIS) – provide information;
- involvement with EYDCPs.

Curriculum development

- guidance and planning for a play-based curriculum;
- assessment, evaluation and recording development;
- organization;
- information – local and national initiatives/changes, e.g. *Birth-to-Three Matters, Foundation Stage Guidance*;
- resources.

Supporting practitioners, children and parents

- advise and support staff – be a motivator;
- welcomed and valued support;
- valuing diversity;
- exemplar teaching;
- a sounding board;
- supporting children and parents.

Quality control

- involvement in pre- and post-OfSTED inspections;
- involvement in OfSTED feedback/Action Plans.

Relationships

- developing good working relationships – two-way process;
- communication and collaboration;
- rapport/mutual respect;
- praise/morale booster/reassurance;
- enthusiastic professional.

The range and the diversity of mentor teachers' involvement and the challenges that they faced indicated the scale of the work involved: 'The range of activity varies so much – aspects of the job rely so much on the needs of the setting' (Mentor teacher B).

Over time, evidence that the programme had a goal beyond the immediacy of the individual setting emerged. The global issue became more apparent with experience. Knowledge and information were important but the notion of a professional critical friend broadened and deepened the role. The role also allowed the mentor's 'self' to develop as well as that of the practitioners and the settings. The programme: 'broadened contact with other people and that raises one's own confidence' (Mentor C). So the role has changed over time: 'It has been an evolution not a revolution and has become more professional' (Mentor D).

Mentor teachers' belief that their involvement was leading to an improvement in standards in settings was supported by their own professional development and that was in a more global context of the establishment of vision and mission.

The growth and development of the programme and the role of the mentor were not achieved in isolation. The vision was inculcated by a range of support mechanisms for the mentor teacher. Local authority mentor training days provided a framework for the developing role which 'was appropriate and pitched at a sensible level. It enabled the ... mentors to team-build quite quickly' (Mentor E). Training days provided the opportunity to share information and ideas. There were opportunities to raise issues or express concerns – they became a forum for addressing general challenges and issues rather than specifics and went some way to developing a more coherent and cohesive role for mentors. An understanding of and confidence in the role were significantly strengthened by this peer group support. The introduction of 'surgeries' – mentor teachers meeting with a member of the inspectorate on a one-to-one basis – was very productive. Much emphasis was placed on the collegiality developed among the mentors. The importance of sharing experiences and consulting when there were issues or challenges was highlighted.

Support in the form of resource files and documentation including the plethora of new legislation when appropriate and available was seen as essential to the day-to-day working with settings. Such resources provided the frameworks for improving practice and raising standards within current policies and legislation. The rapidly changing context needed to be clearly understood. Mentor teachers did not overlook the fact that practitioners' experience and expertise were also an important aspect of their own knowledge base.

Much of the development of the mentor role in working with practitioners in the settings was attributable to the variety of activities that took place. Although knowledge, experience and understanding of the role were essential in working with practitioners in the settings, the most important element of the collaboration was the development of good relationships. These require time and effort by both mentors and practitioners and are determined by shared professionalism – and that also needs time to blossom. The mentor role certainly required time, tact and diplomacy.

Mentor teachers had to overcome the occasional problematic issue of practitioners who were reluctant to be involved – some settings were suspicious and hostile with involvement seen as 'interference'. Others felt intimidated, nervous, vulnerable and threatened. Those anxieties were linked to the lack of knowledge and understanding of the role of mentor which was perceived to be a negatively critical one rather than one of critical friend.

Reflection point

4   When someone has been in a position to support you, did you feel confident, anxious, threatened . . .? What is the basis of these feelings? How did you act to build upon the positive ones and overcome the less positive feelings?

Three key features emerged from the developing programme:

1   The range of activity undertaken was closely linked to the development of relationships.
2   Where good relationships were established, the activity itself was very productive leading to: discussions with staff; reviews of documentation; supporting planning and assessment; modelling practice; in-service training in settings; supporting pre- and post-OfSTED inspections; working with children; involving outside agencies; and providing up-to-date information including new initiatives.
3   The question of time was always an issue. The very individual needs of settings required more or less time to support programme development. It was also a logistical challenge that was almost impossible to resolve.

There were aspects of mentor involvement that provided the basis for success in raising the quality of provision in settings. Mentors needed continually to improve, extend and develop their:

- personal and professional development;
- own practice;
- own knowledge, experience and expertise;
- abilities to reflect upon their own practice.

Both practitioners and mentors felt that quality early years provision could be achieved by:

- developing a richness of activities for all children;
- discussing early years practices openly;
- working towards common goals;
- having a greater awareness of early years issues;
- raising the profile and status of early years work.

Such achievements could only be reached by close collaboration with the practitioners in the settings. Mentor teachers needed to do the following:

- encourage and support enthusiastic and dedicated staff;
- develop practitioner professionalism;
- extend practitioner knowledge and expertise and their experience base;
- encourage and promote reflection;
- motivate practitioners.

Mentor teachers also recognized the evolutionary nature of the programme within a global and visionary perspective and also the importance of developing appropriate activities for each setting. Personal and professional development could be somewhat overshadowed by the need to provide for the very individual demands of each setting. Professional development and the vision of the programme needed to be constantly brought to the fore so that it was not lost in the minutiae of the sharing of knowledge and its practical application in the settings.

A brief evaluation

The success of the mentoring programme lay in a belief that it would have a significant and positive effect on settings, practitioners and children because of its collaborative and supportive nature. Optimism was key, together with the value that each participant placed on her own contributions. The collaborative process – motivation, encouragement and respect – helped practitioners view involvement in very positive terms and led to increased confidence and feelings of worth. Professional rapport provided another collaborative opportunity for success and was influential in supporting and improving quality practices.

A continuing thread throughout the development of the programme was the importance of support for practitioners – motivation, encouragement, confidence building, sharing good practice, improving practice and collaboration. Sharing professional expertise ran alongside the empathetic relationships fostered between each mentor and practitioner.

Reflection points

5   How often do you and your colleagues really collaborate to improve and enhance practice? What importance do you all attach to this?

6   How do you make time to discuss the issues and challenges involved?

A framework for a vision of the future – a mission statement

Handy (1994) described the 'kings' and 'prophets' of organizations – the kings have power while the prophets hold the principles. The kings would be 'the people who make things happen, but every king needs a prophet, to help ... keep a clear head amidst the confusions. No one, however, would want the prophet to run the show' (1994: 19). The reference to 'kings' and 'prophets' was central to the issue of interaction between mentor teachers and practitioners. The early years programme was based on that interaction at the levels of philosophy and principle as well as at the practical, informational and knowledge-based levels. One of the key features of the programme was the need for movement in personal positioning. Both mentor teachers and practitioners' involvement had to be underpinned by a united view of early childhood education (Ball 1994; Edwards and Knight 1994) and the development of self as pedagogue (Soler et al. 2001).

For any support programme to have a lasting impact upon the quality of early years provision, a number of underlying issues and principles would need to be part of the professional development of all those involved. These included a shared philosophy; expertise and experience; relationships; professional practice, professional development/training and change.

A *shared philosophy* meant working towards the same ideals/vision in harmony. Harmony could be realized in the practitioner/mentor teacher collaboration in providing together a quality environment for children's learning and development. The evolution of professional communities – the mentor teachers and practitioners in their settings with multi-disciplinary 'others' – was arguably crucial to the formation of a shared philosophy to underpin quality provision which, in turn, involved change and adjustment.

Second, continual emphasis on the issues of *expertise and experience* among both mentors and practitioners, was important to development and to creating a two-way process. The development of the collaborative use of expertise and experience encourages ownership of a programme. Ownership provided motivation to engage in delivering a quality early years curriculum with children's learning central to the quality equation. Anning and Edwards maintained: 'A collective focus on pupil learning allows the development of a professional discourse which centres on the professional actions of colleagues so they create contexts and plan and evaluate actions taken to support children's learning' (1999: 149).

To move forward with colleagues, communication, co-operation, respect and support are vital and they can only grow, evolve and advance if the expertise and experience of everyone is recognized. A 'facilitator' role for the mentor addressed the mechanisms for dissemination of good practice. Collaborative initiatives between mentor teachers also provided a forum for developing dynamic approaches to mentor training.

In terms of *relationships*, the challenge for mentor teachers was to continue to develop positive and constructive relationships with practitioners based on shared philosophies, expertise and experience. The skills and abilities necessary to foster those positive relationships increased confidence to further the process of improvement and raise standards in settings. The skills involved – trust, empathy, motivation and inter- and intra-personal relationships – were vital, although sometimes challenging! The fundamental links between shared philosophies of education, the expertise of those involved in establishing quality provision and the development of positive relationships between mentor teachers and practitioners, were the factors underpinning *professional practice*.

Gammage and Swann have suggested that 'high quality childhood provision ... [is] dependent upon high quality professional practice' (1998: 15). Relationships are a key element in that equation. The development of the mentor's role involved acting as a facilitator in exposing and developing the skills and abilities necessary to establish good working relationships with practitioners in all settings.

The complexities of expanding understanding of theory and practice in early years education and care were addressed through *professional development/training*. A co-ordinated programme of training initiatives, workshops and conferences provided a framework for everyone's professional development. A study in effective pedagogy (Moyles et al. 2002) confirmed the importance of the reflective practitioner as one in which she is 'clear about principles underpinning early years pedagogy and reflects regularly on current thinking about children's learning and development in relation to effective pedagogy, internal and external initiatives and is committed to training and development' (2002: 44).

Professional development involved the wider community and included the collaboration, co-operation and interactions between mentors/ practitioners, local authority advisors/inspectors, and other experts. Barth's (1990: 45) 'community of learners' formed the basis of the professional development process.

The very nature of professional development implies a notion of *change* – one of the few certainties in life. Professional development involved change and adaptation, the acceptance of which supported improvement and raised standards. The imposition of national and local initiatives, though, provided a challenge in reconciling one's *own* and *outside* aims and objectives but co-ordinated and co-operative professional development opportunities had to be maintained.

Conclusion

The vision for the future must focus on children and maintaining high quality early years learning and care environments. The challenge for all those involved highlights the main issue of professionalism. Moyles et al. (2002: 89) suggest that:

> If we want professionals, then professional understanding itself needs to be nurtured, to be allowed time to develop and opportunity to be applied. Educational improvement depends upon practitioners feeling they WANT to make a difference: upon them feeling empowered and professional.

That offered an interesting vision. Helping practitioners to adopt pedagogical principles and practices (Siraj-Blatchford 1999) is at the heart of creating and sustaining professionals. The StEPs project (Moyles and Adams 2001) provides pointers to the process of developing professionalism and serves as a useful reference for programme development. Government initiatives such as the Early Years Professional Status (EYPS) qualification provide a route to improved professional status for practitioners.

The vision, the mission and the process were key factors in raising standards and improving quality of early years provision in the Worcestershire mentoring strategy. It required commitment and enthusiasm, passion and belief. Mentor teachers and practitioners needed to see themselves as 'a professional body of practitioners who can speak with authority on the special nature of the education and care of young children and their own roles in those programmes' (Moyles et al. 2002: 93).

Mentor teachers needed to engage energetically in the facilitator role in developing that professional practitioner culture, ensuring that practitioners acquired the knowledge, skills, resources and confidence to develop high quality learning environments in which all children would have the opportunity to flourish. Mentor teachers maintained an overview while concurrently supporting the needs of individual settings. The differing roles of the mentor teachers and practitioners in continuing to strive for improvements have been crucial to successful improvement.

The reference to 'kings' and 'prophets' (Handy 1994) was particularly apt. Practitioners had the power to make things happen. They were the 'kings' of their domains but had the global picture and shared vision needed to be a major part of the development. Quality early years provision was developed through common pedagogic principles and practices. The 'prophet' role of the mentor teacher needs to be maintained. Such a collaboration of practitioner and mentor, of king and prophet, has the potential for providing a unique opportunity for developing high quality early years provision. The effective pedagogue is at the heart of the development as part of a community of learners. Quality is attainable but not without effort. There is a role for the inspirational visionary but it is tempered by the place of the corporate image in the guise of national initiatives.

The challenges and issues behind the role of mentor teacher have been revealed. Essentially there needs to be a vision, a mission and a method for mentor teachers and practitioners to collaborate in achieving high quality education and care for all children.

Points for discussion

- How far is it possible for practitioners in different settings to act as mentors to each other?
- What are the skills you think are vital if you are to trust another practitioner and work alongside them to develop your own skills, knowledge and understanding?
- What are the issues and challenges in your setting related to developing yourself as a professional 'educarer'?
- What can leaders and managers do to support the processes?

References and further reading

Anning, A. and Edwards, A. (1999) *Promoting Children's Learning from Birth to Five: Developing the New Early Years Professional.* **Buckingham: Open University Press.**

Ball, C. (1994) *Start Right: The Importance of Early Learning.* London: The Royal Society for the Encouragement of Arts, Manufactures and Commerce.

Barth, R.S. (1990) *Improving Schools from Within: Teachers, Parents and Principals Can Make a Difference.* San Francisco: Jossey-Bass Publishers.

Daloz, L. (1999) *Mentor: Guiding the Journey of Adult Learners.* **Huboken, NJ: Jossey-Bass/Wiley.**

Department for Education and Employment (1998) *Early Years Development and Childcare Partnership: Planning Guidance 1999–2000.* Suffolk: DfEE Publications.

Department for Education and Skills (2006) *KEEP: Key Elements of Effective Practice.* Norwich: HMSO.

Department of Education and Science (1990) *Starting with Quality: The Report of the Committee of Enquiry into the Quality of Educational Experience Offered to 3- and 4-Year Olds (The Rumbold Report).* London: HMSO.

Edwards, A. and Knight, P. (1994) *Effective Early Years Education.* Buckingham: Open University Press.

Eyles, J.G. (2002) The development of quality early years provision: raising standards, improving practice: an encounter with the hydra-headed creature that is the change process. Unpublished Doctor of Education thesis, University of Leicester.

Gammage, P. and Swann, R. (1998) *Issues in Early Childhood Education.* Nottingham: Education Now.

Handy, C. (1994) *The Empty Raincoat: Making Sense of the Future.* London: Hutchinson.

Moyles, J. and Adams, S. (2001) *StEPs: Statements of Entitlement to Play: A Framework for Playful Teaching.* **Buckingham: Open University Press.**

Moyles, J., Adams, S. and Musgrove, A. (2002) *SPEEL: Study of Pedagogical Effectiveness in Early Learning.* DfES Research Report 363. London: DfES.

Pascal, C., Bertram, A.D. and Ramsden, F. (1997) The Effective Early Learning Research Project: reflections upon the action during Phase 1, *Early Years,* 17(2): 40–7.

Pascal, C., Bertram, A., Ramsden, F., Mould, C., Saunders, M. and Georgeson, J. (1996) *Evaluating and Developing Quality in Early Childhood Settings: A Professional Development Programme.* Worcester: Amber Publications.

QCA/DfEE (2000) *Curriculum Guidance for the Foundation Stage.* London: QCA.

Robins, A. (ed.) (2006) *Mentoring in the Early Years.* London: Paul Chapman.

Siraj-Blatchford, I. (1999) **Early childhood pedagogy: practice, principles and research**, in P. Mortimore (ed.) *Understanding Pedagogy and its Impact on Learning*. **London: Paul Chapman.**

Soler, J., Craft, A. and Burgess, H. (eds) (2001) *Teacher Development: Exploring Our Own Practice*. **London: Paul Chapman in association with The Open University.**

Sure Start (2002) *Birth-to-Three Matters: A Framework to Support Children in their Earliest Years*. London: Sure Start.

UNICEF (1991) *The United Nations Convention on the Rights of the Child*. Geneva: UNICEF.

9   Birth to three

The need for a loving and educated workforce

Tricia David

Abstract

This chapter sets out to challenge some of the thinking about babies and young children which has caused us to be 'where we are' in relation to how we provide early education and care for those aged between birth and 3 years old.

First, recent changes to policy and legislation will be outlined, then a brief résumé of the history of provision in England for these very young children will be given and its relationship to the employment of women outside the home. The chapter then explores the assumptions that have been made in the past, both about young children and those who work with them. Research will be presented which should lead parents, politicians and practitioners to reconsider those assumptions. The ways in which other recent English government initiatives and policies demand our attention are also presented and emphasis is placed on the education and training of practitioners.

Finally, some of the most urgent challenges remaining for practitioners are listed, in particular, their key role as advocates for a humane and informed way of being for and with children between birth and age 3 years.

Introduction: issues concerning Early Childhood Education and Care (ECEC) provision for children from birth to 3 years

This chapter focuses on the earliest stages of childhood – birth to 3 years – and discusses some of the issues which have resulted in the neglect of the education, training, qualifications, pay and conditions, of those who work with children in this age group.

In particular, it will explore whether babies and very young children are valued as people and as learners, and I will do this in the context of social and historical aspects of ECEC provision and recent government policies including:

- *Every Child Matters;*
- *The Early Years Foundation Stage;*
- *Early Years Practitioners.*

Provision outside the home for the birth-to-3 age range

Historically, the UK has been slow in developing ECEC provision for children under 5 years (David 1990) and, in particular, provision for children from birth to 3 years still eludes many parents. So although the New Labour Government has fostered a growth in this field since its first election to power in 1997, there is still much work to be done to improve both the quantity and quality of that provision across the country.

Some would argue that the question is not just about improving provision but of contesting the push to increase levels of provision, particularly for children younger than 3 years (Fenton 2006). The 'push' was in part a response to the increasing number of women with young children who wish or need to continue in paid employment soon after the birth of their children and in part the UK government's desire to reduce the number of families on benefits through encouraging mothers to seek employment.

In the past, the development of such provision was discouraged by the UK's *laissez-faire* family policies and because of attitudes to women working outside the home based on misapplications of Bowlby's theory of maternal deprivation (see Bowlby 1953; Rutter 1972; David et al. 2003). Today the issue is still about how to ensure secure attachments and how to organize ECEC such that a 'key worker' would become one of a child's significant others and would be available to a child throughout the hours their parents need to work. According to Gaunt (2006), a recent survey claiming a third of mothers are unhappy with their children's nursery care and would prefer a well-trained nanny is flawed: more widely based surveys indicate 85 per cent of parents to be satisfied or very satisfied with their childcare. However, even this evidence still leaves 15 per cent – three parents out of every twenty – apparently dissatisfied. This may be a reflection of a lack of sensitivity to the individual needs of parents and children but it may also be a reflection of the lack of education and training of those who work with very young children, mentioned earlier. In particular, there are anxieties that young entrants to the work, who also happen to have had little experience or training, cannot respond appropriately to either babies or parents (Sue Palmer, Radio 4 Today programme, Saturday 21 October 2006).

Latest developments: *Every Child Matters* and *The Ten Year Strategy*

Lord Laming's report in 2002 on the tragic and cruel death of Victoria Climbié at the hands of her carers, stressed the need for prevention and better co-ordination of mainstream services. This report was the catalyst to the 2003 Green Paper *Every Child Matters* (HMT 2003), which has at its heart five key themes:

- being healthy;
- staying safe;
- enjoying and achieving;
- making a positive contribution;
- economic well-being.

The subsequent 2004 Children Act and the *Every Child Matters: Change for Children* (DfES 2004) implementation paper indicate a vision for early child-hood education and care (ECEC) provision indicating:

- the development of integrated education, health and social care, through children's centres, extended schools and improved services for young people;
- better support for parents;
- better qualified staff;
- targeted services planned and delivered within a universal context. (Pugh 2006: 10)

In 2004, a ten-year strategy *Choice for Parents: The Best Start for Children* (HMT 2004) was published, linking its aims with those of the 2004 Children Act and *Every Child Matters* (HMT 2003). The strategy includes aspects concerning the childcare workforce. Drawing on research evidence, the Treasury stated:

> The single biggest fact that determines the quality of childcare is the workforce ... The current childcare workforce includes many capable and dedicated people. However ... qualification levels are generally low ... a step-change is needed in the quality and stability of the workforce. Working with pre-school children should have as much status as a profession as teaching children in schools.
>
> (HMT 2004: 44–5)

It seems churlish that I, a protagonist of 'joined-up' working for almost 40 years (David 1994a, 1994b), should urge reflection on why it is the Treasury and not one of the departments closer to the action that is setting this agenda. At last we could finally be moving towards relevant and comprehensive services for children and families. However, sustainability may prove impossible – for example, Hawker (2006) points out that the parents of those 2-year-olds who would benefit most from nursery group attendance are those least likely to access it because of the prohibitive costs. Campbell-Barr's (2005) study cast doubts on the desirability of employment among some groups of mothers, and providers are finding the current level of funding for the extension of free early education to 38 weeks, 15 hours per week, does not support demands for high quality provision (as defined by agreed criteria) (Hawker 2006). So does the Treasury recognize the need to invest in our youngest children or will ECEC and out-of-school provision continue to be seen as a drain on the country's economy? Capitalist societies which have a much better record for individual social health and well-being are said to have developed in a broader social context, rather than a narrow *laissez-faire* one where reciprocity and civic morality are neglected (David 2006).

If the provision of ECEC services is primarily seen as 'care' so that parents can work, thus reducing the need for benefit payments and even contributing to tax revenues, perhaps the Treasury is expecting a profit. If the provision is seen as primarily for the children to gain confidence, to learn through play and to provide a firm foundation for later learning, make friends and be aware of their membership of a supportive community, then any rewards to the Treasury may be much longer in coming.

Reflection point

1   What factors do you consider to have led to a reticence to invest public money in ECEC services for children in the birth-to-3 age range?

Thinking about babies and very young children: the importance of loving relationships

Despite the phenomenal achievements of children in this age group – most have learnt to walk, talk, 'mind read' (know what makes close members of their family 'tick' and how to use this to placate or aggravate them – see Dunn 1999; David et al. 2003), and the admission that research evidence in the field of developmental psychology during the first half of the last century has underestimated young children's abilities (Deloache and Brown 1987), misconceptions and false assumptions continue to permeate societal views.

Similarly, assumptions about those who work with children fail to recognize the complex and skilled nature of caring for and educating children during this first phase of life. Becoming a competent and responsive mother is often regarded as instinctive (for females) and this assumption has been extrapolated to mean that early childhood practitioners can do their job instinctively too, as most are women. As shown by the Treasury's statement (HMT 2004), it is only recently that the need for development of education and training in this has been acknowledged. Meanwhile the pay and conditions of employment in the field continue to reflect those old assumptions, rather than reflecting a society keen to invest in its future citizens at a time when the foundations of their attitudes, skills and concepts are being laid.

However, one important assumption held by many about young children – their need for love and affection – has been reinforced by recent research (Gopnik et al. 1999) and it is interesting to note that further advances in research are indicating that it is loving interactions with familiar, significant others (children as well as adults) which stimulate the production of certain brain-influencing chemicals in the bloodstream (Anderton 2006).

One key reason why familiarity is important in this early phase is that the adults who are the carers need to have a deep understanding of each individual child and the family, as well as being known and trusted by them in their turn. This is because they need to be able to respond sensitively to the child's likes, dislikes, expressions (both bodily and vocal) and to be able to cater for inter- and intra-child differences (Bronfenbrenner and Morris 1998; see also Chapter 15). In other words, practitioners need to be able to understand the ecology of child development (Bronfenbrenner 1979) and how the contexts in which children develop affect that development, as do their own inborn differences. Cultural, linguistic and religious differences mean that each child is born into a unique family and milieu. Practitioners need information about parents' points of view and these can only be gained by sharing knowledge, being willing to listen, respecting difference and providing 'a commitment to provide a service of equal quality to all their children' (Draper and Duffy 2006: 159).

Similarly, Michael Lamb and his colleagues at the US National Institute of Child Health and Human Development have studied various aspects of children's lives and they stress that researchers must always examine: 'the interface between endogenous and exogenous processes, children's conceptions and perceptions of their experiences, and the ways in which knowledge of developmental processes can inform social policies and practices' (Lamb 2006: 1). I would argue that this also applies to practitioners. They must be capable not only of examining those endogenous (within the child/ intra-child) and exogenous (outside the child – contextual or environmental) processes, they must also be able to analyse whether or not social policies are informed by that knowledge.

More recently, Robert Putnam has become one of the 'gurus' invited to discuss social issues with UK government leaders. He is now to spend five years at Manchester University, forging links with Harvard in the USA. In his book *Bowling Alone*, Putnam (2000) identifies social capital ('the connections among individuals', 2000: 19) as absolutely crucial to children's successful development in life, arguing that while the effects of poverty and poor educational facilities are also important, parents who are enmeshed in a supportive family and social network and trust their neighbours, provide a better context for growing and learning than those without these benefits. In other words, the loss of community networks is likely to be damaging to families with young children.

Projects aimed at restoring community networks include those involving Family Liaison Officers (FLOs), or Family Liaison Workers. What seems to have been important to the success of the FLOs has been their approachability and their ability to bridge the home–school divide. However, such innovative projects are not without challenges, for example, irrespective of their levels of training, qualifications and the respect and appreciation of their communities, FLOs sometimes report a sense of being under-valued by other professionals (Powell and Stow 2004), although their relationships with headteachers may have been influenced by individual expectations, personal styles and backgrounds (Powell and Soan 2004). Clearly their role is very complex, as Anning (2005) has pointed out in relation to certain early childhood professions.

What should ECEC do?

Following a meeting in 1997 of Ministers of Education of member states of the Organisation for Economic Cooperation and Development (OECD) at which discussion focused on life-long learning, a project was set up to explore and report on provision outside the home for children in the years from birth to primary school admission. Two reports (OECD 2002, 2006) have been published, covering 20 member states. Using evidence gathered, Bennett (2003, 2004) has highlighted the narrow nature of thinking about young children's learning as typified by the pre-primary style curriculum of the UK *Foundation Stage*, compared with the social pedagogy model of, for example, the Scandinavian countries and Germany.

Those of us in the field of early childhood in the UK need to reflect on the extent to which assumptions about young children and their place in our society mean what we offer them – even if playful – is utilitarian, directed at fulfilling pre-set goals, resulting in downward pressure on children in all phases. We should be challenging thinking among politicians, colleagues and parents, urging them to understand the ways in which a social pedagogic model of working with such young children can still address important aims but is differently lived and experienced by both children and practitioners (see, for example, Edwards et al. 1998; Oberhuemer 2004; Rinaldi 2006).

Reflection points

2   Can you tease out the value placed on young children by the two models – pre-primary and social-pedagogic – of early childhood education and care?

3   What do you think ECEC for children from birth to 3 years should be for? What implications would your view have for practice, for example, what would provision look like? What would adults do with and for the children?

The *Birth-to-Three Matters* Framework and the (new) *Foundation Stage*

Following the implementation of the *Curriculum Guidance for the Foundation Stage* (QCA/DfEE 2000) for children from 3–5 years old, the government commissioned the development of a 'curriculum' for the birth-to-3 phase. The director of the project suggested a better term would be a 'framework' to support work in this phase and in 2002 the DfES Sure Start Unit launched the *Birth-to-Three Matters* pack, distributing copies of the 16 laminated cards, booklet, poster, video and CD-ROM, proposing four aspects of early childhood: *A Strong Child; A Skilful Communicator; A Competent Learner*, and *A Healthy Child*. The pack was intended to help workers in this phase gain knowledge about child development, issues in early childhood, ideas about effective practice, and about how children learn through play. They were also encouraged to reflect on meeting diverse needs (see Chapters 3 and 4) and to access research information. Although anecdotal evidence reported by numerous colleagues suggests the Framework was welcomed in the field, within two years the DfES announced a new *Early Years Foundation Stage* (DfES 2006) was to be instituted to bring together the birth-to-3 and the 3–5 foundation stage.

This proposal was greeted positively because those in the field recognized the need for continuity of experience for children. It was expected that the *Birth-to-Three Matters Framework* would be incorporated into new guidance in England, but there have been widespread fears that this will not be the case and that the change will result in more prescription, with inappropriate goals to be reached, resulting on further downward pressure on young children and even on babies.

In particular, the anxieties sprang from decisions concerning the imposition of a method of teaching literacy through synthetic phonics. The Rose Report (2006) suggests the teaching of phonics should be 'brisk' and 'discrete' and Bromley (2006) believes this means practitioners should use their own experience and expertise to decide if and when children are ready for such sessions. The problem is that most young children recognize the importance of print literacy if they grow up in a print-rich/print-dependent society. They want to take part in literacy activities, because they are very good at detecting what gives a person power, so if they come from a home or community where print literacy is valued, they do not need encouragement to take part in activities that make sense to them because they are relevant and based on their own experiences. But in the main, the activities that 'make sense' to young children are not about the detail of literacy, or phonics, they are about the 'big picture' of literacy, such as what it is for, how we use print and what meaning it carries (see David et al. 2000; Chapter 17).

Unfortunately many practitioners lack the confidence and training to defend their own judgements about what they do and they fall into the trap of believing inspectors want to see formal literacy sessions on phonics (David et al. 2000). Only when practitioners in the field are sufficiently educated and trained to be able to articulate the reasoning and research behind their practice will they feel able to interpret reports, policy and prescriptions in the ways Bromley suggests. Work such as hers is a crucial ingredient in those developments of practitioner expertise. Bromley urges practitioners to observe the children with whom they work, to be and to become knowledgeable about those children in particular and about child development and how children learn, so that they will be able to make appropriate decisions in planning and practice (see Chapter 12).

Meanwhile, Duffy believes we may well have reached a time when one can detect a return to seeing the child as central to the process of ECEC and during KS1. She hopes the new EYFS will 'mark a fundamental change in the way the curriculum for the youngest children is conceptualized' (Duffy 2006: 87).

The remaining challenges concerning practitioners

It will have become clear in the course of this chapter that the education and training of ECEC practitioners are high on the list of priorities for the field. As HM Treasury stated, many of those already working in group or home settings with very young children have great experience and expertise but opportunities to gain qualifications have been severely limited and often entailed prohibitive costs. Owen (2006) has also detailed the complexities and contradictions of the tangle of training courses already in existence.

Whatever their level of training, one of the key aspects of working effectively with young children is being adept at observation, so as not to under- or over-estimate what a child can do, nor to misinterpret what a child is trying to express. The ability to intervene appropriately at a particular moment in a child's play depends on sensitivity to what one knows about that child and observation of the child's behaviours, and bodily, facial and verbal expressions. However well qualified and experienced, we sometimes get this wrong, so we also need the ability to reflect on our practice and learn from the failures as well as from the successes (Moyles and Adams 2001).

It is hoped that the new Early Years Professional status and the ultimate aim of having a graduate in every ECEC group setting will result in growing confidence and competence among all practitioners, since these people will form the vanguard of those able to articulate the rationale for learning through play and conversation and for the mix of child-led and adult-led activities.

From among these practitioners the new heads of Children's Centres will be recruited and their training will need to equip them with abilities to deal with the complexity of their role as discussed by Anning (2005) and Moyles (2006). It seems likely that such heads will come from a variety of service backgrounds and while Owen (2006) points out the need for training equivalent to that for headteachers, she also urges us to remember the long-standing debate concerning the importance of qualified teacher status and its implications for parity of pay and conditions for staff in the ECEC sector. Furthermore, nursery schools have been endorsed by both research (Sylva et al. 2004) and by OfSTED, so it could be argued that the involvement of qualified teachers should continue to be an essential ingredient in this multi-professional field for the sake of both children's learning and staff conditions. But teacher education and training in England for the early years also needs reconfiguring if it is to encompass understandings about children in the birth-to-3 phase.

Once these high levels of training are in place, will practitioners be sufficiently able to address the concerns of Sir Richard Bowlby and his colleagues (Bowlby 2006)? These concerns involve the need for the development of close, warm and sensitive relationships between very young children and their carers, and sometimes the necessary rotas, shifts and staff changes impinge on such bonding.

Other issues include parents as partners, sustainability, and the mindset, or attitudes that can lead to a 'top-down curriculum', including inappropriate formal teaching of such young children. Some practitioners in the birth-to-3 phase feel uncomfortable with the terms 'education' and 'teaching' and I have argued elsewhere (David 2007) that they need not be squeamish about seeing what they do to help babies and toddlers learn through play as being educational and requiring subtle and appropriate teaching.

As a group, early years people need constantly to return to the debate about what early childhood education and care is 'for' in our society. After many years of being privileged to be with young children and ECEC practitioners, parents, researchers and policy-makers in England and many other countries, I have come to the conclusion that each society, perhaps unwittingly, sets tasks for its children, including those in this first phase. However, the children set their own tasks too – some concur with the tasks set by their society or community. Babies and toddlers come into the world primed to be curious and sociable. So they want to take part in their society and they watch and work out what it is we 'do' together, how we communicate, share our lives, love, laugh, live and die.

Our own personal vision, our constructions of early childhood and what we think the earliest years are 'for', are based on our own values. As Nutbrown (2006: 100) states, we need to challenge policy and the language used in policy documents when they do not accord with 'a holistic and developmental view of children's early learning'. In order to be able to do this, each of us needs to be able to articulate our philosophies, values and visions and understand how they have been formed.

Having articulated these to ourselves and shared them with colleagues, we can begin to take up the role of advocates for young children. One way of challenging the thinking of others is to juxtapose the treatment of young children with that of businessmen, for example, or older children. One of my favourite ways of getting people to recognize the improving, but still regrettably fragmented nature of ECEC provision is to ask how they think parents would react if secondary school pupils had to move schools several times between 11 and 16, as well as sometimes attending one school during the morning and another during the afternoon. This clearly has not been thought strange for babies and young children, despite people in this phase of life having less facility in the use of language to understand what is happening and why, compared with older children.

Reflection point

4   What other indicators can you list that would show babies and young children to be valued in contemporary UK society?

Conclusion

The conclusions we reached in the research review for *Birth-to-Three Matters* (David et al. 2003: 143) were as follows:

- Above all, children need loving, responsive, sensitive key persons around them, people who recognize their fascination with and curiosity about what is going on in their worlds, who will cater for their drive to explore and problem-solve through active learning, and who will provide opportunities to play, make friends and share experiences, and yet allow time for them to be deeply focused alone but near others, as well as ensuring all their health needs are met.

- Children need to be respected as people in their own right.
- Children need to live in a society which is informed about their development and learning, and which is involved and delighted in their amazing abilities.

We also threw out a challenge which perhaps sums up the huge responsibility laid upon early years practitioners: 'The question that remains for debate, however, is how, as a society and as a field, we set about ensuring the fulfilment of these apparently obvious and simple conclusions' (David et al. 2003: 9). While that challenge was intended for the whole of society, not just for practitioners, one of the most important indicators that will demonstrate we value all our young children will be according to ECEC practitioners higher levels of education and training, pay and conditions.

Points for discussion

- How far are social policies, as you understand them, informed by knowledge of the within child/intra-child and outside the child/contextual/environmental processes?
- What training opportunities are available to you? How do you decide on which training to focus for yourself?
- Does your setting operate a 'key worker' system? If so, what are the benefits to children? If not, what advantages would such a system provide?

References and further reading

Anderton, M. (2006) *The Science of Parenting*. London: Dorling Kindersley.

Anning, A. (2005) Investigating the impact of working in multi-agency service delivery settings in the UK on early years practitioners' beliefs and practices, *Journal of Early Childhood Research*, 3(1): 19–50.

Bennett, J. (2003) Starting strong: the persistent division between care and education, *Journal of Early Childhood Research*, 1(1): 21–48.

Bennett, J. (2004) Curriculum issues in national policy making, keynote address at EECERA Conference, Malta, 2 September.

Bowlby, J. (1953) *Child Care and the Growth of Love*. Harmondsworth: Penguin.

Bowlby, R. (2006) The proof of attachment theory, *The Daily Telegraph*, Saturday, 21 October, p. 6.

Bromley, H. (2006) All about phonics, *Nursery World*, 106(4040): 13–20.

Bronfenbrenner, U. (1979) *The Ecology of Human Development*. Cambridge, MA: Harvard University Press.

Bronfenbrenner, U. and Morris, P. (1998) The ecology of developmental processes, in W. Damon and R. Lerner (eds) *The Handbook of Child Psychology*, vol.1: *Theoretical Models of Human Development*. New York: John Wiley.

Campbell-Barr, V. (2005) The economy of childcare, unpublished thesis for submission, University of Kent at Canterbury/CCCU.

David, T. (1990) *Under Five – Under-Educated?* Milton Keynes: Open University Press.

David, T. (ed.) (1994a) *Working Together for Young Children: Professional and Voluntary Work with Families*. London: Routledge.

David, T. (ed.) (1994b) *Protecting Children from Abuse: Multi-professionalism and The Children Act 1989*. Stoke-on-Trent: Trentham Books.

David, T. (2006) The world picture, in G. Pugh and B. Duffy (eds) *Contemporary Issues in the Early Years*, 4th edn. London: Sage.

David, T. (2007) Beginning at the beginning, in J. Moyles (ed.) *Beginning Teaching: Beginning Learning*, 3rd edn. Maidenhead: Open University Press.

David, T., Goouch, K., Powell, S. and Abbott, L. (2003) *Birth-to-Three Matters: A Review of the Literature*, DfES Research Report 444. London: DfES.

David, T., Raban, B., Ure, C., Goouch, K., Jago, M., Barrière, I. and Lambirth, A. (2000) *Making Sense of Early Literacy: A Practitioner's Perspective*. Stoke-on-Trent: Trentham Books.

Deloache, J.S. and Brown, A.L. (1987) The early emergence of planning skills in children, in J. Bruner and H. Haste (eds) *Making Sense*. London: Methuen.

DfES (2004) *Every Child Matters: Change for Children*. Nottingham: DfES Publications.

DfES (2006) *Early Years Foundation Stage: A Consultation Document*. London: DfES.

Draper, L. and Duffy, B. (2006) Working with parents, in G. Pugh and B. Duffy (eds) *Contemporary Issues in the Early Years*, 4th edn. London: Sage.

Duffy, B. (2006) The curriculum from birth to six, in G. Pugh and B. Duffy (eds) *Contemporary Issues in the Early Years*, 4th edn. London: Sage.

Dunn, J. (1999) Mindreading and social relationships, in M. Bennett (ed.) *Developmental Psychology*. London: Taylor and Francis.

Edwards, C., Gandini, L. and Foreman, G. (1998) *The Hundred Languages of Children*. New Jersey: Ablex.

Fenton, B. (2006) Day nursery may harm under-3s, say child experts, *The Daily Telegraph*, Saturday, 21 October, p. 1.

Gaunt, C. (2006) Childcarers slate 'biased' survey, *Nursery World*, 106(4042): 5.

Gopnik, A., Melzoff, A. and Kuhl, P. (1999) *How Babies Think: The Science of Childhood*. London: Weidenfeld and Nicolson.

Hawker, D. (2006) Joined up working – the development of children's services, in

G. Pugh and B. Duffy (eds) *Contemporary Issues in the Early Years*, 4th edn. London: Sage.

HMT (Her Majesty's Treasury) (2003) *Every Child Matters* (Green Paper). London: HMSO.

HMT (2004) *Choice for Parents: The Best Start for Children*. London: HMSO.

Lamb, M. (2006) Child development in context. Available at: http://nichddirsage. nichd.nih.gov:8080/ar2004/pages/1ce/ssed.htm (accessed 30 November 2006).

Moyles, J. (2006) *Effective Leadership and Management in the Early Years*. Maidenhead: Open University Press.

Moyles, J. and Adams, S. (2001) *StEPs: Statements of Entitlement to Play*. Buckingham: Open University Press.

Nutbrown, C. (2006) Watching and listening: the tools of assessment, in G. Pugh and B. Duffy (eds) *Contemporary Issues in the Early Years*, 4th edn. London: Sage.

Oberhuemer, P. (2004) Controversies, chances and challenges: reflections on the quality debate in Germany, *Early Years*, 24(1): 9–21.

OECD (2002) *Starting Strong*. Paris: Organisation for Economic Cooperation and Development.

OECD (2006) *Starting Strong II*. Paris: Organisation for Economic Cooperation and Development.

Owen, S. (2006) Training and workforce issues in the early years, in G. Pugh and B. Duffy (eds) *Contemporary Issues in the Early Years*, 4th edn. London: Sage.

Powell, S. and Soan, S. (2004) Friend or FLO? Professional Identities of school-based Family Liaison Officers, paper presented at the British Educational Research Association Conference, UMIST, September.

Powell, S. and Stow, W. (2004) *Final Report on the Evaluation of Kent Children's Fund Family Liaison Officer Service*. Available at: http://eppicentre.ac.uk

Pugh, G. (2006) The policy agenda for early childhood services, in G. Pugh and B. Duffy (eds) *Contemporary Issues in the Early Years*, 4th edn. London: Sage.

Putnam, R.D. (2000) *Bowling Alone: The Collapse and Revival of American Community*. New York: Simon and Schuster.

QCA (Qualifications and Curriculum Authority)/DfEE (Department for Education and Employment) (2000) *Curriculum Guidance for the Foundation Stage*. London: QCA.

Rinaldi, C. (2006) *In Dialogue with Reggio Emilia*. London: Routledge.

Rose, J. (2006) The Rose Report: Independent Review of the Teaching of Reading. Available at: www.standards.dfes.gov.uk/rosereview/report.doc (accessed 31 March 2006).

Rutter, M. (1972) *Maternal Deprivation Reassessed*. Harmondsworth: Penguin.

Sylva, K., Melhuish, E., Sammons, P., Siraj-Blatchford, I. and Taggart, B. (2004) *The Effective Provision of Pre-school Education (EPPE) Project: Technical Paper 12 – the Final Report*. London: DfES/Institute of Education, University of London.

SECTION THREE
ENABLING ENVIRONMENTS

Introduction to Section Three

Janet Moyles

> The environment plays a key role in supporting and extending children's development and learning.
>
> (EYFS Principle 3)

Introduction

Perhaps this is one area – Enabling Environments – where we have taken for granted that practitioners know and understand how to provide appropriate materials, resources and experiences for babies and young children. However, in research conducted earlier this decade, Moyles and Adams (2001) found that while practitioners in nurseries were providing exciting experiences for children, they were less secure in their knowledge of the learning which underpinned these activities. Later collaborative research resulted in similar findings (Adams et al. 2003) in relation to the reception class.

Observing children in order to learn about their learning (see e.g. Hobart and Frankel 2004) is now established practice and enshrined in many new policy documents. But we need also to remember to observe the learning environment itself, how it works for everyone who uses the setting. I remember well in one nursery I visited where collection time for children at the end of day was a nightmare: everyone acknowledged it as such but no-one did anything about it! We get extremely familiar with our everyday lives and don't have the time to question everything that happens. But a brief observation of the difficulties revealed pushchairs to be the main problem and it was relatively simple to make provision for these to go elsewhere. It is clearly vital to make space, time and opportunity for parents to exchange information or enquire about children's progress and they often want to do this at the beginning or end of the day so these occasions need to be as trouble-free as possible.

Observation directly informs our planning of both learning and teaching opportunities and experiences (Hargreaves and Wolfe 2007) and of the physical context in which it occurs – it is the very essence of 'enabling environments' and of the assessment of children's development and learning. The importance currently laid upon physical development and large body movements (vital for healthy development but also necessary to combat the rising obesity problem in young children – see information on the ASO website http://www.aso.org.uk) means that the outdoor environment deserves and requires similar thoughtfulness to that of the indoor environment (see, for example, Cartright et al. 2001; Bilton et al. 2005).

Planning requires knowledge on the part of practitioners, knowledge usually acquired by observation, whether of children or of the context. Children should also know that and why you are observing them – it is respectful and courteous and nothing less than we expect of children! Planning with children also makes them real partners in the learning journey, giving them a sense of empowerment and instrumentality. As Bertram and Pascal (2002: 93) assert, children's learning is supported when they are given responsibility for making their own decisions and operating reciprocally with others. It increases their sense of belonging and interconnectedness and allows them opportunities to negotiate authority as well as positively affecting their dispositions to learn social competence and self-concept.

The implications for the organization and management of a play-based environment now firmly advocated in policy documents are significant and need considered thought and attention if we are to provide child-initiated opportunities as well as playful teaching experiences. By 'playful teaching' I mean those fun activities which are controlled by the adult to provide specific learning – this, to me, is very different from spontaneous child play. Practitioners can use many strategies for directing children's focus upon the learning while still ensuring that the task is retained as a playful one in their eyes. A playful environment, whoever is in 'control', has many potentially messy resources which need to be maintained and sustained in an orderly manner. The right to play always requires responsibilities to be fulfilled by the children as much as by the practitioner in relation to tidying away, of course.

I really like the concept of a 'learning journey' embedded within this section. If we truly believe in life-long learning – and that the first few years of a child's life are significant in the development of a life-long learner (see Gopnik et al. 2001; Bruer 2002), then from birth we are truly engaging with children in a journey of discovery, excitement and blossoming understanding. To do this, we need to consider every angle of children's learning and developmental needs, from home backgrounds and transitions to the child as citizen (Council of Europe 1996). We need to ensure that children are always at the heart of our planning and that the environment in which we and they work and play is happy and fulfilling, contributing both to the learning and the well-being of the child (see Geddes 2005 – although related to school learning it has much to say to practitioners in early years settings).

This section has four chapters, all very diverse, but exploring issues of important and immediate concern to all early years practitioners, those of transitions, outdoor adventures, observation and documentation of children's experiences and the importance of multi-disciplinary working and the wider context. In Chapter 10, Hilary Fabian writes about the transition from home to setting to school. She compares the experiences of children, parents and practitioners in the UK with those in Lapland, explaining that such transitions mark a significant change in both countries in the way that a child participates in the family and the community because commuting between home and setting demands adjustment and brings about changes in identity, relationships and roles.

In Chapter 11, Elizabeth Carruthers – again comparing two international contexts, Norway and the UK – explores how far children's outdoor experiences offer them a sufficient sense of adventure. She makes a strong case for stating that all children benefit from challenging and adventurous outdoor experiences, particularly children with special needs, and looks specifically at the idea of Forest Schools. The latter will be of considerable interest to those settings who do not have their own outdoor environment but who, nevertheless, must still provide for challenging outdoor experiences.

Those who are Reggio Emilia advocates will welcome Chapter 12, in which Paulette Luff considers how observation and documentation of children's experiences can enhance planning and provision. She emphasizes that the Italian term implies something much more lively and vivid than that with which we might be more familiar in England, and that documentation is not an end in itself but a tool for educators. Paulette is clear that through documentation, practitioners can achieve shared understandings and use the records as a basis for action in providing directions for children care and education.

The final chapter in this section (Chapter 13) is an exciting and innovative contribution by Deborah Albon who takes food and eating as the basis for considering the organization of the learning environment. She suggests that food and eating is a key area of childhood practice which is often less planned for or considered when compared to other areas, yet is vital to children's health and well-being. Deborah feels that it also provides a forum for multi-professional practices and community engagement.

As we have seen, this is quite an eclectic but very interesting section with many overlaps with the two previous ones. We have already covered much about working together and exploring children's care and education needs and been witness to some interesting international comparisons.

References

Adams, S., Alexander, E., Drummond, M-J. and Moyles, J. (2003) *Inside the Foundation Stage: Recreating the Reception Year*. London: Association of Teachers and Lecturers.

Bertram, T. and Pascal, C. (2002) Assessing what matters in the early years, in J. Fisher (ed.) *The Foundations of Learning*. Buckingham: Open University Press.

Bilton, H., James, K., Marsh, J. and Wilson, A. (2005) *Learning Outdoors: Improving the Quality of Young Children's Play Outdoors*. London: David Fulton.

Bruer, J. (2002) *The Myth of the First Three Years: A New Understanding of Baby Brain Development and Lifelong Learning*. New York: Free Press.

Cartright, P., Scott, K. and Stevens, J. (2001) *A Place to Learn: Developing a Stimulating Learning Environment*. Lewisham: Lewisham Arts and Library Service.

Council of Europe (1996) *Child as Citizen*. Strasbourg: Council of Europe.

Geddes, H. (2005) *Attachment in the Classroom: The Links between Children's Early Experience, Well-being and Performance in School*. New York: Worth Publishing.

Gopnik, A., Meltzoff, A. and Kuhl, P. (2001) *The Scientist in the Crib: What Early Learning Tells Us about the Mind*. London: HarperCollins.

Hargreaves, L. and Wolfe, S. (2007) Observing closely to see more clearly: observation in the primary classroom, in J. Moyles (ed.) *Beginning Teaching: Beginning Learning*, 3rd edn. Maidenhead: Open University Press.

Hobart, C. and Frankel, J. (2004) *A Practical Guide to Child Observation and Assessment*, 3rd edn. Cheltenham: Nelson Thornes.

Moyles, J. and Adams, S. (2001) *StEPs: Statements of Entitlement to Play*. Buckingham: Open University Press.

10 The challenges of starting school

Hilary Fabian

Abstract

Parental expectations of their children and of attendance at settings and schools can present challenges for all concerned during the transition process. Children usually expect to do well and look forward to starting, but hopeful beginnings need nurturing if they are to come to fruition. This chapter identifies many of those hopes, particularly those to do with learning, and outlines ways that educators can begin to increase the likelihood of a successful transition for all those involved. Expectations of transition are divided into three broad areas of challenge: social and cultural issues; familiarization and context issues; and curriculum and learning issues. The chapter draws on examples from a small-scale comparative study between Lapland in northern Finland and north Wales to illustrate different approaches to the curriculum and the challenges for parents, pupils and practitioners as children make the move to school.

Introduction

The start of schooling has been perceived as one of the major challenges of early childhood (Ghaye and Pascal 1988; Margetts 2003). However, it is not just children who are involved in the transition: children, parents and educators are all involved with this change (Dockett and Perry 2004). If it is to be successful, then it needs to be a process of co-construction through participation between the institution and the family communicating and working together (Griebel and Niesel 2002). In order to understand the complexity of transition, an ecological concept can be used (Bronfenbrenner 1979) comprising a series of nested structures (microsystems) linked together in a network (the mesosystem) and influenced by the wider society (the macrosystem): in other words, an interlocking set of systems comprising home, early childhood services and school, which provide a bridge between experiences and form a basis for on-going social interactions. The ability to manage a successful transition therefore involves not only the individual child but also the social systems of each setting.

The transition to a setting or school marks a significant change in the way that a child participates in the family and the community because commuting between the family and school setting demands adjustment and brings about changes in identity, relationships and roles. More than this, however, are the expectations of children, their parents and educators who all have high hopes at the start of the child's schooling (Fabian and Dunlop 2007). So how can children be helped to make a successful transition? It might be helpful to start with a definition of school success.

Ladd's definition of success in school is very straightforward, and encompasses several aspects of children's adjustment to school:

> A child can be seen as successful in school when she or he (a) develops positive attitudes and feelings about school and learning, (b) establishes supportive social ties with teachers and classmates, (c) feels comfortable and relatively happy in the classroom rather than anxious, lonely or upset, (d) is interested and motivated to learn and take part in classroom activities (participation, engagement), and (e) achieves and progresses academically each school year.
>
> (2003: 3)

These are aspects which are reflected in the UK's *Every Child Matters* outcomes (DfES 2003a) which put the emphasis on the child to adapt to the organization rather than bringing his/her own culture to the setting (Brooker 2002).

As well as taking account of *Every Child Matters*, this chapter draws on the findings of a small-scale study that explored children's, families' and educators' perspectives about the transition to school in Lapland and Wales (Fabian and Turunen 2006). Twenty-four children were asked about their expectations of school; 15 parents and 11 educators of prior-to-school children were interviewed to ascertain their views about transition, particularly in relation to curriculum continuity. In asking questions about the curriculum, a range of issues arose, because all those involved tended to view the transition as a whole rather than as a curriculum issue in isolation. The following sections identify some of the challenges for each group and raise questions that can be asked in any country about young children starting school.

Challenges for children

Most children look forward to going to school and settle quickly, but for a few it is a frustrating time that causes confusion such as not knowing where to go; anxiety about the rules of the classroom, as well as surprises such as everyone wearing the same school uniform (Fabian 2002).

Children enter the institutional world with already developing concepts of themselves (Donaldson 1978; Chapter 13) and by the time they start formal school children are thinkers and have a clear idea about what they like and dislike about learning. They see the school curriculum as a promise of something more than their prior-to-school experiences. They expect a richness to the learning that is greater than that previously experienced; that it will take them in new directions – unknown at this stage – but that there will also be some familiarity about the activities and the daily routines. For example, in Wales, children expected that play would continue as before 'with Lego and play dough' but that there would be additional activities such as 'Spiderman, spellings, letters and shapes'. In Lapland, children also expected 'to play outdoors and indoors, draw and paint, play games, listen to music, skate and ski' just as they did in pre-school but that these activities would be extended into 'learning about days of the week, manners and doing exercises'. These children expected to continue to learn in a similar way once they started school; to 'learn by doing, learning by themselves, remembering'. They also expected the learning environment to offer new and exciting challenges but one where it was safe to express ideas, ask questions and experiment with different approaches.

However, starting school can present curriculum challenges to children in the UK and Lapland as they generally move from a play-based curriculum which helps to develop independence and which flows with the child's agenda, to one in which the teacher directs the learning. They had an inkling that this would happen and asked if there would still be opportunities to go outside and appreciate their natural surroundings – for example 'to see butterflies'; and they wanted to know if there would be dressing up clothes at school. This gives a clear indication that they expected learning to involve play and be thematic. One of the challenges in becoming a school pupil is to transfer what has been learned in the familiar environment of the early childhood setting to the unfamiliar setting of school – to transpose 'symbolic capital' to school (Webb et al. 2002).

While these children were confident in their understanding about what takes place at school, some children in the study will continue to experience a diversity of contextual and cultural influences from their 'old' life as they return to their prior-to-school setting for after-school clubs or are collected by a familiar childminder. As they enter school, children often leave behind places or people who are familiar and face the challenge of making new friends and understanding new cultural contexts (Brooker 2002). They have developed their identity in a social and cultural environment with an emphasis on relationships, the contexts of those relationships and the cultural meaning of those relationships. However, on starting school, children might not be with their friends and will have to mediate new relationships often in unfamiliar surroundings.

Children will have gained expectations about school from relationships with friends, older siblings and other family members, but they might not realize that they are expected to adapt to a more formal way of working.

Reflection points

1   What will children learn about change from the process of starting school?
2   What adjustments will children have to make to fit in with the school systems and environment?

Challenges for parents

At the start of school parents tend to view their child's education in a more serious way (Griebel and Niesel 1999). They have high expectations and also anxieties about their child's behaviour and success; they want their children to acquire skills, knowledge and values that they believe to be important (Tizard and Hughes 1984); are concerned about the ratio of adults to children, playtime and lunchtime (Dowling 1988; Cleave and Brown 1991); and want their child to be happy and confident (Dowling 2000). In Wales, they were also concerned about how their children would cope with a longer day and whether or not their children would be respected and recognized as an individual. All this amounts to a growing pressure on schools to bring about an inclusive curriculum and meet a range of individual needs.

Parents undergo a transition – being a parent of a child at school – and are also concerned about their own role in supporting their child's education. For example, in Wales, they asked whether or not they should be helping with reading before their child starts school. Parents wanted to know how to collaborate to help their child develop and what partnership meant in practice, particularly as they see the availability of teachers decreasing as their child grows older. Parents in Lapland held similar views. They felt comfortable in the prior-to-school setting as they were familiar with the building. They had great confidence in the staff because they always had time for parents, could meet the family's wishes and take their needs into account.

Socially isolated and/or single parents sometimes dread the prospect of their children starting school because the familiar would disappear: they would not know the staff in the new setting, would be unsure of their own future role and would have a gap in their own lives (Fabian 2003). Indeed, Dunlop and Fabian (2005, 2007) found that some parents planned to have another baby once their child started school in order to fill the gap.

Parents felt that the knowledge staff gained of their child was more important than the curriculum. In Lapland, educators devise an individual curriculum for children when they enter the early childhood setting. However, 36% of parents did not recognize that there was an individual plan for their child, based on the initial discussion with the staff. For others, the discussion was highly positive and parents felt they had a great deal of influence over the individual curriculum for their child. The most useful areas that parents identified in this personalized curriculum were social skills, developing friendships, play, daily routines, and specific subject skills, such as language, that would extend an already developed area. However, there was little conception of how the individual curriculum is used in the transition from early education to school. While the individual curriculum was considered a good starting point because it gives the basis for individual support of the child, parents hoped the staff at school would have time to read their child's transfer record and hoped it would not only reflect their child's ability but also the essence of their child. Some parents wanted to have a discussion with the pre-school teacher before the start of school as well as meeting the next teacher, thus co-constructing the transition.

Reflection points

3   How are parents participating in your setting in planning the curriculum for
    their children? How are parents helped to match expectations to reality?
4   How is the curriculum in your setting helping parents to see the continuity of
    their child's learning from one phase of education or setting to another?

Challenges for educators

Sometimes schools are 'fed' by a number of settings often with a range of organizational systems. For these schools, the challenge is recognizing the variety of settings from which children come and the concomitant variety of past learning experiences that have to be anticipated in order to accommodate and establish familiar routines for children. In other cases, the early years service is on the same site with the constituent parts of the system being interlinked and interdependent because the reception and early years educators visit each other's settings on a regular basis or have a system of looping (Gaustad 1998) where the children stay with one teacher for two years. In Lapland, the early years setting in the study was linked by a door to the school through which children visited the school for music and other lessons so staff and children got to know one another. The physical transition was not seen as an ordeal for children or families, even if the pedagogies were different.

Pedagogical differences between early childhood services and schools raise a challenge for teachers who usually expect children to be ready for school (Broström 2002). But what is 'ready'? Is it to do with competencies, skills and abilities? Learning is sometimes characterized by goals which reflect cultural perspectives such as those proposed in the *Early Learning Goals* (QCA 2000) or *Every Child Matters* (DfES 2003a) in the UK. Claxton and Carr (2004: 89) suggest that charting possible directions of growth and providing guidance to progress learning attributes are more important if children are 'to respond in a learning-positive way'. For this to occur, not only do children need to know about what takes place at school, how they are going to learn and how they are going to be assessed, but educators also need to be aware of the role they play in influencing learning. So instead of the child being ready for school, the school needs to take responsibility for being ready and creating a match between children and school (Lam and Pollard 2006). This raises issues concerning finding out about children's prior learning, knowing where to start in order to build on prior-to-school experiences to inform planning and design the child's learning. It might also avoid the problem that Stephens and Cope (2003) identified which was that the school expected the child to fit in with them and if children had difficulty with the transition, then teachers ascribed problems to the child, not to the school.

Multiple communications

Another challenge for educators is ensuring that everyone is involved and communicating with each other in a way that is understood. Parents and children want sufficient and accessible information and opportunities to understand the school environment, its curriculum and where they fit into the organization. Teachers want to know about the children's learning and previous experiences from parents and early years educators. If information is too substantial, given very rapidly or the terminology used is unfamiliar, then it can be confusing, cause misunderstanding and anxiety and hinder the transition process. One of the issues for educators is how and when to present information to parents – by brochure, website or meetings – to meet everyone's needs. Educational inclusion is as much about perceptions as it is access, so if parents think that they or their children do not match the norm, they might think that they will be seen as problematic.

Reflection points

5   How does the curriculum or pedagogy support the continuity of a child's learning during the transition to school?

6   What are the most effective ways that educators and parents can communicate to support children during the transition process?

This next section addresses ways of supporting transitions by going beyond those in the *Common Core of Skills and Knowledge for the Children's Workforce* (see Section 4: 16–17, DfES 2005) to look at social and cultural and familiarization and curriculum issues.

Social and cultural issues

In choosing a school, parents are also choosing values and beliefs, and have decided that they want their child to be part of the philosophical culture of that school. However, children also bring their own social capital with them which suggests that we may carry forward factors influencing our lives. If little capital accrues to a child at the first transition, subsequently there may be less on which to draw (Dunlop 2007), so schools need to capitalize on the strengths that families have transferred to their child, while also helping them understand the language of school.

Well-being and pupil performance go hand-in-hand (Laevers et al. 1997). Children learn effectively if they feel safe and if they feel comfortable emotionally in the classroom (DfES 2003b, http://www.everychildmatters.gov.uk/ete/personalisedlearning/). It is therefore important to help children feel that they belong to the school community by providing opportunities for social interaction, helping children to make friends and learn the rules of the classroom (Bulkeley and Fabian 2006). This in turn facilitates acceptance and helps children to develop a positive attitude regarding their identity as a schoolchild belonging to a particular school.

Friendships and relationships are central in helping children to learn well and profit from school (Fabian and Dunlop 2005) but at the start of school children have to cope with loss of friends from their prior-to-school environment and develop social relationships in the new class. To confirm their sense of self-esteem, a significant feature that helps children with starting school, and identified in several studies (Fabian 2002; Margetts 2003; Dockett and Perry 2004), is the ability to mix with other children and to start school with a friend.

Working with parents and colleagues in prior-to-school settings is a further significant aspect in bringing about a successful transition to school. Colleagues can learn from and with one another about their philosophy of educating and about individual children's needs. By building and cultivating networks both with parents and staff, expectations of school can be clarified, communication improved and parents helped to gain confidence to participate in their child's learning.

Reflection points

7 Who will help children at lunchtimes and playtime? Are there ways to support social interaction?

8 How can visits help children to understand the way in which learning takes place at school?

9 How can parents be kept up-to-date with their children's learning?

Familiarization issues

The new context usually means children have to adjust to changes such as the size of building, number of pupils in the class, different teacher–pupil ratios, different classroom layouts, a wider range of ages and often a different route to school. Teachers' beliefs about what is important at the start of school are reflected in the ways in which they introduce children to the school environment and learning at school. Broström (2002) found that the most frequently used method was the school inviting the child to visit the class before school starts and the teachers visiting the children in their early childhood settings. However, it is what takes place during those visits that makes a difference.

Parents in the Welsh study recognized the contribution that they made in supporting their children, and identified ways to help their children overcome insecurities and fears of their new surroundings such as helping them to develop independence and routines, for example, by 'being able to do up his shoe laces' and 'go to the toilet on his own', and talking to their children about what they might do and see at school. However, there is a danger that the picture that parents give their children of school does not live up to expectations, and children are left to handle the difference between the rhetoric and the reality (Dunlop 2001). Parents thought that the experience of eating a school meal with their child during a visit would give their child confidence. Staff felt children should have a more prolonged transition process and wanted support in developing their own skills in discussing parents' and children's wishes, in helping children respond to change and supporting them in their new, and sometimes challenging, environment.

Understanding the ways in which learning takes place is a major issue. At school there is greater importance given to outcomes and targets; sometimes homework in the form of reading and number activities; being taught subjects rather than areas of learning; and often a change in the teaching method. Parents are more likely to be able to support their child's learning if they are aware of the ways in which children learn at school and the support that they can give at home.

Curriculum issues

In Lapland, a personalized curriculum which involves an individual meeting between educators, children and their parents at the start of a child's formal education aims to take account of the child's individuality and parents' views on aspects such as the child's experiences, current needs and future perspectives, interests and strengths, and individual need for support and guidance. In Lapland, this included the concept of 'self' and emotional life; social, motor and cognitive skills; linguistic development; perception of the environment; working habits; self-expression; and music. In the UK, the *Every Child Matters* initiative (DfES 2003b) outlines a personalized approach to supporting children which means:

- tailoring learning to the needs, interests and aspirations of each individual;
- tackling barriers to learning and allowing each child to achieve their potential (http://www.everychildmatters.gov.uk/ete/personalised learning/).

It is focused on giving all children the support they require, whatever their needs, abilities, background or circumstances. By engaging parents in supporting their children's learning and progression, an understanding develops of formal and informal learning; academic and social learning; and the expectations and achievements of their child.

The difference in pedagogical styles and the curriculum content between early childhood services and school can cause problems with continuity. In Wales, the individual records were sent to school but only if the parents wanted this to happen. In Lapland, the staff ensured the child's individual plans were transferred to the school. Staff in Wales thought it would be helpful if teachers visited the nursery to meet the children and talk with them individually and discuss previous learning. In Lapland, transition activities for children with special educational needs depend on the child's individual circumstances. Whatever the need, there is intensive co-operation between parents, the future teachers and therapists to create the individual curriculum. In the UK, the *Common Assessment Framework* provides a simple process for a holistic assessment of a child's needs and strengths, taking account of the role of parents, carers and environmental factors on their development. Practitioners then are well placed to agree with the child and family about what support is appropriate (DfES 2003c, http://www.everychildmatters. gov.uk/deliveringservices/caf/).

Discussion

Every Child Matters has 'Ready for School' as a sub-heading under 'Enjoy and Achieve'. Readiness suggests a set of physical and cognitive skills that a child should possess to be ready to start school rather than a developing child who has abilities in a range of areas. There is consensus, however, based upon a wealth of research, that a child's readiness for school depends on his/her levels across five distinct but connected domains:

- physical well-being and motor development;
- social and emotional development;
- approaches to learning;
- language development;
- cognition and general knowledge (Rhode Island Kids Count 2005).

Most teachers want children to be healthy, confident, active and attentive, able to communicate their needs, feelings and thoughts, enthusiastic and curious when approaching new activities (Arnold et al. 2006). They also place importance on skills such as the ability to follow directions, not being disruptive in class, and being sensitive to others (Rhode Island Kids Count 2005). As Young (in Arnold et al. 2006: 7) says: 'The child who is ready for school has a combination of positive characteristics.' Starting school marks a boundary which demands that development has reached a particular point. Issues which affect children's intellectual capabilities, academic achievement and behaviour, include the home environment, poverty, care and nurture, food, safety, motivation, language and the child's view of themselves as a learner. Not being ready at a particular time can have a detrimental effect on future learning and self-esteem. So, rather than ensuring readiness for school, Broström (2002) suggests that schools become 'child-ready' to meet the wide range of individuals that enter at the set time. This is a school where 'staff members are welcoming and appreciative of children's efforts, ensure their safety and sense of security, and provide effective learning opportunities which enable children too interact effectively with their world' (Arnold et al. 2006: 19).

Educators and parents often have different ideas of school readiness. Teachers put more emphasis on the social domain, whereas many parents emphasize academic readiness. For example, in my study, parents had confidence that the prior-to-school setting gave their child a good start to their education socially but wanted their child to be prepared for more formal learning as the start of school approaches. Practices that establish and foster relationships among important individuals in the child's life are likely to reap the most benefit for the child (Early 2004). Starting school, therefore, is best supported by practices that engage the parents (and often grandparents) and early childhood setting prior to the first day of school in developing an understanding of how learning takes place at school, sharing information and identifying gaps, overlap and progression.

Conclusion

The start of primary school is a transition for children, parents and educators in children's life-long learning journeys. Children are agents in the transition process as they bring what they learned from home and early childhood settings to school, and have to be active in adapting and responding to the transition. They anticipate the school curriculum as being exciting, rewarding and different but also somewhat familiar. They expect school to be fun, but they are nervous about the unknown and the possibility of having to do things they do not want to do. Parents consider they have greater influence in the prior-to-school setting, have high expectations for their child's success at school and see partnership with school as the way of fulfilling this. Parents consider that the confidence their children gain at nursery has a significant impact on their child's ability to make friends and understand school. Although parents are unsure about curriculum content, they are more concerned that their child is able to maintain their own identity and individuality. Educators are faced with challenges to smooth the transition in terms of organizational systems, curriculum and pedagogy. A major challenge for all is communicating information to understand each other's perspectives.

Social and cultural aspects are central in supporting children in the transition to school and can be improved by developing communication networks and supporting children in developing friendships to gain a sense of belonging to the school community. Teachers usually help children become familiar with their physical surroundings; parents support the preparations for school by attempting to give their child greater independence (see Chapter 14). Personalized learning is becoming more common but discussions and profiles between early childhood settings and schools permit further enlightenment of educational goals at transfer. In the UK, the *Common Assessment Framework* will also help to improve integrated working by promoting co-ordinated service provision, thereby significantly advantaging the minority where further support is necessary.

A successful transition to school is achieved when all those involved understand their role in discussing the child's experience, strengths and needs and in planning the transition process. The well-being of the child then becomes a prerequisite for successful interaction and learning. The policy of *Every Child Matters* to co-ordinate services to maximize success among children as they enter school promotes integration of prior-to-school and school-age services. However, co-ordination is required to ensure that the transition process begins well before the first day of school to give sufficient time for key relationships to form and for continuity of learning to take place.

Points for discussion

- If a transition pattern was plotted for a child who attends several settings in the course of a week (for example, a breakfast club, school or nursery, after-school club, childminder, an activity organized by parents and so forth), how might the child be helped to link the learning from each of these settings?
- How might information about formal and informal learning be transferred between settings? How can settings ensure that children are not lost in the transition in terms of their learning? How is curriculum continuity managed from early childhood services to school?
- If active learning is important, then how do children become active learners in their transition to school? How are children involved with the decisions about their transition?

Acknowledgements

Many thanks to Tuija Turunen from the University of Lapland who worked with me on the research in Lapland and Wales. For additional support, see *International Journal of Transitions in Childhood*: http://extranet.edfac.unimelb. edu.au/LED/tec/

References and further reading

Arnold, C., Bartlett, K., Gowani, S. and Merali, R. (2006) Is everybody ready? Readiness, transitions and continuity: lessons, reflections and moving forward, background paper prepared for *Education for All Global Monitoring Report 2007 Strong Foundations: Early Childhood Care and Education*. Paris: UNESCO.
Bronfenbrenner, U. (1979) *The Ecology of Human Development: Experiments by Nature and Design*. Cambridge, MA: Harvard University Press.
Brooker, L. (2002) *Starting School: Young Children Learning Cultures*. Buckingham: Open University Press.
Broström, S. (2002) Communication and continuity in the transition from kindergarten to school, in H. Fabian and A.W. Dunlop (eds) *Transitions in the Early Years: Debating Continuity and Progression for Children in Early Education*. London: RoutledgeFalmer.

Bulkeley, J. and Fabian, H. (2006) Well-being and belonging during early educational transitions. Available at: http://extranet.edfac.unimelb.edu.au/LED/tec/journal_vol2.shtml

Claxton, G. and Carr, M. (2004) A framework for teaching learning: the dynamics of disposition, *Early Years*, 24(1): 87–97.

Cleave, S. and Brown, S. (1991) *Early to School: Four Year Olds in Infant Classes*. London: NFER/Routledge.

DfES (2003a) *Every Child Matters* (Green Paper). London: HMSO.

DfES (2003b) *Every Child Matters: Change for Children*. Available at: http://www.everychildmatters.gov.uk/ete/personalisedlearning/ (accessed 7 November 2006).

DfES (2003c) *Every Child Matters: Change for Children*. Available at: http://www.everychildmatters.gov.uk/deliveringservices/caf/ (accessed 11 December 2006).

DfES (Department for Education and Skills (2005) *Common Core of Skills and Knowledge for the Children's Workforce*. London: DfES Publications.

Dockett, S. and Perry, B. (2004) Starting school: perspectives of Australian children, parents and educators, *Journal of Early Childhood Research*, 2(2): 171–89.

Donaldson, M. (1978) *Children's Minds*. Glasgow: Penguin.

Dowling, M. (1988) *Education 3-to-5: A Teachers' Handbook*. London: Paul Chapman.

Dowling, M. (2000) *Young Children's Personal, Social and Emotional Development*. London: Paul Chapman.

Dunlop, A.W. (2001) Children's thinking about transitions to school, paper presented at the 11th Annual Conference of the European Educational Research Association, Alkmaar.

Dunlop, A.W. (2007) Bridging research, policy and practice, in A.W. Dunlop and H. Fabian (eds) *Informing Transitions in the Early Years: Research, Policy and Practice*. Maidenhead: Open University Press/McGraw-Hill Education.

Dunlop, A.W. and Fabian, H. (2005) Transition day: who are the stakeholders? Inset day organised by Dumfries and Galloway, 1 December 2005.

Dunlop, A.W. and Fabian, H. (2007) *Informing Transitions in the Early Years: Research, Policy and Practice*. Maidenhead: Open University Press/McGraw-Hill Education.

Early, D. (2004) Services and programs that influence young children's school transitions. http://www.excellence-earlychildhood.ca/documents/EarlyANGxp.pdf (accessed 30 October 2006).

Fabian, H. (2002) *Children Starting School*. London: David Fulton.

Fabian, H. (2003) Managing the start of school for children from dysfunctional families, *Management in Education*, 17(5): 30–2.

Fabian, H. and Dunlop, A.W. (2005) The importance of play in the transition to school, in J. Moyles (ed.) *The Excellence of Play*, 2nd edn. Maidenhead: Open University Press.

Fabian, H. and Dunlop, A.W. (2007) The first days at school, in J. Moyles (ed.) *Beginning Teaching, Beginning Learning*, 3rd edn. Maidenhead: Open University Press.

Fabian, H. and Turunen, T. (2006) How might the transition of five-year-old children be supported by the curriculum? A comparative study between Wales and Finland. *OMEP UK Updates*, 120: 2–6.

Gausted, J. (1998) Implementing looping, *ERIC Digest* 123. Available at: http://eric.uoregon.edu/publications/digests/digest123.html

Ghaye, A. and Pascal, C. (1988) Four-year-old children in reception classrooms: participant perceptions and practice, *Educational Studies*, 14(2): 187–208.

Griebel, W. and Niesel, R. (1999) From kindergarten to school: a transition for the family, paper presented at 9th European Early Childhood Education Research Association European Conference on Quality in Early Childhood Education, 1–4 September, Helsinki, Finland.

Griebel, W. and Niesel, R. (2002) Co-constructing transition into kindergarten and school by children, parents, and teachers, in H. Fabian and A.W. Dunlop (eds) *Transitions in the Early Years: Debating Continuity and Progression for Children in Early Education*. London: RoutledgeFalmer.

Ladd, G.W. (2003) *School Transitions/School Readiness: An Outcome of Early Childhood Development*. Available at: http://www.excellence-earlychildhood.ca/documents/LaddANGxp.pdf (accessed 30 October 2006).

Laevers, F., Vandenbussche, K.M. and Depondt, L. (1997) *A Process-oriented Child Monitoring System for Young Children*. Leuven: Centre for Experiential Education, Katholieke Universiteit Leuven.

Lam, M.S. and Pollard, A. (2006) A conceptual framework for understanding children as agents in the transition from home to kindergarten, *Early Years*, 26(2): 123–41.

Margetts, M. (2003) Children bring more to school than their backpack: starting school down under, *European Early Childhood Education Research Journal: Transitions' Themed Monograph Series*, 1: 5–14.

QCA (Qualifications and Curriculum Authority)/DfES (2000) *Curriculum Guidance for the Foundation Stage*. London: QCA/DfES.

Rhode Island Kids Count (2005) *Getting Ready: Findings from the National School Readiness Indicators Initiative: A 17 State Partnership*. Available at: http://www.gettingready.org/matriarch/MultiPiecePage.asp_Q_PageID_E_318_A_PageName_E_NationalSchoolReadinessIndicat

Stephens, C. and Cope, P. (2003) *European Educational Research Journal*, 2(2). Available at: http://www.wwwords.co.uk/pdf/viewpdf.asp?j=eerjandvol=2andissue=2andyear=2003andarticle=5_Stephen_EERJ_2_2_webandid=86.128.16.233 (accessed 7 November 2006).

Tizard, B. and Hughes, M. (1984) *Young Children Learning*. London: Fontana.

Webb, J., Schirato, T. and Danaher, G. (2002) *Understanding Bourdieu*. London: Sage.

11 Children's outdoor experiences
A sense of adventure?

Elizabeth Carruthers

Abstract

This chapter affirms that children have the right to be outside because, besides being a wonderful springboard for learning, that is where they want to be most of the time. Outside is distinctly different from inside and one of the questions put forward is; should the curriculum be the same outdoors as indoors? The introduction depicts the difference between children's experiences outdoors in the past and the present. A strong case is presented, showing that all children benefit from challenging and adventurous outdoor experiences, particularly those with special needs. Norwegian kindergarten experiences are discussed with reference to their aims and pedagogical views. The importance of the Forest School movement in England – which gives children a more natural and exciting outdoor experience – is compared to the sometimes reduced experiences of outdoors offered in some schools and early years settings. The challenges to teachers of providing an awe-inspiring outdoor experience are outlined. Finally, we consider the importance of children knowing about the natural world to protect it for the future.

Introduction

In the mid-1950s, British school outdoor areas were black-topped empty spaces. Here children had an allotted time to play and, without much adult supervision, children were allowed a break. This had parallels with prison yard time – a stark greenless space to exercise. If one observed the children, however, they made up their own games and interacted with the different groups in the playground. Outside school they had the freedom of outdoors, for example, street play and going to parks and places that appealed to children, which were often wild natural environments. In the school holidays, children would often spend hours away from home playing with, for example, rope swings over water, and in any kind of streams and wooded areas. And they did all this mostly without adults present. The only place to play would be outdoors; it was just the common place. All the children in the street would know each other and brothers and sisters would play together with all the street kids. Children would plan games and events, for example, going on a picnic, using prams to carry food and drink for the gang. These street games and socializing would continue in the playground. Children had their own culture and there was little adult influence. Now perceived problems, such as traffic and fear of crime or abduction leave parents in anxiety-ridden states which mean children are kept at home 'safe from harm'. A survey of children's play experiences (Wild about Play 2005) has revealed that play in highly natural areas is now relatively uncommon.

Reflection point

1   If children have no real experiences of natural outdoor areas, then how can they truly understand conservation and other environmental issues?

In the UK, the *Early Years Foundation Stage* framework (DfES 2006) emphasizes the need for children to play outdoors which should be integrated into everyday planning. The framework suggests that the best outdoor practice is when children can have unlimited choice to go outside. Woonton (2006) firmly claims that if children are given a choice, they prefer to be outside for a large proportion of their time. The early childhood pioneers in England, for example, Susan Isaacs (1932) and Margaret McMillan (1919), saw the garden as the main part of the child's nursery experience. McMillan viewed the inside as a shelter and the outside as being the main part of the child's education in which they seemed totally involved:

> More than any other place our children love the great heap of stones and builders' rubbish left behind. To put up some kind of house to fix some kind of tent and to sit inside – that is the aim of and desire of all the children. And the making of this house is a more popular occupation than any other, except of course the making of mud hills and trenches and the filling of dams and rivers.
>
> (McMillan 1919: 26)

Presently there is a growing body of practical advice and advocacy for outdoor play in England (Tovey 1999; Ouvry 2000; Bilton 2001). The UK Secretary of Education, Alan Johnson stated: 'Every young person should experience the world beyond the classroom as an essential part of learning and development' (Johnson, cited in the *TES* 1 December 2006).

Giving children access to the outdoors will help achieve many government objectives on the *Every Child Matters* agenda (DfES 2003). This includes children's health, citizenship and reduction of deprivation, crime and unemployment. For children growing up in an economically deprived or inner city area, it is particularly beneficial. OfSTED (2006) has recommended that all pupils should experience the benefits of outdoor education. However, *Learning Through Landscapes* (2005) estimates that school grounds are used to only 30% of their potential. The culture of the present-day British school timetable and exam pressures only give children limited time periods outside. There are some very extensive school grounds with wooded areas but some schools give children a very restricted opportunity to experience these. The inside timetable takes over and the pressures of sit-down testing becomes the focus.

Reflection point

2   As a nation, we are aware of the benefits of outdoor experiences for children and we are moving towards giving children more opportunities for outdoors especially in early years' settings, but is it enough?

Outdoor education in many early years settings means outdoor play in the immediate outdoor space. This outdoor play can be very restricted because of fear of litigation and the staff's lack of knowledge and training in environmental education (Maudsley 2005). Going outdoors beyond the setting and into wild and natural places is less common and a recent Sure Start report concluded that children's outside experiences in early years settings lacked a sense of adventure (Sure Start 2006). The child's own culture, within the outdoors, where a sense of adventure prevailed in the 1950s and before, is something that is less likely to be encouraged today; instead early years staff concentrate more on safe things to do outside (Maynard and Waters 2006).

What is the pedagogy of outdoors?

If we look at the kindergartens in Norway, the culture there is to be outside. They have Outdoor Kindergartens and the buildings are built in natural areas; the children go outside all day and engage with the environment. The children use the natural resources in the woods to play. A study of Norwegian kindergartens (Moser and Foyn-Bruun 2006) revealed that the kindergartens had no defined theory of pedagogy, nothing was written down. When headteachers of these kindergartens were asked the question 'Why do children go outside?' they answered, 'It is good for children and that is obvious.' The study then asked the kindergarten headteachers to elaborate on this, outlining their reasons. The headteachers of the study further stated that the children needed to be outdoors because of the following:

- children are natural beings; they are born with the desire to be outside;
- the development of physical aspects and motor skills;
- the importance of using all the senses (outdoors stimulates all the senses and more);
- the strengthening of health, both physical and mental health for children and staff (less stressful, less noisy);
- developing hardiness (e.g. withstand climate changes, weather, wind, etc.; the children learn to cope with pain);
- it enhances self-esteem;
- everyday children face new challenges.

The perspectives these headteachers had of the children seemed to be more from a viewpoint based in nature. In these Norwegian kindergartens there is no abundance of play equipment outdoors but children experience wooded areas with rivers and streams every day. Nature plays a large part in the Norwegian culture – it is a way of life. It is interesting to note that one of the reasons often put forward by schools and pre-schools in Britain for not taking children outside is that it is too cold, too windy or that it is raining: yet it is much colder in Norway especially in the winter where the mornings are very dark.

The rise of the Forest School movement – the beginnings of a culture change in outdoor education

The rise of the Forest School in Britain is a highly significant movement in attempting to give children consistent access to natural phenomena. This movement started in 1995 at Bridgewater College in Somerset. The nursery nurse students were inspired by a visit to Denmark where they observed that children spent 80 per cent of the nursery day outside in the natural environment. Some Danish kindergartens have no permanent base: these are known as 'walk in nurseries'. The children meet the teachers at a specific meeting place and take public transport to an area of woodland before returning to meet their parents back in the town or city. They spend the day exploring, playing and cooking in the woodland. The Bridgewater students set up their own woodland space for children in the College crèche and organized the training of adults in forest skills. Significantly, they disseminated their Forest School knowledge to other settings and even some education authorities who, in turn, have initiated their own Forest School programmes. These Forest Schools are convinced of the holistic benefit of natural experiences to children. It is the regular access that is important where the children can build up their skills, knowledge and confidence in the outdoors, revisiting experiences. Most of those involved with Forest Schools agree that children are encouraged to stretch themselves beyond the usual boundaries set by the classroom, giving them a challenging environment (Doyle 2006).

There is a notable shift now in the British education culture – perhaps because of the need to move away from sedentary lifestyles and to counteract the rise in child obesity, we are moving towards giving children more and better outdoor experiences. We are just in the beginnings of our thinking on the outdoors and although there are pockets of extremely excellent provision, such as the Forest School movement mentioned above, outdoor spaces still tend to be adult-built with lots of 'stuff' (Maynard and Waters 2006). Many obstacles face us in providing stimulating outdoor experiences for children but one of the main challenges is that many educational settings were not built with outdoors in mind and school learning was presumed to be, for the most part, inside.

The Norwegian headteachers, when asked about their curriculum for the outdoors, stated that 'Nature is a curriculum' that does the following:

- influenced the learning process;
- was an arena for the autonomous child;
- gave freedom to children and staff;
- gave a specific quality to play;
- enhanced social relations;
- because of the changing of seasons, gave everything a different lens.

(Moser and Foyn-Bruun 2006)

Nature to these Norwegian kindergartens is a pedagogical space with distinctive and genuine qualities: nature is awe-inspiring matter.

Reflection points

3 If outdoors is distinctly different from indoors, should we be looking at the curriculum in the same way?

4 When we plan our play provision outside, should we also be asking ourselves: 'Is there any adventure, freedom, ecology, wonder and awe-inspiring matter? And is it worthwhile going outside if there are not these phenomena?'

There is a commonly used phrase in England that we should 'mirror the provision indoors to that outdoors'. This train of thought has led, for example, to books, pencils, construction and puzzles being available out-doors. Ouvry (2000) suggests that what is offered indoors should complement what is happening outdoors and the outdoor experience will be on a much grander scale. Perhaps it could be argued that these are indoor materials and that we should look at the outside in a 'distinct outdoor way'. The *National Curriculum* and the *Early Years Foundation Stage* documents can easily be translated outside and all the traditional subject areas can be 'covered'.

Waters supports the view that children need to be supported in their connections with the natural world: 'By having an affiliation with the natural world we are more likely to take care of it and ensure its survival, which in many respects loosely guarantees our survival' (2005: 17). It is not enough therefore just to go outside because many of the outside environments set up for children are artificially fabricated and for the most part are compensatory. Many schools and pre-schools become victims of commercial companies selling plastic landscapes, like man-made fibre grass or other very brightly coloured ground coverings with equipment that is not moveable and these result in the children losing interest because these materials do not have countless properties such as natural environments do.

Reflection point

5   What can we as practitioners do to make the outside worthwhile for children?

Moving towards richer outdoor experiences

Case study 1: A planning meeting for staff at a Children's Centre

Sarah observed that some of the children were swinging from the coloured ribbons dangling from the trees. Sue said she was concerned about the safety of the children and was dubious about the ribbons holding the weight of the children. Sarah was wondering whether we could tie a strong rope to the branch of the tree and the children could then swing safely. Helen said the children could get burns for the rope; what about a trapeze bar? Jeannette said we already had a trapeze bar on the climbing apparatus; a rope would give a different experience. Sally agreed the rope would give the children a different and a more adventurous experience. Helen said they will burn their hands. Kelly said they probably will not climb the rope and there will not be much of a chance of burns. Elizabeth said, 'It depends whether we want to take the risk or not.' Sarah said, 'I can buy the rope from a shop near me.' Jeanette said, 'Let's vote – rope or trapeze?' Most people voted in favour of the rope. Sarah, being the outdoor co-ordinator organized the rope to go on the tree. The rope was not used as one of the teachers complained that it was not safe for the children and they might hurt themselves and she was not willing to take the risk.

Case study 1 exemplifies some of the challenges, issues and dilemmas of creating outdoor spaces for children that give opportunities for needs and interests. Safety has become an over-riding factor in everything we do, to the extent that we have become too safe. The culture is now unsafe because children are not involved in safety issues and do not learn to keep themselves safe and be aware of danger. Children do need the opportunity to understand how to keep themselves safe and be aware of the safety of others. The Royal Society for the Prevention of Accidents are concerned that children's outdoor play spaces are too safe and children are finding them uninteresting. David Yearly of the RSPA (Sure Start 2006) states that outside play environments need to be as safe as necessary but not as safe as possible. In Case study 1, the staff were willing to take risks, although further thinking on this has to be developed so that everybody feels that children are safe. The staff are also really observing children and planning from their needs and interests. Data on children's interests at this Children's Centre have found that the children's preferred play space was outside 95 per cent of the time and so the Centre have appointed an outdoors co-ordinator from within the existing staff structure. The Centre is serious about outdoor experiences for children. To develop the wild and adventurous side of outdoors, they have secured a site in a forest near the city. The children go in small groups once a week and as the staff grow more experienced they will expand this programme to offer more sessions for children and their families together. This is only the beginning of giving these inner city children quality childhood experiences outside. One of the principles of the Centre is the belief that children have the right to childhood. This shift in taking the children outdoors is believed to be a step in giving them real childhoods but in doing this, besides the challenge of safety, there are many other challenges including:

- The culture of the setting needs to change.
- Staff need to be given opportunities for professional development focused on aspects of outdoors.
- Staff need to be willing to go outdoors.
- The need to reclaim and add to existing outdoor play areas.
- The need to rethink teachers training programmes. If we are advocating that children should have access to outdoors most of the time, then teachers at present are not trained for this. Maynard and Waters (2006) stated that the tendency for teachers was to over-formalize outside and give a prescribed 'safe' set of activities that would be better suited indoors.
- Our biggest asset is parents who, when shown the benefits of outdoors and realize that this was a great part of their own childhood, are only too willing to support the school and pre-school in the

adventurous move outside. Making time initially to get parents on board is a challenge worth taking.

How inclusive are children's outdoor experiences?

All children need play that is exciting and challenging and to be guarded against over-protection. Perhaps some parents would fear the exposure to inclement weather for our more vulnerable children. However, Bilton (2005) notes that when children go outdoors more often, instances of ill health lessen. It was thought that because children had access to outdoors more frequently rather than spending most of their time in stuffy classrooms that the risk of infection was kept to a minimum. The outdoors can provide a child with special needs with access to risk-taking and adventure and they may not normally be given these opportunities. Outdoors is a multi-sensory environment and for blind children, for example, it unfolds for them many stimulating experiences. It could be argued that there is a greater need for children with special needs to experience the outdoors. Life can be very restricting for children with a physical disability but, if given the chance to go outside as much as all the other children, then they can experience awe-inspiring moments, as testified by the Norwegian children's experiences. Carlin states, 'Life is not measured by the number of breaths we take, but by the moments that take our breath away' (Carlin, cited in Woonton 2006: 23).

It is this kind of awe and wonder that is the right of every child – as we see in Case study 2.

Case study 2: A child in school

Sophia is a Year 1 child who has cerebral palsy and has difficulty in walking but loves to challenge herself and is gaining confidence in this area. Her school has provided a wooden bridge that has an uneven surface for the children to go over. There are also winding and secret pathways with overhanging plants. Sophia is supported as she willingly goes over the bridge and ventures along the pathways, smelling the aroma of hanging honeysuckle and lavender plants. Throughout the term she manages to steady herself on the bridge and eventually manages to go over the bridge unaided. The school have developed additional playtimes for a small group of children, like Sophia, who want to try things that they do not feel confident about, especially with more able-bodied children running about. The staff observe the children with special needs in playtimes with the other children to see how they use the skills developed in the additional playtimes.

In Case study 2, the children with special needs benefit from the outside environment and the careful planning of the staff. The school has provided a challenging environment and all children access the outdoor equipment with a level of independence and, therefore, they are confident to take on new challenges.

What is the zone of children's outdoor experience?

Looking at children's outdoor experiences, we can see that there are different zones of experience, the immediate one being home garden and school or nursery outdoor play space. The second zone is community spaces which, in some cases, could include wild spaces. The third zone is beyond the community and often involves transport for the children to forest, beach or hill areas. Children clearly need more than occasional access to all of these to truly get the best and fully realize their own potential in learning experiences outside.

A lot of children's experiences of outdoors might only be in their back garden, the school playground or a walk to the park, with occasional trips to the outer zone of forests, mountains and beaches. Encouraging regular access to all the zones has implications for planning, funding and community and parent support.

Within the immediate zone of the outdoor area next to a setting, access can be a challenge because not every class in school or pre-school has immediate access to outdoors. Ouvry (2000) reminds us that the desire and drive to make the changes necessary for children to go outside need to be there and many educators and early years practitioners are not excited about outdoors. Some adults are what Waters (2005) describes as bio-phobic, meaning that they have a hate for the outdoors and they will find excuses not to go outside. However, many foundation classes in England have pioneered different ways to give children regular access to the immediate outside environment, as in Case study 3.

Case study 3: Foundation/Year 1 class, village school

Mrs Billings' Year 1/Foundation class has no immediate access to the playground – it is used mainly for the older children. Mrs Billings has informed the headteacher of the need for her class to have more freedom to experience the outdoors and have an easier way to access the outdoors. After a few meetings with parents and staff, the head gave permission for a hilly area of the playground to be levelled and landscaped for the children. The children were involved in planning the layout. A section of the hill was roped as a climbing area. A large sit-in sand pit was created for all weathers. A parent donated several water barrels and a water area with pipes and funnels was developed with a tap as a water source. Some parents helped the children dig an area for flowers and plants. At the edge of the play area there was a wild garden; a stile, a gate and a tunnel were made for the children to choose how they were going to enter this area. A door was built on the side of the classroom and a path made from the door to this newly built outside area. The classroom assistant or teacher now accompanies children to this area every day for long periods of play. This outside area has grown and developed and become a vital part of the children's learning experience.

There is a deep concern about the educational experiences of boys (Connolly 2004). Studies reflect that boys' play is not supported at school or in early years settings (Holland 2003). Boys tend to under-achieve or fair less well than girls. Boys favour superhero play incorporating battles and killing dragons and other superheroes. They are less likely to want to sit down and do sedentary activities. Boys' interests in action and adventure are often seen as negative behaviour by the mainly female teaching staff (Millard 1997). Presently the *Early Years Foundation Stage* (DfES 2006) is promoting and focusing on teachers' awareness of engaging boys. More access and opportunities to go outside and connect with larger spaces that can accommodate boys' interests may help teachers develop a more boy-friendly environment.

Is children's access to knowing and understanding animals in their natural habitat being endangered?

> The grace of a high-flying bird. The roar of wind in the trees: At one time or another in our lives, nature touches you ... and me ... and all of us in some personal, special way.
>
> (Cornell 1978: 8)

Children given opportunities to be in contact with animals display a deep curiosity and desire to know about the animals they encounter. Within educational settings there are now so many restrictions on keeping animals that this has resulted in a lack of first-hand experiences for children in seeing, touching and knowing about real animals. Furthermore, organizations that are protecting animals are alarmed about the lack of children's experience of the outdoors and, therefore, access to wildlife which subsequently results in a lack of understanding of the need to preserve wildlife. The Royal Society for the Protection of Birds (RSPB 2006: 5), in a discussion paper, stated: 'Out of classroom learning in the natural environment should be an integral part of every child's education.'

In this paper it is emphasized that children are losing connection with the natural environment and there is an urgent need to resolve this. If this is not addressed, the consequences could compromise our society's ability to understand and deal with environmental challenges in the future, such as climate change.

Conclusion

There is a need nationally to move further towards protecting children's right to play outside. Outside play in a school or early years setting is only a part of providing worthwhile outdoor experiences. The present set curriculum and objectives in England can benefit children going outdoors *only* if they add aims, for example, of awe, adventure, wonder, risk and challenge. Senge (1990: 21) reminds us that education at a deep level involves 'a movement of mind'. To really embrace and support valuable and sustainable outdoor experiences for children, we need to rethink our whole traditional indoor-orientated education curriculum. Fjortoft and Sagerie (2000) emphasize that it is the actual (natural) environment outside that is beneficial: their research revealed that children who play in the forest tend to demonstrate better motor skills than children who play in a traditional playground. More importantly, there is an urgency to provide young children with wild environmental experiences and to let them know how beautiful the natural environment is to protect it for the future and for all the children of the earth.

Points for discussion

- Do the children in your setting access all three outdoor zones regularly?
- How adventurous is your setting's immediate outdoor environment?
- Are all children given equal opportunities and access to challenging experiences outside?
- How many of your staff have recently been on professional development days on outdoor issues? How would you assess your staff's knowledge of outdoor education?

References and further reading

Bilton, H. (2001) *Outdoor Play in the Early Years*. London: David Fulton.
Bilton, H. (2005) *Playing Outside: Activities, Ideas and Inspiration for the Early Years*. London: David Fulton.
Connolly, P. (2004) *Boys and Schooling in the Early Years*. London: RoutledgeFalmer.
Cornell, J. (1978) *Sharing Nature with Children*. Los Angeles, CA: Ananda.
DfES (Department for Education and Skills) (2003) *Every Child Matters* (Green Paper). London: HMSO.
DfES (2006) *The Early Years Foundation Stage: Consultation on a Single Quality*

Framework for Services to Children from Birth to Five. Nottingham: DfES Publications.

Doyle, P. (2006) Nature makes the best teacher and classroom, *Early Years Education*, 8(3): 3–10.

Fjortoft, I. and Sagerie, J. (2000) The natural environment as a playground for children, *Landscape and Urban Planning*, 48(1/2): 83–97.

Holland, P. (2003) *We Don't Play with Guns Here.* Berkshire: Open University Press.

Isaacs, S. (1932) *The Nursery Years.* London: Routledge.

Jordan, E. (1995) Fighting boys and fantasy play: the construction of masculinity in the early years of school, *Gender and Education*, 7(1): 69–86.

Learning Through Landscapes (2005) Supergrounds for schools, *Play Today*, 46: 25–31.

Maudsley, M. (2005) *Playing on the Wildside*. Gloucester: Playwork Partners.

Maynard, T. and Waters, J. (2006) Learning in the Outdoor Environment: a missed opportunity? paper presented at the 16th EECERA conference, Reykjavik, Iceland.

McMillan, M. (1919) 'Nursery schools', *The Times Educational Supplement*, 13 February, p. 81.

Millard, E. (1997) *Differently Literate: Boys, Girls and the Schooling of Literacy.* London: Falmer Press.

Moser, T. and Foyn-Bruun, E. (2006) Small children condemned to freeze? The pedagogical foundations of Nature and Outdoor Kindergartens in Norway, paper presented at the 16th EECERA conference, Reykjavik, Iceland.

Office for Standards in Education (2006) *Early Years: Safe and Sound.* London: OfSTED.

Ouvry, M. (2000) All about outdoor learning, *Nursery World*, 5 April, pp. 15–22.

Qualifications and Curriculum Authority (2006) *Early Years Foundation Stage.* London: QCA.

RSPB Education Policy Department (2006) Out of classroom learning policy, discussion Paper, 24 November.

Senge, P. (1990) *The Fifth Discipline.* New York: Doubleday.

Sure Start *Magazine* (2006) Playgrounds are not adventurous, 12: 3–4.

Times Educational Supplement (2006) Cash and badges to boost safety, 1 December, p. 9.

Tovey, H. (1999) A unique education experience, *Early Years Educator*, 1(7): i–vii.

Waters, P. (2005) A 'hole' lot of fun to be had at out-of-school clubs, *PlayRights*, XXV(1–2): 16–19.

Wild About Play (2005) Available at: http://www.playwork.co.uk/ wildaboutplay/ (accessed 14 January 2006).

Woonton, P. (2006) Taking risks is vital for providing truly inclusive practice, *Early Years Education*, 8(3): 23–5.

12 Written observations or walks in the park?

Documenting children's experiences

Paulette Luff

Abstract

In this chapter it is acknowledged that the process of observing and documenting children's activities can be complex and challenging. In the light of the requirement for English early years professionals to base planning for children's learning on observations of children's interests and abilities, the issue is raised of how this can be achieved effectively. The origins of the practice of documentation in the early years are first considered, before looking at arguments both for and against an emphasis on this aspect of professional work. Some practical suggestions are then made for approaching documentation creatively and productively in order to understand and celebrate children's achievements. While it is recognized that documentation is not an end in itself but a tool for educators, the importance of sharing understandings gained through documentation is vital. A focus throughout the chapter is on using documentary records as a basis for action in providing directions for children's care and education.

Introduction

The chapter title is taken from a letter to *Nursery World* magazine (Cunningham 2006). The correspondent protests against the proliferation of paperwork for practitioners in early childhood settings and claims that parents prefer staff to spend time with children not charts. I must say that I sympathize with this reaction and agree that any aspect of our work with young children should not be undertaken unquestioningly. As early years professionals, we must take a thoughtful and reflective approach towards the activity of observation and documentation and carefully consider its value for young children and their families and for ourselves.

Observation has been described as the 'foundation of education in the early years' (Hurst 1991: 70). In the UK, we follow a rich tradition of observing children and using written accounts of these observations to understand children's play and learning. Susan Isaacs' (1930, 1933) observations of children at the Malting House School clearly demonstrated how accounts of children's chosen activities can provide illuminating information for the adults who work with them. Her ideas about the value of basing education upon child observations are also evident in the design of Infant Admission Record cards and her recommendations for their use in Wiltshire schools (Isaacs et al. 1936). Early childhood education pioneers Friedrich Froebel and Maria Montessori likewise emphasized the importance of observing children to ascertain their abilities and interests and encouraged the use of insights gained from such observations as a basis for planning future learning. In contemporary practice, too, a main aim of our observations is to discover what children already know and understand in order to provide experiences which build upon and extend their existing abilities and ideas. The Possible Lines Of Direction (PLOD) charts, developed at the Pen Green Centre (Whalley 1993), provide an effective method of carrying out observations from which plans are made to correspond with children's dominant interests. With increasing access to technological tools such as digital cameras, camcorders, dictaphones and scanners, we are able to provide additional evidence to support and document our observations of children. Successful practice at Wingate Community Nursery School, highlighted in the *Celebrating Young Children* project (DfES 2006) and work in other UK settings – for example, Fortune Park Children's Centre (Driscoll and Rudge 2005) – show how early years professionals can capture and share evidence of children's learning and use this to inform planning and teaching.

Our current use of observation and documentation to promote children's learning is influenced by inspirational practice in international contexts. Carr (2001) describes how the tradition in many early childhood settings of parents and practitioners exchanging informal observations about children, at the beginning and end of the day, has become formalized in the learning story approach to documenting learning, in New Zealand. These learning stories record, reflect and promote positive learning outcomes in accordance with the strands of the Te Whāriki curriculum: well-being, belonging, communication, contribution and exploration (New Zealand Ministry of Education 1996). It is from the early childhood programmes of Reggio Emilia, in Italy, that we have adopted the concept of 'documentation'. In marked contrast to a typical British understanding of the word documentation, with its suggestion of dusty historical papers or excessive bureaucracy, the Italian term implies something much more lively and vivid. In the municipal early childhood centres of Reggio Emilia, documentation takes the form of photographs, written observations, children's drawings or paintings and transcripts of audio-taped conversations. This on-going record-keeping aims to capture the 'progettazione' (open-ended project work) in progress, enabling the teachers to see and hear the children's meaning-making, to understand the children's current thoughts, questions and strategies, and to form hypotheses about possible directions for future learning (Rinaldi 2006). Documentation goes beyond the unidirectional activity of practitioners recording and analysing child observations to become a dynamic collaborative enterprise in which the child is an active participant and parents and others may become engaged.

There is a key difference between the practice of documentation in Reggio Emilia and the use of their ideas in England. Theirs is a collective society and those values are reflected in the approach to documentation. In Reggio Emilia the sole focus is upon the project work in progress and the ideas of the group of children working on that project. No individual child records are kept and so the production and analysis of documentation concentrates solely upon the children's thinking, and possible directions in which to take their learning. English early years practitioners face a more challenging dual task, as they aim to implement and evaluate group learning activities and also to base planning on individual interests and abilities and record each child's progress.

The processes of planning for learning using documentation are, therefore, highly complex. An additional challenge, for English early years professionals, is a requirement to work in two potentially contradictory ways. On the one hand, as in the Te Whāriki and Reggio Emilia approaches, open-ended learning opportunities are to be planned according to careful looking at, and listening to, children's actions and responses and yet, on the other hand, staff and children are expected to work towards specific, pre-set learning outcomes. As skilled early years practitioners we must, therefore, gain confidence in demonstrating how specified criteria can be met through flexible, holistic ways of working. We also need to find means of using structured guidelines, such as the *Early Years Foundation Stage*, as frameworks for our observation and documentation. It is unsurprising that some people feel daunted by these tasks.

A case against documentation?

Most people who choose to work with children do so because they enjoy interacting with babies and young children and not because they gain pleasure from producing evidence of those interactions. In many English nurseries, staff complete charts recording feeding, sleeping and nappy changing; sign accident and incident books and medication records; prepare daily summary reports for parents; maintain observational records of each child's progress; and develop long-, medium- and short-term curriculum plans and associated evaluations. Practitioners reading this chapter can probably add to that list and may sympathize with one early years worker's comment, 'We'll need secretaries soon!' For some people, documenting their professional practice is rewarding, for others, it is a chore but, for most, it is a fact of life. Experienced childcare workers may look back to the 1970s and 1980s as a golden age when work and play with children took precedence over desk work, or they may welcome the introduction of systematic record-keeping and reporting as tools to support effective childcare and education.

There is no doubt that documentation is time-consuming and most early years staff have heavy work loads and limited time to keep and use records. With nurseries open for long hours, strict adult–child ratios need to be maintained at all times and a variety of other tasks completed. It is challenging for practitioners to take time to document learning, to quote one teacher's comment: 'you rarely get a chance to step back ... and to watch what the children are doing' (Keating et al. 2000: 449). In order for observations and other documenting of learning to occur, it has to be seen as central to the process of working with children. Early years practitioners have to be committed to making records, take time to discuss them and relate the findings to their practice. This process is greatly assisted when managers of settings support staff in these endeavours and facilitate non-contact time so that practitioners can develop and reflect upon their observations and other records. In the infant toddler centres and pre-schools of Reggio Emilia, the central importance of pedagogical documentation is recognized and six hours of every teacher's time each week is allocated for producing, analysing and discussing this work.

Practitioners with limited time to document learning can, nevertheless, be observant and responsive to children without writing everything down. Some might claim that this is sufficient: 'We need to look at ways of making our profession value the information in our heads, rather than words on paper' (Shauna, Child Care Centre Director, cited in Grieshaber et al. 2000: 48). In many nurseries there are wonderful instances of early years practitioners who are sensitive to cues from children and constantly react in thoughtful ways to encourage their learning. K., for example, working with babies, sees 15-month-old S. stretching up to put a toy car in a garage, which is on top of a storage unit. K. goes across to her and S. turns to K. and says 'Car'. K. says, 'S. is playing with the car?' and lifts the garage down onto the floor. S. smiles at K. with quite a cheeky, pleased expression on her face and kneels to play with the garage. Nothing is documented but K. works observantly with S., and the other babies in her care, using what she sees to respond well and enhance their experiences throughout the nursery day.

There are also those who consider that young children are the objects of too much scrutiny and that making children the objects and subjects of our constant adult gaze could be an exercise of power and control (MacNaughton

2003). A first-year early childhood studies student raised the following thought-provoking questions: 'Why do we constantly judge children? ... Why is it important for us to analyse everything a child does?' Although I advocate the use of documentation in professional practice, and in the remainder of the chapter will argue for its use, it should not be accepted unthinkingly. Paperwork which is seen as an end product, designed to measure and compare children's attainment and demonstrate the practitioners' ability to perform for external scrutiny, is probably of limited educational use, whereas documents which capture work in progress, and reveal ways in which children and adults are making meanings, can be a very useful basis for developing understandings of care and learning.

Reflection point

1   What priority do you think should be given to documentation?

A case for documentation?

If time in a busy early years workplace is to be spent on observation and the associated documentation, we have to be certain of its value both to young children, promoting the quality of the care and education they receive, and to ourselves as professionals in enhancing our understanding of our work. For documentation to be worthwhile, it must support and enrich the learning of both children and the practitioners who work and play with them. If the documentation completed in an early years setting is literally a paper exercise – a duty completed in order to have the required records in place when an external inspector calls – it is probably of little value. If observation is reduced to ticking checklists of pre-identified learning goals, it will provide very limited insights into the richness of children's learning. This restricted form of documentation may also lead to a negative focus upon outcomes that have not yet been achieved, rather than a respect for all the skills and knowledge that the children have acquired. Here I offer four arguments in favour of constructive, thoughtful documentation.

First, observing and documenting learning can be a way of valuing and listening to children. Peter Elfer (2005) suggests that emphatic, respectful, close observation can be an effective way of hearing young children's powerful communications and taking account of their perspectives, as required by The Children Act (HMSO 2004) and the United Nations Convention on the Rights of the Child (1989). In Reggio Emilia, too, documentation is seen as a way of building relationships with children and discovering the messages they convey about themselves through their actions (Rinaldi 2006). In an

English early years setting, 3-year-old T. and 4-year-old S. were observed sitting at a table, paper in front of them and pens in hand, role playing a staff meeting. Their talk as they played, about whether the children liked the garden, showed their awareness of the decision-making process at their day nursery and their potential to contribute to discussions about their learning. Cathy Nutbrown (1996) describes young children, such as T. and S., as wide-eyed and open-minded with an awesome capacity to observe and learn from those around them and to master all the complexities of early learning. This corresponds with Loris Malaguzzi's (1998: 78) image of children as rich in potential with 'surprising and extraordinary strengths and capabilities linked with an inexhaustible need for expression and realisation'. An observant approach to documentation challenges us to adopt this highly positive view of the child. It requires young children to be seen and respected, setting their own priorities for learning, with an ability to handle, develop and make sense of complex ideas.

Second, work on observation and documentation can be an important source of learning for early years practitioners as we seek to understand the language of children and appreciate their thinking. Mary Jane Drummond (2003) suggests that starting to inquire into children's learning is potentially fascinating, inspiring and likely to challenge teachers' practice. In the municipal infant and toddler centres and pre-schools of Reggio Emilia, analysis of the meanings to be found in documentation is considered to be an essential aspect of every teacher's continuing professional development. Written observations and other forms of documentation allow information to be presented and exposed to scrutiny and there is always something to be discovered and learned. A single observation, a photograph, a video clip, or a more extensive collection of documentation may provide the basis for reflection, linking with knowledge about theories of child development and areas of the curriculum. Where documentation is maintained over time, each individual child's unique progress can be noted and, across groups of children, common patterns of development may be seen to emerge. Analysis of documentation can also be used to assess the effectiveness of teaching strategies and as a basis for planning new teaching methods and approaches. This process of evaluation is not always easy, as observing closely and documenting what children are actually doing, rather than what we think they are doing, may challenge assumptions and lead to a need to reassess our professional judgements.

Third, documentation provides a strong basis for collaborative work. Vygotsky's (1981) theory, that knowledge is co-constructed in relationship with other people and the environment, sees learning and teaching activities as processes of enquiry in which children and adults can be jointly involved. Capturing and presenting the learning taking place in early years settings, through displaying documentation, also promotes communication with children's families. Discussion based upon observations, photographs and children's drawings are likely to be enjoyed by both parents and practitioners. These conversations provide ideal opportunities to talk confidently about what the children are learning and to gain important insights from parents about children's actions and reactions when at home. This collaboration is not always simple, as there is rarely one single possible interpretation of documentary evidence. When discussing observations and documentation with one another, and with children and parents, practitioners must be ready to offer tentative hypotheses, consider multiple possible explanations and be prepared to change their views.

Fourth, observation and documentation that occurs during the learning process, and are seen as integral to it, may raise the quality of educational experiences for all children. Observing what children can do and considering what this may lead on to make teaching exciting and thought-provoking. Where learning activities are based upon children's own abilities, ideas and interests, and then extended by attentive adults, they are likely to be stimulating for those children and sufficiently challenging. The excellence of the ideas and artwork presented in the *Hundred Languages of Children* touring exhibition (of the work taking place in the Reggio Emilia pre-schools) is a testimony to this. In addition, observing different areas of provision and the ways in which the children use the facilities on offer in the nursery environment can help us to appreciate the value and potential of resources and learning areas. A group of nursery school staff reviewed a video tape of children enjoying socio-dramatic play with the ice cream stall. They saw not only the children's effective use of the props provided (ice creams made from balls of different coloured tissue paper and cones and lollies cut from card) and considerable skills in taking the roles of both buyers and sellers of ice cream, but also observed the way in which the children improvised additional props, such as seat cushions for surf boards. This proved a stimulus for discussion of further ways to develop this imaginative seaside play.

Reflection point

2   What do you think is the main value of documenting children's learning?

Effective documentation in practice

In the light of the above arguments, early years practitioners are urged to observe and document because of the value of the process for children and not merely because it is a government requirement. Documentation should enhance our walks in the park with children and not prevent them happening. It is not necessary to record everything, to spend time producing masses of perfect paperwork which is filed away and rarely seen. It is important, however, to recognize that thinking and learning are not easily visible and that our memories are not unlimited. Writing down an observation, photocopying a drawing, or taking a photograph help us to bring learning into view, so that it can be seen, reflected upon and discussed. Three practical approaches to documentation are considered below. Any of these can be adapted, according to available resources, and used in a variety of early years settings.

Photo sequences

By taking a digital camera along to the park, staff may capture a sequence of photographs. These could be of a child gaining confidence on the climbing frame, or a small group of children finding and examining leaves and acorns. On returning to the nursery, even before these pictures are printed, children will love to sit with a practitioner and review the images on a computer screen (or, if available, via a data projector) recognizing themselves, naming other children, remembering and talking about what they did on the walk. As soon as selected images are printed, they can be displayed in simple photograph albums or on the nursery walls, with or without captions. Children can then see and recall their actions, parents and visitors to the nursery have evidence of what happened during the walk in the park and may understand and comment on the learning that occurred, and the staff can use the pictures as a starting point for their discussions, evaluations and the planning of future outings.

Child profiles

A portfolio, or profile, compiled during a child's time attending an early years setting can provide a very positive record of what that child can do and has achieved (Driscoll and Rudge 2005). Kept in a scrapbook, document wallet or loose-leaf folder, such profiles might contain written observations, children's drawings and photographs of the child involved in activities. It is not possible or necessary to record everything in a profile but at key points during the child's time at nursery, as part of a process of regular occasional monitoring, on special occasions, or when something notable occurs, entries can be made. It is likely that a child's key worker will have the main responsibility for keeping the profile but will use it in an open and inclusive way, as an invaluable means of building relationships with the child and family and for creating and sustaining links between nursery and home. Children are proud of their profiles and can take decisions about what goes into them. They may want to include the leaf rubbing they did at the park, or the photograph of them pushing their friend on the swing. Parents are thrilled to see what their children are achieving at nursery and the profile can provide a stimulus to talk about what children are doing at home. The profile may be taken home and parents may add pictures or stories about family events. For parents, nursery staff and other professionals, the profile can be an invaluable document to review the child's strengths, understand their interests, and note the progress that has been made.

Learning stories

Practitioners, parents and children can also all be involved in contributing to learning stories. As with photo sequences and portfolios, this approach focuses upon positive outcomes emphasizing each child's participation and their development of positive dispositions and attitudes towards learning. Observations are made, often recorded on prepared proformas. These provide space for an observation, or learning story, to be recorded and have sections for a short-term review, which allows the practitioner to offer an initial interpretation of the learning story. The observed story is then discussed and interpreted collaboratively and, along with photographs, work samples and comments from the child and parents, becomes the basis for decisions about the next steps for learning (Carr 2001). In this approach, the focus is upon the child as a learner within the early years setting with the recognition that their learning is supported and enhanced by the people and resources which promote the child's activity and thinking. If a notebook and camera are taken on the walk to the park, a simple learning story can be captured: 'W. picked something up off the ground and said, "It's an acorn." He handed it to E. saying, "It's muddy. Can you get the mud off it?" When E. cleaned it and handed it back, he tried very hard to remove the shell from the acorn. He asked E. to break it open and then looked at the seed inside and said, "It's white."' Returning to the nursery, the short-term review may be that W. recognizes the acorn and is curious to find out what's inside. Talking to other staff, to W. and to his mother you may discover that W. is developing an interest in finding natural objects and you then might plan to collect and examine more acorns, to bring them back to nursery to look at more closely, with a magnifying glass, and perhaps plant some acorns to investigate their growth.

Reflection point

3   What forms of documentation do you use? Which other methods might you experiment with?

Conclusion

Whichever approach you take to observation and documentation, it must be one which is useful and rewarding. Mary Bousted, general secretary of the Association of Teachers and Lecturers, discussing inspection of teaching in a speech to the union conference declared, 'It is not the number of lesson observations that counts but evidence of the professional dialogue which has taken place as a result of the observation' (2006: 16). Similarly with documentation, it is not the volume or aesthetic appearance of the documentation that is significant but, rather, the actions that take place as a result of the documentation. These actions may be small: a chat with a child about a drawing; sharing a photograph with a parent; or a brief exchange of ideas about an observed incident with a colleague. Actions may be larger and more ambitious: following up children's questions about where vegetables come from with a year-long allotment gardening project; changing the nursery open day from an exhibition for parents to visit into an opportunity for families to become involved in a community arts event; re-reading Chris Athey's (1990) work and attending a day training course to understand toddlers' play in terms of their developing schemas. Our advice is to start small but to be thoughtful, proactive and open-minded: encouraging children to explore; recognizing and supporting their meaning-making; and celebrating their enjoyment and commitment to learning.

Points for discussion

- Who is documentation for and who contributes to it?
- How do you decide what to document?
- How much time can be spent on observation and documentation? Is it possible to reorganize to create more time?
- How do you analyse and understand the evidence of children's abilities gained through documentation? When and how can you discuss your perceptions and insights with others in order to learn with colleagues and parents?
- Do your observation and documentation provide a basis for effective action?

References and further reading

Athey, C. (1990) *Extending Thought in Young Children*. London: Paul Chapman Publishing.
Bousted, M. (2006) There be dragons: speeches, 2006. *ATL Report*, p. 16.

Carr, M. (2001) *Assessment in Early Childhood Settings*. London: Paul Chapman Publishing.

Cunningham, M. (2006) Letter of the week, *Nursery World*, 106(4045): 30.

DfES (Department for Education and Science) (2006) *Celebrating Young Children* (poster and DVD pack). London: DfES.

Driscoll, V. and Rudge, C. (2005) Channels for listening to young children and parents, in A. Clark, A.T. Kjørholt and P. Moss (eds) *Beyond Listening*. Bristol: The Policy Press.

Drummond, M.J. (2003) *Assessing Children's Learning*, 2nd edn. London: David Fulton.

Elfer, P. (2005) Observation matters, in L. Abbott and A. Langston (eds) *Birth-to-Three Matters*. Maidenhead: Open University Press.

Grieshaber, S., Halliwell, G., Hatch, J.A. and Walsh, K. (2000) Child observation as teachers' work in contemporary Australian early childhood programmes, *International Journal of Early Years Education*, 8(1): 41–55.

Her Majesty's Government (2004) *The Children Act 2004*. London: HMSO.

Hurst, V. (1991) *Planning for Early Learning*. London: Paul Chapman Publishing.

Isaacs, S. (1930) *Intellectual Growth in Young Children*. London: Routledge and Kegan Paul.

Isaacs, S. (1933) *Social Development in Young Children: A Study of Beginnings*. London: Routledge and Kegan Paul.

Isaacs, S., Fildes, L. and Chesters, G. (1936) *Child Guidance: Suggestions for a Clinic Playroom*. London: Child Guidance Council.

Keating, I., Fabian, H., Jordan, P., Mavers, D. and Roberts, J. (2000) 'Well, I've not done any work today. I don't know why I came to school', perceptions of play in the reception class, *Educational Studies*, 26(4): 437–54.

MacNaughton, G. (2003) *Shaping Early Childhood*. Buckingham: Open University Press.

Malaguzzi, L. (1998) History, ideas and basic philosophy, in C. Edwards, L. Gandini and G. Forman (eds) *The Hundred Languages of Children*, 2nd edn. Greenwich, CT: Ablex.

New Zealand Ministry of Education (1996) *Te Whāriki. He Whāriki Mātauranga mō-ngā-Mokopuna o Aotearoa: Early Childhood Curriculum*. Wellington: Learning Media.

Nutbrown, C. (1996) Wide eyes and open minds – observing, assessing and respecting children's early achievements, in C. Nutbrown (ed.) *Respectful Educators – Capable Learners: Children's Rights and Early Education*. London: Paul Chapman Publishing.

Rinaldi, C. (2006) *In Dialogue with Reggio Emilia*. London and New York: Routledge.

United Nations (1989) *Convention on the Rights of the Child*. Available at: http://www.ohchr.org/english/law/pdf/crc.pdf (accessed 15 December 2006).

Vygotsky, L.S. (1981) The genesis of higher mental functions, in J. Wertsch (ed.) *The Concept of Activity in Soviet Psychology*. Armonk, NY: M.E. Sharpe.

Whalley, M. (1993) *Learning to Be Strong: Setting up a Neighbourhood Nursery Service for Under-Fives and Their Families*. Sevenoaks: Hodder and Stoughton.

13 Food for thought: The importance of food and eating in early childhood practice

Deborah Albon

Abstract

This chapter aims to highlight the challenges and issues that present themselves in an area that is rarely out of the news at present: food and eating. The importance of food and eating to early years' pioneers is traced, notably Margaret McMillan, and I consider current policy in the UK and internationally; emphasizing how food and eating could be a key way that practitioners embrace a multi-disciplinary agenda. In particular, readers are encouraged to reflect upon the reasons why food and eating practices are important, not only for the direct impact they have on children's health, but also for the cultural and symbolic importance they have in people's lives.

Introduction

Children's dietary intake seems to be rarely out of the news at the present time. This is not just in the UK but world-wide. Examples include Jamie Oliver, the celebrity chef's campaign to improve the quality of school meals in the UK (www.feedmebetter.com); the Vive la Gourmandise campaign in France – a campaign to fight obesity but with a key aim to restore the Gallic pleasure in eating (Sage 2006); and the Community Childhood Hunger Identification Project (CCHIP) in the United States (Dani et al. 2005) – to name but a few.

While these campaigns have different foci, and I could have chosen numerous other world-wide campaigns and programmes, what they share is a concern for children's diet and eating. In minority world countries, the concern is primarily regarding the quality rather than the quantity of their diet, whereas both are causes of concern in much of the majority world. It should be noted that much public policy seems to be directed at improving young children's health via healthy eating in early years' settings at the present time. Yet we should not be seduced into thinking that concern for young children's diet is a new phenomenon; early childhood pioneers such as Margaret McMillan were writing and campaigning for an improvement in both nutrition and the mealtime experience of young children over a hundred years ago.

My passion for including a chapter relating to food and eating in this book comes from my belief that it is a key area of early childhood practice, which is often less planned or considered when compared to other areas of practice. Like many other early years practitioners, I have enjoyed shopping, preparing and cooking food with children; pretending to eat meals as part of role play; growing food; sharing food at mealtimes and snack-times; helping to develop children and parents' knowledge of healthy eating; as well as participating in celebration meals and picnics.

I can think of numerous anecdotes from my own practice, which suggest that the area is important to parents and children too. Among the many examples, I can recall a 4-year-old in conversation with his best friend, when having his first ever lunch in school, saying excitedly 'I never thought the day would come when I'd have my own lunch-box.' In addition, I cannot count the number of times that parents on home visits and during settling in periods have discussed their anxieties about the prospect of their child eating meals at nursery. Our personal memories, both good and bad, are important as these inevitably help to develop our interests – personal and professional – in some areas more than others.

Much is said in early childhood practice of the importance of a holistic approach; the importance of seeing both care and education as inseparable and equally important; and the importance of developing multi-disciplinary practice (Pugh 1988; DfES 2003; Frost 2005). My aim in this chapter is to consider some of the issues and challenges that this presents, and to show how practice in the area of food and eating could have an important part in demonstrating our commitment to these areas. I will be arguing that early years settings have a strong role to play in the development of children's bodies as well as their minds. In short, I aim to provide 'food for thought' and stimulate thinking on this crucial area of practice.

This chapter aims to consider the following:

- Why is food and eating a key issue in early childhood practice?
- Food and eating and multi-disciplinary practice: the challenges and issues.
- What might early childhood practitioners do to improve practice in the area of food and eating?

Historical perspectives

Before considering the key issues that present themselves regarding food and eating today, I provide an historical perspective on the subject. The importance of food and eating can be seen in the work of many important early childhood pioneers, such as Comenius (1956) and Rousseau (1979). What is especially interesting, is that in texts that were, and still are, considered to be educational tracts, food and eating play a significant part. In other words, it would seem that many of the founders of early childhood philosophy and practice that we know today believed that food and eating were an important part of a child's learning and development.

Margaret McMillan could be described as a food and eating champion of the late nineteenth and early twentieth centuries. For her, the child's body was of primary importance as she believed there was a direct link between physiology and learning (Steedman 1990) – something that is endorsed by many today, as we will see later. In particular, her focus was upon the health inequalities that existed between the rich and the poor. This can be seen in the following quotation: 'Below every strike, concealed behind legislation of every order, there is this fact – the higher nutrition of the favoured few compared with the balked childhood of the majority' (McMillan, quoted in Steedman 1990: 15). Importantly, McMillan believed that children's health and nurture should be promoted through the education system as opposed to through public health institutions. For McMillan, it was indefensible to expect a hungry child to learn and she was the principal campaigner behind the 1906 School Meals Act.

Her philosophy of the importance of seeing the child's bodily needs as requiring to be met in order that they can learn can be seen in the following quotation, 'Our mental life is conditioned by the physical, who can separate these?' (McMillan, quoted in Steedman 1990: 208). In practice, at the Rachel McMillan nursery school in Deptford, McMillan encouraged children to grow food in the garden for the kitchen and promoted an education which was framed around the needs of the body as well as the mind.

Reflection point

1   Consider the concerns of Margaret McMillan. Are there any similarities with current concerns?

McMillan's concern regarding health inequalities is echoed today, both nationally and globally. In the UK, for instance, there are a significant number of children who do not have access to a healthy diet (Blackburn 1991;

Doyle and Hosfield 2003). Not only this, the mass feeding of children which was a result of the 1906 Act, was also abhorrent to McMillan. The conditions in which the child ate were as important as the food itself. When we think of the way many school meals are served, we might wonder what progress we have made.

We can see that a concern with children's diet and meal-time experience is not new in early childhood philosophy and practice. Indeed, early childhood pioneers such as Margaret McMillan placed great importance on this area. In encouraging practitioners to look carefully at both the quality of the food they offer young children as well as the meal-time experience itself, we can draw strength from the fact that historically, early childhood practice has a long tradition in seeing this as an important area.

Why is food and eating a key issue in early childhood practice?

Food and eating is a key issue in early childhood practice. In the present day, every early childhood setting provides some sort of meal, snack or drink for the children in their care, be they organized along sessional or full day care lines. As many early childhood settings expand their services to support the needs of working parents, young children are increasingly eating meals away from home. It would seem, then, that early childhood settings have an important responsibility to ensure that children both are well fed and have a positive meal-time experience.

In health terms, a consideration of food and eating in early childhood settings is crucial in two important respects: first, early childhood is viewed as a crucial period in laying down the foundations of good health in later life and, second, it is seen as being a vital period in forming the healthy eating habits that will ensure this good health continues (Alles-White and Welch 1985; Pelto 1987; Radcliffe et al. 2002).

More specifically, a diet too high in sugar has been linked to dental caries and childhood obesity (Yudkin 1971). Indeed, childhood obesity, which is also linked to a diet too high in fats and an overly sedentary lifestyle, is viewed as a significant factor in the increased prevalence of type two diabetes and later heart disease (Wardley et al. 1997).

But we should not see food and eating as being purely about investment in a child's future health; there are now known to be links between the food and drink a child imbibes and his or her learning. Dani et al. (2005) argue that some children in Western countries eat a nutritionally impoverished diet that may adversely affect their learning and behaviour, as well as putting them at risk of chronic illness. They demonstrate the link between nutrition and brain functioning, showing that a deficiency in essential fatty acids, for instance, produces symptoms akin to attention deficit/hyperactivity disorder (ADHD). Furthermore, studies have shown that a diet rich in minerals, vitamins, and protein is linked to improved cognition and behaviour (Scrimshaw 1998).

The consumption of breakfast is also linked to young children's ability to learn. Dani et al. (2005) point to studies in the United States carried out in relation to the Community Childhood Hunger Identification Project (CCHIP). Children who obtained a nutritional breakfast as part of the Universal Free Breakfast Programme (USBP) were shown to have improved grades and behaviour. While these studies were carried out on older children, the benefit of eating a nutritious breakfast is seen to be important for people of all ages. Dani et al. (2005: 261) conclude:

> Meeting nutritional requirements throughout childhood is essential for full intellectual and behavioural development. An inadequate diet, in turn, negatively impacts on learning and behaviour in multiple ways. It is thus unfortunate that many children are not receiving an adequate diet and may thereby be compromised in their learning ability and at risk of behavioural problems. Parents and teachers need to be aware of how children may be impacted by their diet, and educate them about the enormous benefits of good nutrition.

Reflection points

2 How aware are you of the link between diet and learning?

3 Do you share this information with children and families? If so, how?

While this section has so far considered the importance of food and eating from a health perspective, then a link to learning perspectives, there is also an emotional dimension to the subject. Frances Chaput-Waksler (1996) asked a group of students to write about their childhood memories. What surprised her was that rather than writing about supposedly 'big things', the students wrote about issues such as mealtimes and the strategies that they, as children, used to subvert adult demands. This led her into thinking that these supposedly 'little things' were actually very important.

Reflection point

4 Consider your experiences of food and eating at nursery or school, and the impact these have had on you. Try to recall what makes these good or bad memories.

What this shows us is that food and eating should not just be thought of in terms of how diet affects a child's health and ability to learn; food and eating experiences are also significant cultural events, which have a symbolic importance in people's everyday lives (Lupton 1994; Albon 2006). Ben-Ari (1997) argues that food and drink events are important ways in which adults manage how children become part of a culture beyond that of the home.

Reflection point

5   Think about a young child's food and eating experiences. As he or she gets older, these experiences are likely to widen, with each experience having differences in expectations of behaviour often implicit within them. After all, how we might behave in a canteen is different to how we might behave at a family celebratory occasion at home, as there are different, unwritten cultural ideas that govern how we are to behave in different contexts.

Finally, food and eating are an important issue in early childhood practice because while early years settings do not have the same intimacy of the home, neither do they fall into the public domain in the way that a restaurant might do. This is because food and drink events are especially significant in places such as early years settings because they are performed on a daily basis as part of an everyday routine with familiar people in a familiar place (Mennell et al. 1992). Routines are a crucial area of early childhood practice and mealtimes and other food events such as snack times are a key example of this. For Manning-Morton and Thorp (2003), routines such as mealtimes are 'key times for play' (taken from the title of their book) and, as such, are deserving of early years practitioners' attention in terms of careful planning, for instance. Viruru (2001) describes food and mealtimes as making a significant contribution to the 'rhythm' of the day in early childhood settings.

Food and eating and multi-disciplinary practice: the challenges and issues this presents

So far in this chapter, I have shown how a healthy diet is vital to children's health and optimum learning. I have also argued that food is of primary cultural and symbolic importance. In other words, I have highlighted the principal role food plays in children becoming part of the wider world. Food and eating, then, is an issue that cannot be viewed purely from a health perspective or an education perspective, as a range of theoretical and professional approaches can be drawn upon in both its study and practice (Albon

2005). This is also reflected in the number of people who have a professional interest in children's dietary intake.

Reflection points

6   Make a list of people and or groups who have a responsibility for promoting healthy eating for young children and their families in your area. What professional disciplines do they come from? I hope, in thinking about this question, that you can see that there is a wide range of professionals, from many agencies, who aim to promote a healthy diet for young children and their families. I hope too that you included early years practitioners in your list as they play a crucial role in both providing a healthy diet for children and educating them about food and eating (sometimes educating their families too).

Much policy and practice seems to be geared towards the importance of developing an holistic approach to working with young children and their families at the present time. The *Every Child Matters* agenda (DfES 2003) highlights promoting health alongside education as being important for schools and early years settings to target. In addition, it makes explicit the need for different agencies to work together to ensure children stay healthy. Therefore, we can see that responsibility for children's health is not just the premise of doctors, nurses, dieticians and the like, but is the responsibility of all professionals who come into contact with children and families.

In the UK, the National Healthy Schools Programme (NHSP) was set up in 1999 and guidance is now available to help schools achieve the standards (DfES/DoH 2005). Robinson (2006) reports on initiatives in Kent linked to the NHSP, which involve joining up a range of professionals with local knowledge in order that schools are supported in improving children's diet. The Healthy Schools Programme coordinator for Kent set up a Healthy Eating Strategy Group (HESG), bringing together a dental officer, community dietician, teachers, council official with responsibility for school meals and others, with an aim to support schools, who, with the communities they serve, identify their own needs regarding the healthy eating agenda. The coordinator, along with the HESG, has helped to develop school food policies, set up fruit tuck-shops and breakfast clubs, developed courses on healthy eating for parents and more recently, is beginning to look at projects on growing fruit and vegetables (Robinson 2006). This is but one of many initiatives across the UK.

This multi-disciplinary agenda can also be seen in numerous international projects. In Mexico, for instance, *Progresa/Oportunidades*, a poverty relief strategy launched in 2002, aims to educate parents about nutrition and other health matters, provide a nourishing meal for children alongside their education as well as help mothers into voluntary work. It has reached five million households to date (Molyneaux 2006). In Senegal, too, public policy is directed towards the inclusion of education for young children alongside health promotion strategies aimed at improving the diet of young children and their families (Rayna 2003). We can see, then, that an emphasis on multi-agency and multi-disciplinary working in projects where food and eating have a key role is not confined to the European countries alone, there are projects across the world that are exemplars of this.

But despite the laudable direction of such policy initiatives, in practice, there is often a division between caring for the child's body and educating the child's mind, with the latter having more status. This is a key challenge to multi-disciplinary working. Arguably, this asymmetry is linked to long-standing philosophical debates around mind/body duality and the idea that the body needs to be controlled in order for the mind to be developed (Bell and Valentine 1997). As a result of this, there seems to be a tendency to elevate education over care.

But both educating and caring for children are equally important. Indeed, if we consider the importance of food and eating in early childhood practice, then we would see that ensuring children receive a nutritious diet is crucial in ensuring their healthy growth and development, which in turn can significantly affect their learning. Conversely, we would see that educating children about food and eating is likely to have positive benefits for their current and future health and development. My point, then, is that food and eating could play a pivotal role in developing multi-disciplinary working as a whole range of professional groups have an interest in the area.

Alongside what could be described as philosophical barriers to multi-disciplinary working around food and eating, other challenges also present themselves. These might include:

- practical issues, such as time constraints, which make meeting together across disciplines and agencies difficult;
- the overwhelming number of national and local initiatives that have been, and are being developed around healthy eating;
- an unwillingness to think beyond one's own professional training and role, i.e. someone might have trained as a teacher and think their job should be solely to teach children, viewing developing healthy eating as the job of health professionals. This might, in part, link back to the earlier discussion around the higher status given to developing the mind over caring for the body. On a more practical level, embracing multi-disciplinary working could also be seen as adding further to an already enormous workload.

Reflection point

7   Consider the particular personal and professional challenges that present themselves to you in relation to multi-disciplinary working.

What might early childhood practitioners do to improve practice in the area of food and eating? Issues to consider

This final section aims to consider the ways in which early years practitioners can improve their practice in relation to food and eating. I aim to explore how practitioners can promote healthy eating and an enjoyment of food through both providing a nutritious diet and positive mealtime experience and, second, by educating children about the food that they eat.

One key way early years practitioners can improve their practice is by listening to children and parents with regards to their experiences of food and eating. It is interesting that the report *Starting Early: Food and Nutrition of Young People* (DfES/FSA 2004) highlights the need to involve children in decision-making about food in schools and the National Healthy Schools Programme (DfES/DoH 2005) highlights the need for consultation with parents and children regarding food policy and practice in their setting.

Listening to children can present challenges to practitioners, especially if they believe young children are incapable of rational thought and unable to express their views. Based on this belief, such practitioners may believe that, as adults, they should act in children's 'best interests', leaving the child's voice not sought and unheard (Hyder 2002). This view is challenged by the UN Convention on the Rights of the Child and recent perspectives on children's participation (Franklin 2002) and has led to a wide range of projects, which involve children's direct participation. McAuliffe and Lane (2005), for instance, put forward a range of strategies, which encourage practitioners to listen and respond to young children's views of food involving role play, or playing smelling and tasting games, among other suggestions.

Listening to parents' ideas and concerns on healthy eating is vital too (Crawley 2006). Practitioners tend to ask parents whether their child has any specific dietary needs owing to cultural or religious background, or due to an allergy or medical condition. This is an essential part of ensuring a setting is responsive to diversity. However, planning for diversity also means that practitioners should ensure they familiarize themselves with the ways in which food is eaten in individual families and not make assumptions regarding this.

Reflection points

8   Think about the children in your care. Are you aware of the way(s) in which food is eaten in their households? If babies, are they held in a particular way when fed (this may also apply to older children)?

9   As the child gets older, what implements (if any) does the child use and when? Do they eat with other family members or do they eat at a separate time? When are the children used to eating? How do they sit – or do they sit down – to eat? How is food incorporated into the family's cultural celebrations? Are snacks eaten regularly or rarely?

10   Do children help with food shopping, food preparation and cooking at home? How often has the child eaten away from home (if at all) prior to starting in the setting – are you aware of the range of people they eat with and the range of different places they have had a meal or a snack?

These are just a few of the many questions early years practitioners might ask about a child's food and eating experiences as opposed to the actual food the child eats. Remember, the mealtime experience itself is an important one and parents and children are a vital source of information in this area.

Early years settings need to ensure that they provide nutritious meals for children. This should also be extended to snacks that are provided (Crawley 2006). Water should be available at all times but, crucially, children should be shown how they can access it. Individual settings need to decide whether to have a group snack-time, as opposed to a self-service snack time, as there are positive and negative aspects to both. The former allows for easier regulation of hygiene as well as ensuring all children can choose a snack; but is likely to be inappropriate for very young children and can make an artificial division in the session. In addition, there is an underlying assumption that adults need to manage children's bodies as opposed to children being able to decide when they are hungry and thirsty.

Alternatively, having self-service snacks that are available when the children feel they need them does afford the opportunity for children to make decisions about when they are hungry and thirsty – if we think about it, demand feeding with young babies comes from a perspective that sees even the youngest child as capable of knowing and communicating when they should be fed. Arguably, though, an opportunity for a social occasion is lost if this practice is adopted and issues of hygiene and equity (in terms of ensuring all have had a snack) are harder to monitor – especially if the group is large.

Reflection point

11   Think about the early years setting you work in or a setting you know: are children able to have a snack when they want to or is there a more formal coming together for a snack in a group? What reasons do practitioners give for their practice?

Whatever practice is adopted, it is important that practitioners are able to articulate their reasons for working in the way that they do in this, as in any other area of early years practice. Unfortunately, some settings seem to adhere to a snack-time policy on the basis of using the opportunity to introduce more formal learning owing to having a captive audience. Therefore, rather than an informal time to share and talk about the food and drink they are imbibing, young children are introduced to more formal learning as a result of their being grouped *en masse*.

Another important aspect of food and eating is that it lends itself to a range of curriculum areas. Research seems to testify to the importance of creating a meaningful context for children's learning (Donaldson 1978), with cooking experiences, for instance, being seen as having the potential for learning a range of concepts, such as measuring and weighing in mathematics (Pound 1999). While this is very valuable, it is imperative that practitioners do not forget the importance of teaching about food and eating itself. Crucially, then, I am arguing that a key issue for practitioners is to develop a curriculum *about* food and eating as well as *through* food and eating.

Reflection point

12   Think about a cooking activity such as making vegetable soup with a group of 3- and 4-year-old children. What knowledge, skills and attitudes in relation to food and eating could you introduce them to?

Think about what they might learn about where food comes from – is it grown locally or maybe organically? You may even grow some of the vegetables yourself. Think about food handling skills; hygiene and safety with equipment. Think about cookery skills such as chopping and possibly sieving, as well as serving attractively. Think about developing the children's knowledge of how different foods taste and being able to discern between foods. Think about the science of cooking and how the action of boiling and simmering changes the texture and appearance of the soup. Think about developing the children's knowledge about foods that are particularly nutritious. Finally, think about developing children's enjoyment of preparing, cooking and sharing food.

I'm sure you can see that there is a lot to learn about food itself through a cooking activity. Yes, it is an excellent vehicle for some meaningful mathematics work and, yes, we might also talk to children about the colours of the vegetables and such like, but I am advocating that we ensure that we are educating children *about* food, not just *through* food.

Conclusion

This chapter has demonstrated that a consideration of food and eating is of key importance in early years practice. This is because:

1   Healthy eating lays down the foundation for later good health.
2   Healthy eating, alongside other health-related behaviour such as exercise, plays a crucial role in disease prevention as well as the prevention of a range of conditions such as type two diabetes.
3   The early years are a crucial period in laying down healthy eating habits.
4   There is a strong link between nutrition and learning.
5   Not all children have access to a healthy diet at home and even if they do, children who are having mealtimes away from home are getting a significant amount of their nutritional intake in early years settings.
6   Food and eating have a strong emotional and symbolic significance for children and their families.
7   Food and eating are a key way in which children are socialized into the wider world according to the particular socio-cultural and historical context in which they live.
8   Food and eating could be a significant area in the development of multi-disciplinary practice.

To conclude, as long ago as a hundred years ago, Margaret McMillan recognized the importance of food and eating to young children's all-round health, development and learning. Much of public policy today seems to echo her concerns and requires the involvement of a range of agencies to work together for children's health. The challenge is to ensure that food and eating are given their rightful place; that of paramount importance in early years practice.

Points for discussion

- With the early years team you work with, reflect upon the importance you give to food and eating practices in your setting, i.e. the organization of snacks and drinks; mealtimes; special occasion food events; growing and cooking food.
- Are children able to observe food being prepared and cooked and in your setting? Why might it be important for them to observe this?
- Do you educate children *about* food as well as *through* food?
- How involved are parents and children in the decision-making about food and eating in your setting? How can you develop this further?
- Think about how you celebrate special occasions such as birthdays and festivals. Often, cross-culturally, these include dishes with high sugar content. Reflect as a team on your practice in this area – do you allow children to bring in birthday cakes, for instance, or do you encourage a healthier option? If you do the latter, reflect upon the symbolic significance of foods such as birthday cakes.

References and further reading

Albon, D. (2005) Approaches to the study of children, food and sweet eating: a review of the literature, *Early Child Development and Care*, 175(5): 407–18.

Albon, D. (2006) Sweet memories: an examination of six families' narratives around sweet eating, *Early Childhood Practice*, 8(1): 12–20.

Alles-White, J. and Welch, P. (1985) Factors affecting the formation of food preferences in pre-school children, *Early Child Development and Care*, 21(4): 265–76.

Bell, D. and Valentine, G. (1997) *Consuming Geographies: We Are What We Eat*. London: Routledge.

Ben-Ari, E. (1997) *Body Projects in Japanese Childcare: Culture, Organisation and Emotions in a Pre-School*. Richmond, Surrey: Curzon.

Blackburn, C. (1991) *Poverty and Health: Working with Families*. Buckingham: Open University Press.

Chaput-Waksler, F. (1996) *The Little Trials of Childhood and Children's Strategies for Dealing with Them*. London: Falmer Press.

Comenius, J.A. (1956) *School of Infancy*. Chapel Hill, NC: University of North Carolina Press.

Crawley, H. (2006) *Eating Well for Under-5s in Child Care: Practical and Nutritional Guidelines*, 2nd edn. St Austell: Caroline Walker Trust.

Dani, J., Burrill, C. and Demming-Adams, B. (2005) The remarkable role of nutrition in learning and behaviour, *Nutrition and Food Science*, 35(4): 258–63.

DfES (Department for Education and Skills) (2003) *Every Child Matters* (Green Paper). London: HMSO.

DfES/Food Standards Agency (2004) *Starting Early: Food and Nutrition Education of Young Children*. HMI 2292, London: OfSTED.

DfES/DoH (Department of Health) (2005) *The National Healthy School Status: A Guide for Schools*. London: DoH.

Donaldson, M. (1978) *Children's Minds*. London: Fontana.

Doyle, M. and Hosfield, N. (2003) *Health Survey for England 2001: Fruit and Vegetable Consumption*. London: The Stationery Office.

Franklin, B. (2002) Children's rights and media wrongs: changing representations of children and the developing rights agenda, in B. Franklin (ed.) *The New Handbook of Children's Rights: Comparative Policy and Practice*. London: Routledge.

Frost, N. (2005) *Professionalism, Partnership and Joined Up Thinking: A Research Review of Frontline Working with Children and Families*. Totnes: Blacklers.

Hyder, T. (2002) Making it happen – young children's rights in action: the work of the Save the Children Centre for Young Children's Rights, in B. Franklin (ed.) *The New Handbook of Children's Rights: Comparative Policy and Practice*. London: Routledge. http://www.feedmebetter.com (accessed 2 September 2006).

Lupton, D. (1994) Food memory and meaning: the symbolic and social nature of food events, *The Sociological Review*, 42(4): 664–85.

Manning-Morton, J. and Thorp, M. (2003) *Key Times for Play: The First Three Years*. Maidenhead: Open University Press.

McAuliffe, A.M. and Lane, J. (2005) *Listening and Responding to Young Children's Views on Food*. London: National Children's Bureau.

Mennell, S., Murcott, A. and Van-Otterloo, A.H. (1992) *The Sociology of Food: Eating, Diet and Culture*. London: Sage.

Molyneaux, M. (2006) Mothers at the service of the new poverty agenda: *Progresa/Oportunidades*, Mexico's conditional transfer programme, *Social Policy and Administration*, 49(4): 425–49.

Pelto, G.H. (1987) Cultural issues in maternal and child health and nutrition, *Social Science and Medicine*, 25(6): 553–9.

Pound, L. (1999) *Supporting Mathematical Development in the Early Years*. Buckingham: Open University Press.

Pugh, G. (1988) *Services for Under Fives: Developing a Coordinated Approach*. London: NCB.

Radcliffe, B.C., Cameron, C.V. and Appleton, J.M. (2002) When food comes from home, *Australian Journal of Early Childhood*, 27(3): 38–44.

Rayna, S. (2003) Implementation of the integrated early childhood policy in Senegal, *Early Childhood and Family Policy Series No. 2*. Paris: UNESCO.

Robinson, S. (2006) *Healthy Eating in Primary Schools*. London: Paul Chapman.

Rousseau, J.J. (1979) *Emile (or On Education)*. New York: Basic Books.

Sage, A. (2006) The French way is to let them eat cake, *The Times*, 13 March, p. 13.

Scrimshaw, N.S. (1998) Malnutrition, brain development, learning and behaviour, *Nutrition Research*, 18(3): 351–79.

Steedman, C. (1990) *Childhood, Culture and Class in Britain: Margaret McMillan 1860–1931*. London: Virago.

Viruru, R. (2001) *Early Childhood Education: Postcolonial Perspectives from India*. London: Sage.

Wardley, B.L., Puntis, J.W.L. and Taitz, L.S. (1997) *Handbook of Child Nutrition*, 2nd edn. Oxford: Oxford University Press.

Yudkin, J. (1971) Sucrose in the aetiology of coronary thrombosis and other diseases, in J. Yudkin, J. Edleman and L. Hough (eds) *Sugar: Chemical, Biological and Nutritional Aspects of Sucrose*. London: Butterworths.

SECTION FOUR
LEARNING AND DEVELOPMENT

Introduction to Section Four

Janet Moyles

Children develop and learn in different ways and at different rates and all areas of learning and development are equally important and interconnected.

(EYFS Principle 4)

Introduction

I have to confess that this is probably my favourite area, of course, in the whole of the EYFS principles because it involves us all in thinking deeply about children's play and learning experiences whether in settings or schools. In the DfES *Five Year Strategy for Children and Learners* (DfES 2004: Para 5), even the government is clear that 'Particularly in the earliest years, children learn through play and exploration...'

As practitioners, however, we do need to be clear what we mean by 'play'. It's easy to think that by putting out play resources or giving children hands-on experiences with, for example, drama at story time, that we are providing effectively for children's play and learning. This is only half the story. Children's self-chosen play activities are vital for 'free-flow' play, as defined by Tina Bruce (1991), but it's also possible to be a playful adult, to teach playfully and to connect with children in playful exchanges and interactions which the children may not necessarily deem as 'play' (because of the lack of personal choice) but which importantly contributes to children's overall development and learning in a fun and engaging way, and also allows monitoring and evaluation. When we are undertaking playful teaching, we should acknowledge this to ourselves: when we are making provision for child-initiated play activities, this should also be acknowledged. That way, we can keep the balance between the two approaches appropriate for everyone concerned.

The current links between play, playful approaches, creativity and brain development are exciting (see e.g. Bruer 2002; Healy 2004; Posner and Rothbart 2006). Play is thought to enhance children's resilience, resourcefulness, reflectiveness and reciprocity – all major attributes for citizens of the twenty-first century. One of my favourite lists of play qualities was that given several years ago by Mary Pugmire-Stoy (1992: 3) who asserted:

In play, a child accomplishes many things:

- experiments with people and things;
- stores information in his/her memory;
- studies causes and effects;
- reasons out problems;
- builds a useful vocabulary;
- learns to control self-centred emotional reactions and impulses;
- adapts behaviours to the cultural habits of his/her social group;
- interprets new and, on occasion, stressful events;
- increases ... ideas about self-concept;
- develops fine and gross motor skills.

It can readily be seen that these characteristics indisputably link play with the way individuals learn, decision-making processes and the ability to make connections (all part of this section of EYFS). It's also vital that we trust children's natural learning instincts and not try to force learning upon them during inappropriate phases of development.

Various theories of how, why, what and when children learn have been proffered over the past few decades and are well documented elsewhere (e.g. Wood 1999; Nutbrown 2006; Merry and Rogers 2007). The tendency has been to consider learning as a 'behaviour' in which learners (children and adults) engage. This has sometimes led to the notion that learning only happens when the learner is 'taught' something and in some way responds. With the advent of the thinking promoted by Piaget, Bruner and Vygotsky (Mooney 2000), theories advanced to a consideration that learning behaviour was more to do with a construction and reconstruction by the learner of actions which made sense to them and which could be guided and supported by more experienced others, essentially termed social-constructivism.

New understandings about brain development have established the child as a 'competent learner' in his/her own right. Research on brain studies indicates that learning is something which happens quite individually through the connections made within the brain as a result of some external stimulus received through the senses – in young children, this stimulation is usually play-based. This is called variously *associationism* or (in computer analogy terms) *connectionism* (see Lee and Das Gupta 1995; Smith 2004). Put simply, if we look at something with our eyes and recognize it as, say, a cat, this has only occurred through prior learning and prior brain connections between the features we recognize – head, small pointed ears, green eyes, lithe body, tail, and so on. To this will be added what we have perceived through our ears, e.g. purring, meowing and through our touch, e.g. furry body, razor claws and tiny sharp teeth.

As importantly, however, we will also use our emotional response to the cat – i.e. it scratched and bit me and I am not going to pull its tail again! – in order to achieve understanding. What we have done over time is accrue a concept of 'catness', through gradual exposure to cats and cat-like behaviours and through the gradual building up of a schema for 'cat'. Most importantly, each of us will have our own unique understand of 'cat'. Therefore, an adult concept of cat is likely to be different from a child's concept of cat due to the differing levels of experience over time of adding to, amending, revising and developing the concept.

While brain studies research is extremely complex, it serves to show that adults' and children's capacity for learning, reflection and innovation is both awesome and exciting. Practitioners need to understand the basic functioning of the human brain so as to understand children's development and potential and set this alongside the kind of curricula knowledge required in this section of EYFS.

Being able to perceive the overall patterns, relationships and meaning is an important factor in dealing with what one is attempting to learn (and to teach): 'to understand a topic, one must understand the way its facts fit together to make a certain kind of pattern' (Sotto 1994: 43). In addition, Sotto asserts that a crucial part of learning is 'insight' which only comes when thinking is actually suspended, while the mind immerses itself in a problem, simultaneously with being open to possible solutions. Play and its associations with mastery provide this time and stimulation. This equates well with Claxton's notion of a 'tortoise' mind, meaning not that the mind has slowed down but rather that it has suspended outward activity in order to contemplate a challenge without hurry or anxiety (Claxton 1998). It will only be possible for children to make intuitive and intellectual leaps if they are allowed time and opportunity to reflect on their patterns, meaning and interrelatedness. This is something which pure, non-directed play permits.

This section also includes all the six areas of learning originally found in the *Curriculum Guidance for the Foundation Stage* (QCA/DfEE 2000). These areas must not be conceived of as discrete in any way because all overlap significantly with others, particularly in play. For example, a child in a play context can be simultaneously using language/communication and mathematical knowledge, being creative, exploring their knowledge and understanding of the world, being physically active, solving problems and engaging socially with others, either adults or children. This is what makes play such a powerful and efficient medium for monitoring and assessment of children's knowledge, skills, capabilities and understanding.

The contributions in this final section are very useful in a variety of ways. In Chapter 14, David Whitebread describes his research experiences in developing independence and self-regulation in young children's learning and how practitioners coped with their changing roles. He describes how the learning environment, the choice and design of activities and specific types of adult–child interactions were crucial in children achieving independence.

Dan Davies and Alan Howe challenge us in Chapter 15 to answer the question 'What does it mean to be creative?' They believe that, in recent years, practitioners, particularly those new to the profession, have had few opportunities to explore creative practice, teach creatively or come to understand the nature of children's creativity. They encourage practitioners to try to re-define creative practice in the early years and regain a real sense of creative learning and teaching.

Chapter 16, by Maulfry Worthington, explores the multi-modal dimensions of children's play in the context of mathematics teaching and learning. Maulfry outlines some of the challenges and issues that practitioners have faced in teaching early 'written' mathematics and shows how, through using their own mathematical graphics, multi-modal ways of representation children can be allowed to playfully explore significant aspects of symbols, meanings, interpretation and communication. She asserts that multi-modality extends what we already know of children's early mark-making and the role of visual representations in supporting thinking.

Last – and certainly not least – Marian Whitehead challenges us to think closely about recent government initiatives in relation to children's literacy learning, in particular, phonics. She asserts that literacy is not rooted in only letters and words, but in non-verbal communication and close relationships. Marian feels that a narrow reliance on one kind of phonic approach in the initial teaching of literacy in English will always fail many children because at the heart of reading is a search by children for meaning and understanding. She proffers a powerful argument for a more eclectic approach to literacy which, for the sake of children, effective and thoughtful practitioners will want to reflect and act upon.

This section should leave all readers with plenty to challenge their thinking in relation to the implementation of a curriculum which both supports young children's learning and does so in ways which makes sense to them, and is consonant with both current thinking and authentic child development knowledge.

References and further reading

Bruce, T. (1991) *Time to Play in Early Childhood*. London: Hodder/Arnold.

Bruer, J. (2002) *The Myth of the First Three Years: A New Understanding of Baby Brain Development and Lifelong Learning*. New York: Free Press.

Claxton, G. (1998) *Hare Brain, Tortoise Mind. Why Intelligence Increases When You Think Less*. London: Fourth Estate.

DfES (Department for Education and Skills) (2004) *Five Year Strategy for Children and Learners*. Norwich: DfES Publications.

Healy, J. (2004) *Your Child's Growing Mind: Brain Development and Learning from Birth to Adolescence*. Louisville, KY: Broadway Publishers.

Lee, V. and Das Gupta, P. (eds) (1995) *Children's Cognitive and Language Development*. Oxford: Blackwell.

Merry, R. and Rogers, J. (2007) Inside the learning mind: primary children and their learning processes, in J. Moyles (ed.) *Beginning Teaching: Beginning Learning*. Maidenhead: Open University Press/McGraw-Hill.

Mooney, C. (2000) *Theories of Childhood: An Introduction to Dewey, Montessori, Erickson, Piaget and Vygotsky*. St. Paul, MN: Redleaf Press.

Nutbrown, K. (2006) *Threads of Thinking: Young Children Learning and the Role of Early Education*, 3rd edn. London: Paul Chapman.

Posner, M. and Rothbart, M. (2006) *Educating the Human Brain*. Washington, DC: American Psychological Association.

Pugmire-Stoy, M. (1992) *Spontaneous Play in Early Childhood*. Florence, KY: Delmar.

QCA (Qualifications and Curriculum Authority)/DfEE (Department for Education and Employment) (2000) *Curriculum Guidance for the Foundation Stage*. London: DfES/QCA.

Smith, A. (2004) *The Brain's Behind It: New Knowledge about the Brain and Learning*. London: Network Educational Press.

Sotto, E. (1994) *When Teaching Becomes Learning*. London: Cassell.

Wood, D. (1999) *How Children Think and Learn: Understanding Children's World*, 2nd edn. Oxford: Blackwell.

14 Developing independence in learning

David Whitebread

Abstract

There is currently a resurgence of interest in stimulating and facilitating young children as learners. One strand of this interest relates to fostering 'independent learning' among young children. This emphasis is also supported by the *Early Years Foundation Stage*, and several other recent government guidelines and policy documents.

This chapter first of all presents an overview and critique of the considerable psychological and educational research literature concerned with independent or self-regulated learning. Second, the chapter reports on the findings of the Cambridgeshire *Independent Learning* (CIndLe) project, a two-year research project which has shown that from a very young age children are capable of considerable independence in their thinking and learning.

Aspects of pedagogy which have been shown to be critical in fostering self-regulation in young children are also discussed. These are at the level of the learning environment, the choice and design of activities, and the critical features of adult–child interaction. Four underlying principles guiding pedagogy for self-regulation are also elaborated, and provide a framework for the evaluation of educational practice in the early years which aims to encourage and facilitate independence in young children's learning.

Introduction

There is currently widespread interest in fostering 'independent learning' among young children, as attested by a number of recent publications (Featherstone and Bayley 2001; Williams 2003), by the current enthusiasm for such approaches as Reggio Emilia and High/Scope and by recent official policy guidelines. However, while this aspiration is widely endorsed, there are challenges at a number of levels which militate strongly against its realization in practice, including a lack of clarity at the level of policy, constraining structural factors at the level of classroom practice and insufficient access among early years practitioners to relevant current psychological research concerning the nature of children's learning. This chapter examines the psychological research literature concerned with the development of independent, or self-regulated, learning in young children and, second, reports on the findings of a two-year research project exploring this development and pedagogical approaches to facilitating and encouraging it in early years settings.

What is meant by 'independent learning'?

The education policy context

Recent initiatives, circulars and curriculum documents from various government agencies have given prominence to the idea of independent learning and what it subsumes. In the revised QTS Standards entitled *Qualifying to Teach* (TDA 2006), for example, teacher trainees are required under Standard S3.3.3 to:

> teach clearly structured lessons or sequences of work which interest and motivate pupils and which make learning objectives clear to pupils, employ interactive teaching methods and collaborative group work [and] promote active and independent learning that enables pupils to think for themselves, and to plan and manage their own learning.

In the *Curriculum Guidance for the Foundation Stage* (QCA/DfEE 2000: 3), a stated principle is that there should be 'opportunities for children to engage in activities planned by adults and also those that they plan and initiate themselves'.

It is clear that there is currently a strong commitment to independent learning but also confusion and a need for clear definition. On the one hand, early years practitioners are being asked to provide 'personalized learning' and respond to the *Every Child Matters* agenda and, at the same time, they are being continually bombarded by 'top-down' pressures to force-feed all children with set curricula and formalized 'standards'. In some recent policy guidelines, e.g. the *Early Years Foundation Stage* (DfES 2006), the emphasis has unhelpfully shifted more towards helping children with personal independence skills and becoming an independent *pupil*, i.e. being able to function in a classroom without being overly dependent on adult help. As we shall see, research studies have also generally found that this is the dominant concern for many teachers. This is very distinct, however, from the concern to help children to develop as independent *learners*, i.e. being able to take control of, and responsibility for, their own learning. It is for this reason that the term 'self-regulation' is increasingly preferred, with its emphasis on the learner taking control and ownership. As we shall see, it is also a term which has a strong tradition within the psychological literature.

The context of the classroom

While a commitment to encouraging children to become independent, self-regulating learners is almost universal among thoughtful and committed early years practitioners, at the level of everyday classroom realities there are a range of structural factors which present challenges in bringing this to reality. The need to maintain an orderly classroom, combined with the pressures of time and resources, and perceptions of external expectations from head-teachers, managers, parents and government agencies, can often militate against the support of children's independence.

While many practitioners avowedly seek to encourage children to be independent in their work, to think of their own ideas, and to use their initiative, the classroom ethos they actually generate makes this kind of behaviour very high risk (Galton 1989). Evidence from a study across the Foundation Stage and Key Stage 1 greatly supported this view (Hendy and Whitebread 2000). Early years teachers interviewed shared a commitment to encouraging greater independence in learning among young children, but held a wide spectrum of views about the essential key elements within it, and of their role in fostering the necessary skills and dispositions. They held a dominant concern with the *organizational* element of children's independence, as opposed to any concern with cognitive or emotional areas. Children appeared to become more, rather than less, dependent on their teachers during their first few years in school. Nursery-aged children, for example, were consistently more likely than the older children in the study to suggest they would try to resolve problems themselves. Older children were more inclined to ask their teacher. Later in the chapter more recent research in early years settings in the UK and elsewhere, including work from the CIndLe project, will be presented showing that approaches can be developed, even within existing constraints, which enhance independent, self-regulated learning.

Reflection points

1   What do you understand by 'independence' in children?
2   In your setting do you focus on independence in organizational issues or consider children's independence in thinking? What evidence do you have for your response?

Psychological approaches to self-regulated learning

If early years practitioners are successfully to foster independent learning in their settings, a clear understanding needs to be developed by them of the skills and dispositions involved in self-regulated learning, and of the pedagogical practices which are most likely to foster these. The remainder of this chapter will, therefore, review briefly the relevant research literature from developmental psychology before we proceed to examine research exploring educational practices which might be helpful in this area.

Within cognitive developmental psychology in the past 30 years or so there has been a very considerable body of research evidence related to the development of children as independent learners. It has variously been characterized as 'learning how to learn' (Nisbet and Shucksmith 1986), 'reflection' (Yussen 1985) 'self-regulation' (Schunk and Zimmerman 1994) and 'metacognition' (Metcalfe and Shimamura 1994), all of which are concerned with children developing self-awareness and control of their own mental processing. The term 'metacognition' was first coined by Flavell in 1979 and, since that time, the significance of an individual's ability to monitor and regulate her/his own cognitive activity has been demonstrated across a wide range of human development (see e.g. Whitebread 1996). It has is also well established that children with learning difficulties commonly exhibit metacognitive deficits (Sugden 1989). Wang et al.'s (1990) review concluded that metacognition was the most powerful single predictor of learning. More recently, Veenman and Spaans (2005) have shown that metacognitive skillfulness makes a unique contribution to learning performance beyond that accounted for by traditionally measured intelligence.

This work has been inspired by two traditions within developmental psychology. First, is the socio-cultural tradition founded on the work of the Russian psychologist, Lev Vygotsky (1978, 1986) who believed that the development of children's learning was a process of moving from other-regulation (or performing a task while supported by an adult or peer) to self-regulation (performing a task on one's own). All learning for Vygotsky starts socially.

A considerable body of research work in recent years has investigated the processes by which adults support children's learning. This research has largely endorsed Vygotsky's approach, and has also identified the elements which make some adults particularly effective in supporting and promoting children's learning. Adults encourage, instruct, ask questions, give feedback, and so on. These various forms of interaction combine so that the skilful adult provides what has been termed 'scaffolding', a temporary support structure which enables the child to successfully carry out any particular task, and thus build skills and understanding. Crucially, however, research has shown that a key characteristic of a good scaffolder is the ability sensitively to withdraw support as the child becomes able to carry out the task more independently, or to take over more of the regulatory role for themselves (for an excellent review of work in this area, see Schaffer 2004).

Learning for Vygotsky can be characterized as a process of internalization, whereby the procedures for successful completion of a task are initially modelled and articulated by an adult or more experienced peer with the child, who gradually becomes able to talk themselves through the task (the common phenomenon of child self-commentary thus takes on particular significance!). Finally, the child can fully self-regulate using internal speech or abstract thought.

The second tradition is the information-processing approach and specifically, the early work in the 1960s and 1970s of John Flavell on the development of children's memory abilities (metamemory) which led to work on metacognition (Brown 1987). Essentially, metacognition is defined as a set of processes enabling us progressively to become aware of and to think about our own cognitions, or mental processes, and, as noted earlier, has been shown to be enormously significant in terms of our development as effective thinkers and learners. In Brown's model it was characterized as consisting of three related elements:

- 'metacognitive experience': the on-line monitoring or self-awareness of mental processing, and reflections upon it;
- 'metacognitive knowledge': the knowledge which is gradually accumulated about one's own mental processing, tasks and cognitive strategies for dealing with tasks;
- 'self-regulation': the metacognitive control of mental processing, so that strategies are developed and used appropriately in relation to tasks.

There have been two significant later developments in this area of research. First, there has been a broadening of notions of self-regulation from the purely cognitive concerns of Vygotsky, Flavell and Brown to include emotional, social and motivational aspects. The work of those such as Goleman (2005) on emotional intelligence, for example, is part of this trend. Understandings emerging from neuroscience also support a model which integrates emotional and cognitive aspects of self-regulation (Gerhardt 2004). The development of metacognitive and self-regulatory functions appears to be related to developments in the frontal lobes (Barkley 1997).

Second, there has been the recognition of metacognitive processes in very young children. Bronson (2000) demonstrates that the development of metacognitive and self-regulatory processes is fundamental to the whole range of young children's psychological growth. She describes in detail extensive research which has explored the emotional, prosocial, cognitive and motivational developments in self-regulation throughout the different phases of early childhood.

The CIndLe Project: young children as self-regulating learners

In my recent research (the Cambridgeshire Independent Learning project) focusing on self-regulation in young children (Whitebread et al. 2005), the team worked with 32 Foundation Stage teachers over two years and collected approximately 100 hours of video, and numerous other occasional observations. From this data, 705 events have been recorded and documented that show evidence of self-regulatory and metacognitive behaviour. As the average duration of these events is a number of minutes, and in some cases as much as 20–30 minutes, this average rate of incidence of around seven events per hour is a striking testimony of the pervasiveness of self-regulatory and metacognitive behaviours in children in the 3–5 age range.

As part of this project, a checklist of self-regulatory behaviours (*CH*ecklist of *I*ndependent *L*earning *D*evelopment – CHILD 3–5) was developed, consisting of 22 statements describing the most common and significant achievements in cognitive, motivational, emotional and social areas of development within the 3–5 age group (see Table 14.1). A number of the statements from the checklist were present in as many as a third of all the recorded events. For example, the statements of abilities for which the most numerous observations were recorded included the following:

- can control attention and resist distraction;
- can speak about how they have done something or what they have learnt;
- can make reasoned choices and decisions;
- develops own ways of carrying out tasks.

Of these 705 self-regulatory events documented in the project, 582 (i.e. 82.6%) contained an element specifically of metacognitive activity. This provides initial and substantial evidence of the clear ability of young children to engage in a wide range of metacognitive and self-regulatory activities.

Table 14.1 Checklist of independent learning development 3–5

Statement	Exemplar event	Description
		EMOTIONAL ELEMENTS OF INDEPENDENT LEARNING
Can speak about others' behaviour and consequences	Warning about paper clips	Three children are playing in the workshop area. A girl that appears to be leading the game is explaining to the rest of the group how dangerous paper clips can be, modelling the correct way of using them.
Tackles new tasks confidently	Counting to 100 Making big sums Counting backwards Counting forever	A sequence of events representing a clear progression in the way children spontaneously set up and solve increasingly more challenging mathematical tasks after being provided with enough cognitive structuring by the teacher.
Can control attention and resist distraction	Fixing a bike	A child has entered the workshop area and has decided that he is going to fix the bike that has been placed as part of the setting. The child remains on task for an extended period of time using different tools and checking the outcomes of his actions.
Monitors progress and seeks help appropriately	Building a bridge	A group of children have decided to build a bridge to get to a castle but the bridge keeps falling down. The 'builders' actively seek the advice of other children who stop in front of the construction to see what is happening.
Persists in the face of difficulties	Finding the screwdriver	A girl has entered Santa's workshop area. She is looking for the screwdriver to make some toys. She actively looks for it and asks for the other children's help. After 15 minutes where she appears to have been engaged in other activities, she finally finds it. 'I found the screwdriver!'
		PROSOCIAL ELEMENTS OF INDEPENDENT LEARNING
Negotiates when and how to carry out tasks	Planning the game Playing in small group	A group of children have been encouraged to create a game using a hoop and a ball. The children actively discuss who is going to hold the hoop and who is going to throw the ball. They all agree they have to take turns. 'Otherwise it wouldn't be fair' says one of the children. They try out the game before teaching it to the rest of the class.
Can resolve social problems with peers	Negotiating number of children	Too many children are in the workshop area. A child becomes aware of the situation and acts as a negotiator trying to determine who can stay and who has to leave. He uses different questions to solve the problem: 'Who doesn't want to be here?', 'Who's been here the longest?'

Table 14.1 *continued*

Statement	Exemplar event	Description
Is aware of feelings of others; helps and comforts	Making cards	A girl helps a boy make a card. She doesn't 'do' it for him but has been asked to show him what to do. During the sequence she is very helpful and 'keeps an eye on him'. She does not take over, yet seems to take pride in the helping process.
Engages in independent co-operative activities with peers	Three Little Pigs crisis	Children are playing Three Little Pigs in the role play area. A 'crisis' has been introduced. The Big Bad Wolf has stopped the electricity getting to the house. The children are exploring using torches and working out what to do.
Shares and takes turns independently	Taking turns	A group of girls are playing a lottery game. They spontaneously take turns asking: 'Whose turn is it?' and reminding each others: 'It's your turn now!'
COGNITIVE ELEMENTS OF INDEPENDENT LEARNING		
Is aware of own strengths and weaknesses	Counting beans with Jack	A girl is counting beans using a puppet (Jack). Being aware that there are too many beans to count, she decided to put some of the beans away so Jack can 'count them better'.
Can speak about how they have done something or what they have learnt	Drawing a fire	Two boys sit side by side at the drawing table and discuss how to draw a fire. One says it is a zig-zag shape and draws an example, saying that his mummy told him it was like this. The other disputes this and says it goes little and then very big, drawing small downward lines and long vertical lines. They talk about how fire is spread and how the flames move.
Can speak about planned activities	The castle	Two girls have decided that they want to make a castle in the play area. Being prompted by the teacher's questions they verbalize what they want to put in the castle, the materials they need and what to do first.
Can make reasoned choices and decisions	Writing an animal story	Two boys collaborating on a story decide between them that they want it to feature a particular animal so send someone in search of a picture to copy.
Asks questions and suggests answers	Skeletons	A group were interested in skeletons, and the nursery nurse helped them to draw around one another and copy pictures from books to fill their skeletons. The children felt the bones in their bodies as they drew. They asked questions about the bones and in some cases one child answered another's question.
Uses a strategy previously modelled	Peer support in writing	Two boys support another with his writing when they see him struggle. They communicate clearly, using strategies they have heard from their teacher, and are sensitive to his feelings.

Table 14.1 *continued*

Statement	Exemplar event	Description
Uses language previously heard for own purposes.	Writing messages	Two girls help a boy who also wants to write. They track what he is doing and point to an example of a message (written by a child) on the wall and draw attention to the individual letters, naming them for the boy.
		MOTIVATIONAL ELEMENTS OF INDEPENDENT LEARNING
Initiates activities	Making computers	Two children decide to make a computer out of a cardboard box. The work collaboratively together and persist when things don't go well e.g. working out how to join the box (computer screen) to the table.
Finds own resource without adult help	Goldilocks and the Three Bears	The children have decided to recreate the story of Goldilocks and the three bears. They have found three boxes of different sizes for the beds, three bowls and spoons for the bears and a pot to book the porridge.
Develops own ways of carrying out tasks	Making books	One child made a 'book' by sellotaping together three small sheets of computer paper. She drew simple illustrations and asked her teacher to write the story for her. It was a perfect story. 'The cat was lost. The flower was lonely. The dog had no friends. The sun came out and cheered them all up.' The book was read to the class and by four weeks later half the class had made books using the same method.
Plans own tasks, targets and goals	Christmas wrapping	A group of children have turned the play area into Santa's workshop. They have decided that they are going to wrap presents; they have found resources, and they have negotiated their roles.
Enjoys solving problems and challenges	Building a bridge	The teacher has set up a problem: the children need to get a treasure located at the other side of the room, crossing a river filled with crocodiles. The children decide to build a bridge and they co-operate to achieve their plan.

Reflection points

3   Look at Table 14.1: which aspects can you recognize in children in your setting? Which aspects are absent or minimal?

4   Looking at the emotional element of Table 14.1, what examples do you have of
children in your setting exhibiting these traits?

You could continue to look at aspects of CHILD 3–5 in relation to children in your
setting to decide how independent the children really are!

The pedagogy of self-regulation

As we noted earlier, explanations of the origins and development of self-
regulation, and the role of parents and educators within this, have often been
cast within a Vygotskian framework (e.g. Schunk and Zimmerman 1994).
Collins et al. (1989) provided an extensive review of approaches which they
termed 'cognitive apprenticeship' models of teaching and learning whereby
adults help to make the processes of learning explicit to children.

Several other useful pedagogical techniques deriving from this broad
tradition have been investigated and developed with primary-aged children.
These include:

- 'co-operative groupwork' (Forman and Cazden 1985): a range of
techniques involving children in collaborative activities which
oblige them to articulate their own understandings, evaluate their
own performance and be reflective about their own learning;
- 'reciprocal teaching' (Palincsar and Brown 1984): a structured pro-
cedure which involves teachers modelling the teaching of a particular task to children who are then asked to teach the activity to their
peers;
- 'self-explanations' (Siegler 2002): an instructional practice which
requires children to give 'how' and 'why' explanations about, for
example, scientific phenomena or the events in a story, and then
asks children to give explanations of their own and an adult's
reasoning;
- 'self-assessment' (Black and Wiliam 1998): a range of pedagogical
ideas involving children's self-assessment of their own learning,
including, for example, children making their own choices about the
level of difficulty of tasks to be undertaken, and selecting their best
work for reflective portfolios;
- 'debriefing' (Leat and Lin 2003): a range of techniques for reflecting

upon an activity or piece of learning including 'encouraging pupils to ask questions', 'making pupils explain themselves' and 'communicating the purpose of lessons'.

Brooker's (1996) analysis of her work with a Year R class over the course of a year provides an excellent example of giving children responsibility for and ownership of their own learning. She began, before the start of the school year and during the first term, by interviewing the children on a number of occasions, asking them, among other things, 'Why do children go to school?', 'What are you good at?', 'What do you like doing best?', and 'How do you think you learn things?' In the spring term she moved on to develop the habit of self-assessment, training herself to withhold the usual excessive praise bestowed on children of this age and instead asking them 'How do you think you got on then?' At the end of the second term she asked the children 'What would you like to learn next term, after the holidays?' and this began a final phase during which, by a process of constant discussion and negotiation, the children gradually acquired more and more ownership of the curriculum and procedures of the classroom. At each stage the children's answers were systematically recorded. Progressively, as the year went on, their views influenced the content and organization of their school day until, by the end of the year, the children were very largely deciding how the classroom would be organized and which activities would be available each day.

Perry and colleagues have been engaged in similar work with young children from kindergarten to Grade 3 in British Columbia (Perry et al. 2002). They engaged in extensive observations in classrooms and interviews with teachers and provided evidence of young children planning, monitoring, problem-solving and evaluating their learning. The pedagogical elements which emerged as being most effective in promoting self-regulated learning in these classrooms involved the teachers in offering choices to the children, opportunities for them to control the level of challenge in tasks and to evaluate both their own work and that of others. Perry's detailed analysis of the classroom discourses of highly effective teachers reveals a complex and highly skilled set of practices. The use of co-operative ways of working, together with an evaluative style that was non-threatening and which focused on understanding, were two significant elements.

The CIndLe Project: four pedagogical principles

Within the CIndLe project, effective pedagogies were also explored to encourage aspects of self-regulation with the 32 Foundation Stage teachers. A variety of activities were trialled, including collaborative problem-solving activities, children teaching one another, activities which required the children to reflect on their learning. However, it soon became clear that we needed to think more broadly and look at the overall ethos of the classroom, and this led to organizing the classrooms in ways which gave children access to resources, allowed them to make choices and gave them responsibility for the activities in particular areas of the classroom (such as the role play area, the craft area, the writing area). Finally, we examined the way we interacted with the children, so that we asked more genuine open-ended and more challenging questions, we explicitly discussed learning, emotions and self-regulation strategies and we engaged in sustained conversations with the children within which we explored and developed their ideas (what Neil Mercer and colleagues have referred to as 'exploratory talk' – Littleton et al. 2005).

The following list is a small selection of some of the general pedagogical points and insights which emerged from the project:

- The children learnt a great deal by watching one another.
- Given the opportunity to make their own choices and decisions, the children were remarkably focused and organized and pursued their own plans and agendas with persistence and sometimes over long periods of time.
- Sometimes when an adult became involved in an activity the children were more inclined to say they couldn't do something, but if they were working with another child they were less likely to question their ability, and often mimicked the other child, gaining confidence in their abilities.
- The most effective response the practitioner gave to a child asking for help was to refer them to another child who has greater competence or expertise in the particular area.
- Sometimes it is best for adults not to intervene in children's disputes and disagreements in collaborative play, but give them time and space to resolve issues themselves.
- Recognition of the important distinction between praise (which produces 'adult-pleasers') and encouragement (which gives information/feedback and supports independence).
- Children differ between those who respond well to open-ended, child-initiated tasks and those who like a supportive structure established by an adult; both kinds of opportunities need to be provided.

Finally, from this work emerged four underlying principles which tied together all of these practices in ways which explain their importance when considered in the light of current research about children as learners. These involve:

- the provision of an emotionally warm classroom environment;
- an ethos in which children feel in control;
- activities which provide cognitive challenge;
- opportunities for adults and children to talk about learning.

Reflection points

5   How much opportunity are children given in your setting to work together in a truly collaborative way? Think about some examples – how did the children respond?

6   Do children get the chance to assess their own learning experiences in your setting? Again, think about examples – how did the children respond?

---

1 Emotional warmth and security – attachment

We have known for a long time about the importance of children experiencing emotional warmth and security. Early work by an American animal psychologist called Harlow with baby monkeys was one of the first pieces of evidence that emotional security allowed babies to be more adventurous and independent. John Bowlby's work in the UK concerned with mothering and early attachment inspired significant research in this area. Secure emotional attachments in young children have been found to be associated with a range of positive emotional, social and cognitive outcomes. The evidence also suggests that this emotional security is the product of the child experiencing early relationships which are emotionally warm, sensitive and predictable (see Durkin 1995, for a review).

Within the CIndLe project, we collected many examples of adults providing emotional support for children in ways which enabled a child to persevere with a task which might otherwise have been abandoned (e.g. putting on a coat!). Practitioners thus enabled the child to learn that perseverance can be a pleasurable experience and lead to a successful outcome. Often, in the absence of this kind of support, either the element of perseverance is lost as adults complete the task for the child, or pleasure is replaced by frustration and the task is abandoned. More generally, to provide emotional warmth and security in the classroom environment, practitioners can:

- provide a model of emotional self-regulation, talking through their own difficulties with the children;
- show that they appreciate effort at least as much as products;
- show an interest in the children as people, and share aspects of their own personal lives;
- negotiate frameworks for behaviour with the children which are seen to be fair and supportive.

2 Feelings of control

Closely related to emotional security is the need for feelings of control. Human beings are quite literally control freaks! Research has established that right from birth we very powerfully enjoy feeling in control of our environment. An early experiment carried out in California by Watson and Ramey (1972) involved the parents of 8-month-old babies being given special cots which came complete with attractive and colourful 'mobiles'. The parents were asked to put their babies in the cots for specified periods each day for a few weeks. In some of the cots the mobiles either did not move, or moved around on a timed schedule. But in other cots the mobile was wired up to a pillow, so that the mobile would move whenever the baby exerted pressure on the pillow. At the end of the experiment, the parents of the babies who had experienced these 'contingency mobiles' wanted to pay the research team large amounts of money to keep the cots because their babies had enjoyed them so much, happily spending long periods of time rolling on and off the pillow and watching the effects on the mobile. Feeling in control of their environment and their learning is fundamental to children developing confidence in their abilities, and the ability to respond positively to setbacks and challenges.

Early years practitioners need to have the confidence to allow sufficient flexibility for a child who has been inspired by a particular experience to pursue that interest. Allowing opportunities for child-initiated activities enhances children's sense of ownership of and responsibility for their own learning. Other practices which are helpful in giving children this feeling of control include:

- making sure that children have access to a range of materials for their own purposes;
- giving children the opportunity to make choices about activities;
- understanding that a beautiful adult-made role play area or display may not be as valuable for the children's learning as one to which children have contributed;
- adopting a flexible approach to timetabling which allows children to pursue an activity to their satisfaction, avoiding unnecessary interruptions.

3 Cognitive challenge

The third underlying principle of good practice which encourages self-regulatory and independent learning is the presence of cognitive challenge. Children spontaneously set themselves challenges in their play and, given a choice, will often choose a task which is more challenging than the task which an adult might have thought was appropriate. Providing children with achievable challenges, and supporting them so they can meet them, is the most powerful way to encourage positive attitudes to learning, and children's independent abilities.

More generally, to promote this kind of cognitive challenge in their settings, practitioners can do the following:

- require children to plan activities;
- consider whether activities planned to be carried out individually could be made more challenging as a collaborative group task;
- ask more genuine, open-ended questions that require higher-order thinking, e.g. why, what would happen if, what makes you say that?
- give children opportunities to organize activities themselves, avoiding too early adult intervention.

4 Articulation of learning

Finally, it is clear that if children are going to become increasingly aware of their own mental processing, the processes of thinking and learning need to be made explicit by adults, and the children themselves need to learn to talk about and to represent their learning and thinking. In his famous nine glasses experiment, the American psychologist, Jerome Bruner, demonstrated that while most 3–5-year-olds could reproduce a pattern of different sized drinking glasses exactly as they had seen it on a 3×3 matrix, only those who could talk about the pattern and had a vocabulary of words such as 'taller', 'fatter', 'thinner', 'shorter', and so on, were able to turn the pattern upside down, or flip it left to right, and produce transformations of it (Bruner and Kenney 1966). The ability to not just reproduce information, but to manipulate and transform it, is of course fundamental to any kind of abstract thinking.

Within the CIndLe project, many practitioners developed techniques to stimulate children's reflections and held extended conversations with them about their learning. These included, for example, taking digital photographs of the children playing or engaging in a task, and then reviewing them with the children on a laptop computer. In situations where they had not been an active participant in the children's imaginative play, they were able to ask genuine questions and stimulate the children to reflect upon their thinking and decision-making during the activity.

Other strategies which are effective in stimulating children to talk about their learning include:

- peer tutoring, where one child teaches another;
- involving children in self-assessment;
- making learning intentions explicit when tasks are introduced, or

discussed either while the children are engaged in the task, or afterwards in a review session;

- modelling a self-commentary, which articulates thinking and strategies; for example, when solving a mathematical problem, or drawing an object from life.

Conclusion

When independent learning has been advocated or discussed in education, often the focus has been on purely organizational issues to do with children being able to get on with their work without being overly dependent on the practitioner. In this chapter, however, I have argued that encouraging children to become independent or self-regulated learners involves more than this and is fundamental to children developing as learners.

There are structural reasons why facilitating genuinely self-regulated learning in early years classrooms is not straightforward. However, the 32 practitioners who worked on the CIndLe project have managed to achieve outstanding results and have found ways of developing their practices which have been enormously beneficial to both children and practitioners. Organizing the classroom environment and organizing learning activities in special ways, with certain styles of interaction and discourse between adults and children and between the children themselves, can make a significant contribution.

Whenever a practitioner moves to give young children more responsibility for their own learning, they have always been deeply impressed by the response from the children, and have seen the benefits very quickly for the children's motivation and learning. When they enter school, the vast majority of young children are voracious in their enthusiasm for life and for learning and, sadly, for many the experience of schooling diminishes rather than supports these appetites. Education has become, for too many of our children, something which is done *to* them, rather than *with* them.

Points for discussion

- What do you understand by the term 'metacognition'? It is often referred to as 'thinking about thinking' but is perhaps best described as higher-order thinking which involves active control over the cognitive processes of learning. With all such terms it's better if you put it into your own words!
- Self-regulation is more obvious, but what do you understand by that term? How is self-regulation apparent in your workplace, for staff and

children? How important is self-regulation to you and your colleagues?

* Think about occasions when you have talked to children about their learning. Was it really about the task and its completion or was the conversation really about learning and the ways in which the child learns?

NB If you would like to know more about the CIndLe project you can access further details, downloadable versions of publications and an order form for the CD-based training resource produced by the project team at: http://www.educ.cam.ac.uk/cindle/index.html

References and further reading

Barkley, R.A. (1997) *ADHD and the Nature of Self-control*. New York: Guilford Press.

Black, P. and Wiliam, D. (1998) *Inside the Black Box: Raising Standards through Classroom Assessment*. London: Kings College School of Education.

Bronson, M.B. (2000) *Self-Regulation in Early Childhood*. New York: Guilford Press.

Brooker, L. (1996) Why do children go to school? Consulting children in the Reception class, *Early Years*, 17(1): 12–16.

Brown, A.L. (1987) Metacognition, executive control, self-regulation and other more mysterious mechanisms, in F. Weinert and R. Kluwe (eds) *Metacognition, Motivation and Understanding*. Hillsdale, NJ: Lawrence Erlbaum.

Bruner, J.S. and Kenney, H. (1966) The development of the concepts of order and proportion in children, in J. Bruner, R. Olver and P. Greenfield (eds) *Studies in Cognitive Growth*. New York: Wiley.

Collins, A., Seely Brown, J. and Newman, S.E. (1989) Cognitive apprenticeship: teaching the crafts of reading, writing and mathematics, in L.B. Resnick (ed.) *Knowing, Learning and Instruction*. Hillsdale, NJ: Lawrence Erlbaum.

DfES (Department for Education and Skills) (2006) *The Early Years Foundation Stage: Consultation on a Single Quality Framework for Services to Children from Birth to Five*. Nottingham: DfES Publications.

Durkin, K. (1995) Attachment to others, in K. Durkin (ed.) *Developmental Social Psychology: From Infancy to Old Age*. Oxford: Blackwell.

Featherstone, S. and Bayley, R. (2001) *Foundations of Independence*. Lutterworth: Featherstone Education.

Flavell, J.H. (1979) Metacognition and cognitive monitoring: a new area of cognitive developmental inquiry, *American Psychologist*, 34: 906–11.

Forman, E. and Cazden, C. (1985) Exploring Vygotskian perspectives in education: the cognitive value of peer interaction, in J.V. Wertsch (ed.) *Culture, Communication and Cognition: Vygotskian Perspectives*. Cambridge: Cambridge University Press.

Galton, M. (1989) *Teaching in the Primary School*. London: David Fulton.

Gerhardt, S. (2004) *Why Love Matters: How Affection Shapes a Baby's Brain*. London: Routledge.

Goleman, D. (2005) ***Emotional Intelligence*, 2nd edn. New York: Bantam Books.**

Hendy, L. and Whitebread, D. (2000) Interpretations of independent learning in the Early Years, *International Journal of Early Years Education*, 8(3): 245–52.

Leat, D. and Lin, M. (2003) Developing a pedagogy of metacognition and transfer: some signposts for the generation and use of knowledge and the creation of research partnerships, *British Educational Research Journal*, 29(3): 383–416.

Littleton, K., Mercer, N., Dawes, L., Wegerif, R., Rowe, D. and Sams, C. (2005) Talking and thinking together at Key Stage 1, *Early Years*, 25(2): 167–82.

Metcalfe, J. and Shimamura, A. (eds) (1994) *Metacognition: Knowing about Knowing*. Cambridge, MA: The MIT Press.

Nisbet, J. and Shucksmith, J. (1986) *Learning Strategies*. London: Routledge and Kegan Paul.

Palincsar, A.S. and Brown, A.L. (1984) Reciprocal teaching of comprehension-fostering and comprehension-monitoring activities, *Cognition and Instruction*, 1: 117–75.

Perry, N.E., VandeKamp, K.J.O., Mercer, L.K. and Nordby, C.J. (2002) Investigating teacher-student interactions that foster self-regulated learning, *Educational Psychologist*, 37(1): 5–15.

QCA/DfEE (2000) *Curriculum Guidance for the Foundation Stage*. London: QCA/DfEE.

Schaffer, H.R. (2004) The child as apprentice: Vygotsky's theory of socio-cognitive development, in *Introducing Child Psychology*. Oxford: Blackwell.

Schunk, D.H. and Zimmerman, B.J. (1994) *Self-Regulation of Learning and Performance*. Hillsdale, NJ: Lawrence Erlbaum.

Siegler, R.S. (2002) Microgenetic studies of self-explanation, in N. Granott and J. Parziale (eds) *Microdevelopment: Transition Processes in Development and Learning*. Cambridge: Cambridge University Press.

Sugden, D. (1989) Skill generalisation and children with learning difficulties, in D. Sugden (ed.) *Cognitive Approaches in Special Education*. London: Falmer Press.

TDA (Training and Development Agency) (2006) *Qualifying to Teach*. London: TDA.

Veenman, M.V.J. and Spaans, M.A. (2005) Relation between intellectual and metacognitive skills: age and task differences, *Learning and Individual Differences*, 15: 159–76.

Vygotsky, L.S. (1978) *Mind in Society*. Cambridge, MA: Harvard University Press.

Vygotsky, L.S. (1986) *Thought and Language*. Cambridge, MA: MIT Press.

Wang, M.C., Haertel, G.D. and Walberg, H.J. (1990) What influences learning? A content analysis of review literature, *Journal of Educational Research*, 84: 30–43.

Watson, J.S. and Ramey, C.T. (1972) Reactions to response-contingent stimulation in early infancy, *Merrill-Palmer Quarterly*, 18: 219–27.

Whitebread, D. (1996) The development of children's strategies on an inductive reasoning task, *British Journal of Educational Psychology*, 66(1): 1–21.

Whitebread, D., Anderson, H., Coltman, P., Page, C., Pino Pasternak, D. and Mehta, S. (2005) Developing independent learning in the early years, *Education 3–13*, 33: 40–50.

Williams, J. (2003) *Promoting Independent Learning in the Primary Classroom*. Buckingham: Open University Press.

Yussen, S.R. (ed.) (1985) *The Growth of Reflection in Children*. New York: Academic Press.

15 What does it mean to be creative?

Dan Davies and Alan Howe

Abstract

After briefly reviewing educators' concerns about the place of 'creativity' in young children's education, this chapter will examine the relationship between practitioner creativity and children's creativity, considering the following issues:

- Can teaching in the early years be considered a 'creative profession'?
- What do practitioners need to know about creativity in order to nurture it in children?

We then move on to challenge a number of 'myths' about creativity in early childhood education:

- Young children are innately creative and require minimal intervention to express this creativity.
- Creativity is synonymous with play.
- Creativity is primarily associated with the Arts.

Introduction

The recent upsurge in the UK government's interest in educational creativity, typified by the commissioning of the Roberts Report (2006) *Nurturing Creativity in Young People*, is a response to serious concerns from the profession that our current education system is ill-equipped to make the most of the creative potential of all children (Craft et al. 2001; Howe et al. 2001). Since 1997, the UK government has identified the significant contribution that the 'creative industries' make to the UK economy and come to recognize that an education system fit for the twenty-first century must not only equip the population with basic skills but also nurture the creativity of young people (Roberts 2006). In recent years practitioners, particularly those new to the profession, have had few opportunities to explore creative practice, teach creatively or come to understand the nature of children's creativity. The challenge is to re-define creative practice in early years education.

Can teaching in the early years be considered a 'creative profession'?

It is not uncommon to hear teachers likened to postal workers with a full sack – they are required to 'deliver' an appropriate curriculum, the latest initiative, high standards and improving results. Preferable metaphors, more likely to motivate and inspire practitioners, are those which align teaching to creativity. Woods' (1996) metaphor is the artist: '[teachers] create and sustain moods ... through skilful deployment of a variety of tones, which make subtle use of time and space'.

When students are learning to be teachers, some will write their plans as if scripting a play – they write their lines, make note of stage directions and list their props before heading off to take the stage. While it might be appealing to describe teaching in these terms, can the claim that teaching is a 'creative profession' be sustained under these circumstances?

A characteristic of the creative professional is that of 'non-conformity' or the ability to go beyond the norm or usual practice. Sternberg and Lubart (1995) have identified this as one of the characteristics of 'creative' teachers. It is, however, a high-risk strategy requiring self-confidence and an investment of time and energy (Yeomans 1996). The need to keep such risks within bounds requires an ability to monitor and evaluate events:

> Professional creativity should not be taken as suggesting some sort of runaway experimentation with what we do together. Rather, it asserts that responsible experimentation and innovation, planned and monitored with the help of colleagues as well as relevant theoretical notions, are desirable activities.
>
> (Ashcroft and James 1999: 25)

Craft (2002) identifies a number of constraints on teachers' professional creativity:

- limitations of terminology (lack of understanding or agreement about what 'creativity' means in an educational context);
- conflicts in policy and practice (the dissonance between what we espouse as educators and what we actually do in the classroom);
- limitations in curriculum organization (a traditional subject-bound curriculum);
- limitations stemming from centrally controlled pedagogy (e.g. the orthodoxy of literacy and numeracy teaching in England).

Within the current culture of conformity in education that Craft identifies, there is the danger that practitioners do not see teaching as a 'creative profession' and those who do have either been driven out, deterred from entering the profession, or had their practice suppressed (Sternberg and Lubart 1995). Craft (2000: 3) acknowledges the frequently adverse conditions within which teachers seek to innovate, and points to the value of 'possibility thinking' in transcending limitations, while maintaining a realistic view of events in and surrounding the classroom. In some respects, there is much less tension between policy and practice within early years setting than there might be in later phases of education when curriculum organization and pedagogy have become bound, certainly in England, by centrally determined orthodoxies embodied in National Literacy and Numeracy Strategies. Nevertheless, the challenge to managers of early years settings is to find ways to support practitioners' creativity through 'giving permission' to innovate and take risks with their practice. In turn, senior staff require the same support from local education authorities and governmental departments. The government response to the Report (DfCMS/DfES 2006) is encouraging in this respect: 'We will ensure that creativity continues to be of fundamental importance in the *Early Years Foundation Stage*. We will also examine ways of recognising and rewarding practitioners and settings which demonstrate particularly effective creative practice' (2006: 6). The form that 'recognition and reward' will take remains to be seen, but this statement points to the fundamental importance of arriving at shared understandings within early years settings of what 'creative practice' actually means.

Reflection points

1   What do you understand by 'creative practice'?
2   Is creative practice nurtured in your setting, for children and practitioners? In what ways?

What do practitioners need to know about creativity in order to nurture it in children?

Having established that early years teaching is a creative profession, it is not difficult to argue that creative teaching is a desirable and worthwhile professional aspiration and therefore contained within most notions of 'good teaching'. OfSTED (2003: 8) found that practitioners who inspire creativity have a clear understanding of what it means to be creative, although they are not always able to put this understanding into words. Creativity can be seen as 'making connections between previously unconnected ideas' (Koestler

1964): a useful definition in the context of early years practice. Creative teaching might then involve making links between:

- areas of learning;
- children's lives and experiences in and out of the setting;
- the setting and the community.

This 'joined-up-thinking' is entirely consistent with the views of many early years educators who advocate that children's learning should be holistic, contextualized and developed from their experiences and interests.

The National Advisory Committee on Creative and Cultural Education (NACCCE 1999) made a useful distinction between 'teaching for creativity' (associated with children's creative development) and 'teaching creatively' (associated with teacher attributes) which need to be understood separately, although it becomes clear that the two are closely related (as in the distinction between 'play' and 'playful teaching' outlined in the Introduction to this book). Practitioners cannot effectively foster children's creativity if their own is being suppressed. NACCCE (1999: 29) went on to propose a working definition of creativity for educators: 'Imaginative action fashioned so as to produce outcomes that are both original and of value', which has enjoyed widespread acceptance; although some take issue with the notion that creativity should always have *outcomes*. The intention of the NACCCE report was to present creativity as a democratic and inclusive concept. In that spirit, *outcome* needs to be viewed in the widest possible way – as an artefact, an idea, a behaviour or action. This, however, still leaves room for the persistence of a number of myths about creativity in early childhood education, some of which we consider below.

Creativity myths in early childhood education

1 Young children are innately creative and require minimal intervention to express this creativity

We have all been surprised and charmed by the unexpected ideas and connections young children make, with a seemingly greater frequency than older children – certainly than adults. We describe them as 'imaginative' when they become engrossed in role-play activities or indulge in flights of whimsical fancy. We secretly envy the unfettered free association and divergent thinking they appear to exhibit, perhaps associating this with the 'zany' creativity of artists who appear to have retained this childlike naïvety which our education system has crushed in the rest of us. But is what we are admiring really creativity or just immature thought processes? Are young children really more creative than the rest of us and just need leaving alone, or are there things we can do as educators to help them develop as creative individuals?

The *laissez-faire* attitude towards children's creativity implied by the statement above derives from a 'nativist' view of childhood (Bruce 1997), first espoused by Rousseau in the eighteenth century and strongly promoted by the (1967) *Plowden Report*, leading to a widespread trepidation among teachers of daring to tread in this 'secret garden'. Yet research into children's creativity suggests that these early expressions may be 'pre-conventional' (Rosenblatt and Winner 1988), in that children below the age of around 6–8 years appear to exhibit unusual ideas because they are unaware of the conventions of thought and representation that we adults take for granted. Once children become aware of conventional ways of thinking (from ages 6–8 to about 10–12) they tend to adopt them – perhaps through social pressure, or because they recognize conventions as useful ways of thinking about the world – leading to an apparent decline in the expression of 'creative' (unusual) ideas. What really counts as creativity, argues Craft (2000), is *post- conventionality,* i.e. being aware of conventions but choosing to go beyond them. This is why, for example, an apparently naïve and childlike painting by Picasso may be regarded as an example of exceptional creativity, whilst a superficially similar representation by a 4-year-old is not. The 4-year-old may indeed have been creative in his or her own terms – by transcending his or her own conventions (what Craft terms 'little c creativity') – but lack of awareness of societal norms means that his or her creativity is at an earlier developmental stage.

The assumption that post-conventionality is inherently superior to pre-conventionality (since it involves awareness of constraints and the ability to transcend them) could be regarded as implying a deficit model of early childhood creativity. However, we would not want to give the impression that young children produce novel ideas because 'they don't know any better'. In many fields, ignorance of convention can produce startling innovation; what Root-Bernstein (1991) has termed the 'novice effect'. He argues that creative adults are often characterized by shifting fields or focuses of attention at regular intervals in their careers, avoiding 'staleness' by putting themselves in the role of novices. Most children are relative novices by comparison with adults, hence the frequent 'freshness' of their responses. At a neurological level this may correspond to greater plasticity and capacity for making connections between neurons in a child's brain (Greenfield 2000) by comparison with the more rigid structures present in later life.

Dust (1999) summarizes the literature on models of creative processes, suggesting that four phases are commonly identified: *preparation, incubation, illumination* and *verification.* When considering children's creativity, we tend to focus on 'illumination' – children's instant responses to situations seeming to arise directly from their fertile imaginations. For example, psychologists tend to measure children's *ideational fluency* (Moran 1988). Ideational fluency tasks require children to generate as many responses as they can to a particular stimulus, such as different uses for a simple object or examples with a common characteristic: 'all the things you can think of that are red'. While measures such as this may provide some indication of children's abilities to generate ideas, they fail to capture or even acknowledge the other phases of creative processes. *Preparation* involves accumulating knowledge, skills, wisdom and research to underpin the value of the idea proposed. It is Einstein's '99% perspiration' lying behind every '1 per cent inspiration'. It is part of what separates pre-conventional from post-conventional creativity. Surely practitioners have a role here in providing children with access to information and experiences that will help them develop the quality of their novel ideas; helping them to understand the nature of conventions so that when they are being original in either their own or wider terms, they can identify this. Similarly with *verification*, teachers can help children evaluate the outcomes of their creativity. Csikszentmihalyi (1990) uses the term 'gatekeepers' to denote those members of a 'creative' field who make judgements about work claiming to be of value. In educational settings such judgements can be shared between practitioners, children and their peers. Incidentally, this social approach to creative evaluation challenges the brain-based model above; we could argue that creativity actually belongs in 'communities', residing in the 'spaces' between individual minds, rather than being sited entirely in the individual (Craft 2000: 149).

Reflection points

3   How do children in your setting show their creativity? Do you see evidence of *preparation, incubation, illumination* and *verification* in their creative activities?
4   How far do you feel that play and creativity are linked? What examples do you have from your observations of children?

---

2 Creativity is synonymous with play

Opportunities for children to play are often associated with the development of their creativity. For example, Bruner et al. (1976) arrived at significant insights into children's play and its role in enabling them to negotiate, solve problems and imagine alternative futures – all attributes closely associated with creativity. Bruner and his colleagues observed children playing with objects in different structured situations. In one such experiment, children were classified in terms of their attitudes to a specially designed toy and the playfulness with which they interacted with it: 'The more inventive and exploratory the children had been initially in playing with the super-toy, the higher their originality scores were four years later' (Bruner et al. 1976: 17).

Significantly, Bruner's 'play' groups outperformed 'taught' groups consistently. One of the fundamental characteristics of play is that it is low risk; we cannot be wrong when playing (Moyles 1989). The security this gives to players enables them to take risks – the experience gives children confidence to be inventive and make mistakes when the situation becomes more structured. Thus the ability to solve problems is linked closely with the freedom to play. But is all play creative? Are there types of play which are more productive in children's creative development than others?

Moyles (1989: 63) identifies *specific exploration* as being that kind of play which looks at what the material is and what it can do, and *diversive exploration* as leading a child to explore what *they* can personally do with the material. For example, a child might manipulate play dough for some time, exploring its properties (specific exploration), then later start to make an animal out of it (diversive exploration). The latter might be identified as offering more opportunity for creativity, but we could equally see both stages as parts of a creative process; the specific exploration as *preparation* (Dust 1999) while the diversive exploration might be associated with *verification* of the idea which has come to the child while finding out what the material can do. Similarly, Hutt's taxonomy of children's play (1979) distinguishes between that which is *epistemic* (problem-solving, exploratory, concerned with skills); *ludic* (symbolic, repetitive, fantasy, concerned with innovation) and *games-play* (rule making and following). At a first glance, ludic play might appear to offer more scope for creativity than the other two. But this may be to confuse imagination with creativity – the mistake made by psychologists in focusing on ideational fluency as representative of the whole creative process of which it is only a part (see above). Further consideration of these categories leads us to anticipate that epistemic play is likely to be more productive in developing the knowledge, skills and strategies necessary for post-conventional creativity. One feature of ludic play that could raise doubts about its creative potential is the presence of *schemas*: patterns of 'repeatable behaviour into which experiences are assimilated and that are gradually co-ordinated' (Athey 1990: 37). For example, a child may be fascinated by putting objects into bags or wrapping them up, while repeatedly drawing enclosed circular shapes (an envelopment schema). Schemas tend not to be isolated patterns of behaviour – they develop in clusters and are part of whole networks of senses, actions and thinking, characteristic of Piaget's 'sensori-motor' stage of development between the approximate ages of 2 and 4. Could repetitive behaviour be creative? Perhaps not in terms of the widely accepted definition of the word from *All Our Futures* (NACCCE 1999): 'imaginative activity fashioned so as to produce outcomes that are both original and of value', although again it could lay the foundations for creativity at a later stage.

In an observational study of pre-school settings, Hutt et al. (1989) noted that children often engaged in stereotypical, repetitive behaviours –

particularly in sand and water play – and that there was little evidence of cognitive challenge. Adult interventions were predominantly monitorial and did not involve sustained conversations. The activities where an adult was present (commonly collage and 'junk modelling') produced more sustained engagement and lively discussions. A consistent theme running through these studies is that educators need to be active and promote the conditions for creative development through play. Play on its own is not necessarily creative! Gura (1992) concluded that a number of learning-relevant conditions were necessary to support high quality play. These factors are closely linked to ideas about creativity already discussed and include:

- enabling children to take risks, be creative and playful in their ideas;
- organizing the physical setting to maximize learning opportunities;
- adult involvement;
- allowing children to share the initiative about what is to be learnt;
- developing effective systems for observation and record keeping, and using these to inform curriculum planning.

With these conditions in place, we suggest that the types of play most likely to offer scope for activity are play with materials and objects, role play and playing games, each associated with one of Hutt's categories above.

Play with materials and objects
Craft (2000, 2002) has proposed the concept of 'possibility thinking' to be at the core of creativity and a foundation for knowledge. She sees that possibility thinking as posing questions and 'a continuum of thinking strategies' from 'What does this do?' to 'What can I do with this?' (Craft 2002: 113). These questions are *generative* in the sense that they lead to new actions and the creation of new knowledge for the learner. Generative questions are the kind that children will 'ask' as they play with materials. Children can be prompted into new patterns of play by presenting them with materials in new ways, for example, by changing the contents of the water tray to promote new thinking. A 'sparkly water tray' contains a range of objects small and large, some of which float, some sink, some reflect and some refract the light, creating changing colours, leading to a range of questions and observations such as: what do these things do when they get wet? This wet mirror is a bit like the one in our bathroom that gets 'steamy'. Is this the same tinsel that was on the Christmas tree? Can I stick the wet sequins to my arm? Why do some sequins float and some sink?

Perhaps the best materials for encouraging possibility thinking are those gathered from nature. Natural materials are of infinite variety and therefore more capable of provoking original responses by comparison with manufactured, uniform resources. What can be done with a pile of autumn leaves?

They may provide a 'habitat' for the toy dinosaurs, they can be scrunched to make a satisfying noise, torn to create confetti, sorted into pretty ones and not so pretty ones … Consider a child mixing wet paints together on a sheet of paper, swirling them with a brush and watching them merge, change colour and drip down the easel. Another child has a lump of clay and adds more and more water to make it 'muddy' – slipping and sliding between her fingers – and then proceeds to make a hand print with the 'mud' rather than make a model like the rest of the table are doing. We may think that such activities are creative play, but just because art materials are involved it doesn't necessarily mean that any activity counts as 'creative'. Notice that in both the above scenarios there is no mention of the child necessarily working towards an end point – a painting or model. An important feature of creative play is that it is centred on what the child wants to do at that moment, not on what an adult might want as a product.

Role play

Playing make believe, pretending and imaging (seeing reality in the mind's eye) are all features of *ludic* play. A key feature of such play is that it is a low-risk way of 'rehearsing' for the real world. In setting up a role-play area practitioners hope to provide children with opportunities to develop their creativity, although in reality this may not always be the case. Broadhead and English (2005) have found that *pre-themed* role-play areas can actually be *less* good at stimulating co-operative play and higher-order learning than practitioners assume. Their research has focused on the setting up in reception classes of open-ended role-play areas or 'whatever you want it to be places'. Two key features of these are:

- play resources that can be used for a variety of purposes;
- extended play periods with regular access so children can become 'expert players'.

However, children cannot create play in contexts they haven't experienced. They need to be provided with knowledge on which to base their creativity. A key ingredient in the above research is the provocation of a theatre performance where the actors 'suggest' ways in which the play-props might be used. Children will mimic adult behaviour whether it is in the contexts of a play or 'real life'. Visitors to the classroom or visits to workplaces can be used to provide new knowledge and ideas about how adults interact and behave. These experiences can in turn stimulate play. For example, a visit to a local garden centre can subsequently involve children in setting up a 'garden centre' area where they can play the adult roles they witnessed during the trip.

Playing games

Playing games with rules might not seem to offer much scope for creativity. Rules that are open to interpretation or allow for creative responses, however, offer a clear structure within which creative thinking can be developed. For example, in earlier writing (Davies and Howe 2002), we describe 'playing the scientist game' with young children, including a set of 'rules' or steps to be followed. The rules are expressed in terms of questions that guide the process of scientific enquiry:

- What have we noticed?
- What are we going to find out?
- What do we think will happen?
- How did we do it?
- What did we find out?

Armed with magnifying aids and note pads, children can be encouraged to be scientists as they make observations, perform 'investigations' and report back their findings. They might be guided to make 'discoveries' by practitioners modelling scientific behaviour themselves. Expert practitioners are able see the everyday through a child's eyes – the shape of a snail trail, the flow of sand, the smell of an apple, and these 'commonplace' observations can promote questions – 'Where is the snail now?', 'Does the sand feel wet?', 'Does an apple core smell different to a whole apple?' By modelling questions, practitioners can show children how to put their natural curiosity into words, which can then form the basis of the rules for the scientist game. Games with a basis in logic can also promote connection-making and creative thinking. A collection of objects from the kitchen or garden can be sorted and linked – 'How are these items different?', 'How are they the same?', 'Can you think of a different way to sort them?'

Reflection points

5   How far does your provision allow children to take risks and bring a creative approach to activities?

6   What activities do you provide to encourage children's natural curiosity to be celebrated and extended?

7   What opportunities for creativity do you provide in your setting within the areas of curriculum, be it EYFS or Key Stage 1?

3 Creativity is primarily associated with the Arts

Although we welcome the renewed interest in creativity within early years education prompted by *All Our Futures* (NACCCE 1999) and the inclusion of 'Creative Development' as one of the areas of learning in the Foundation Stage – now the *Early Years Foundation Stage* (DfES 2006) – we have some reservations about the strong arts bias in both these documents. For example, the *Curriculum Guidance for the Foundation Stage* (QCA/DfEE 2000: 116) states that the area of Creative Development relates to 'art, music, dance, role-play and imaginative play'. This has reinforced the widespread perception among teachers that in order to develop children's creativity, we need to involve them in arts-based activities. Research we undertook with primary trainee teachers (Davies et al. 2004) revealed that they expected art lessons to provide more opportunities for creativity than any other curriculum area, and that they anticipated little scope for creativity in science or mathematics. Once they had analysed observed lessons in these areas against a set of criteria for creative practice, these expectations were frequently confounded!

We have already suggested above that scientific activities can promote creativity. Whether practitioners recognize this may have a great deal to do with their own educational experience, which may have promoted a view of science as a factual body of knowledge about the world, concerned with laws and formulae and 'discovered' through complex experiments, we will find it difficult to recognize the scientific significance of 4-year-olds pushing each other around on wheeled toys. If, on the other hand, we regard scientific knowledge as shifting and tentative – inherently rooted in the 'here and now' of everyday things and events – early years science will appear as a natural component of young children's learning and creative development. Thus children playing the 'scientist game' (see above) can change the questions and interpret the rules in creative ways; this is post-conventional creativity in that they are becoming aware of the conventions of scientific enquiry through 'playing about' with it.

Of course, the early years curriculum is not divided into compartmentalized subject areas called 'science' and 'maths' – it is concerned with children's holistic development and the links between curriculum areas. Here too, science can stake its claim for creativity in its potential for expression through different media. For example, many scientists communicate their ideas by telling us stories. Their stories are about how the world began, how the mountains and seas, animals and plants came to be. They tell us how they carried their work and what they found as they delved, dissected and deliberated over the universe. Many of their stories claim to be 'true' – the authors are usually convinced about this – the readers or listeners need to make up their own minds about that. Some scientist tales may turn out to be false, or better stories take their place. What is important is that we – and the young children we teach – never stop telling the stories.

Conclusion

In this chapter we have argued that teaching in the early years should be regarded as a creative profession, but that it is one in which the nature of creativity in both learning and teaching tends to be ill-defined. In particular, there are a number of myths about creativity in the early years which have tended to perpetuate, and which we have sought to challenge. We hope that this will support practitioners in thinking through the issues.

Points for discussion

- In what ways could early years educators be considered to be 'creative professionals'?
- How can an understanding of children's creativity help practitioners reflect on their practice?
- Which of the above 'creativity myths' are present in our early years setting and how can we go about challenging them?

References and further reading

Ashcroft, K. and James, D. (eds) (1999) *The Creative Professional: Learning to Teach 14–19 Year Olds*. London: Falmer.

Athey, C. (1990) *Extending Thought in Young Children: A Parent-Teacher Partnership*. London: Paul Chapman.

Broadhead, P. and English, C. (2005) Open-ended role play: supporting creativity and developing identity, in J. Moyles (ed.) *The Excellence of Play*, 2nd edn. Maidenhead: Open University Press.

Bruce, T. (1997) *Early Childhood Education*, 2nd edn. London: Hodder and Stoughton.

Bruner, J.S., Jolly, A. and Sylva, K. (eds) (1976) *Play: Its Role in Development and Evolution*. Harmondsworth: Penguin.

Craft, A. (2000) *Creativity Across the Primary Curriculum: Framing and Developing Practice*. London: Routledge.

Craft, A. (2002) *Creativity and Early Years Education*. London: Continuum.

Craft, A., Jeffrey, B. and Liebling, M. (eds) (2001) *Creativity Across the Primary Curriculum*. London: Continuum.

Csikszentmihalyi, M. (1990) The domains of creativity, in M. Runco and R. Albert (eds) *Theories of Creativity*. London: Sage Publications.

Davies, D. and Howe, A. (2002) *Teaching Science and Design and Technology in the Early Years*. London: David Fulton.

Davies, D., Howe, A. and McMahon, K. (2004) Challenging primary trainees' views of creativity in the curriculum through a school-based dierected task, *Science Teacher Education*, 41: 2–3.

DfCMS (Department for Culture Media and Sport)/ DfES (Department for Education and Skills) (2006) Government Response to the Robert's Report. Available at: http://www.culture.gov.uk/Reference_library/Publications/archive_2006/ govtresponse_nurturingcreativity.htm (accessed 15 December 2006).

DfES (2006) *The Early Years Foundation Stage: Consultation on a Single Quality Framework for Services to Children from Birth to Five*. Nottingham: DfES Publications.

Dust, K. (1999) *Motive, Means and Opportunity: Creativity Research Review*. London: NESTA.

Greenfield, S. (2000) *Brain Story*. London: BBC Books.

Gura, P. (ed.) (1992) *Exploring Learning: Young Children and Block Play*. London: Paul Chapman.

Howe, A., Davies, D. and Ritchie, R. (2001) *Primary Design and Technology for the Future: Creativity, Culture and Citizenship*. London: David Fulton.

Hutt, C. (1979) 'Play in the under-fives: form, development and function', in J. Howells (ed.) *Modern Perspectives in the Psychiatry of Infancy*. New York: Brunner/Marcel.

Hutt, S.J., Tyler, S., Hutt, C. and Christopherson, H. (1989) *Play, Exploration and Learning: A Natural History of the Preschool*. London: Routledge.

Koestler, A. (1964) *The Act of Creation*. London: Hutchison.

Moran, J. (1988) *Creativity in Young Children: ERIC Digest*. ERIC Clearinghouse on Elementary and Early Childhood Education, Urbana, IL. Available at: http:// www.kidsource.com/kidsource/content2/Creativity_in_kids.html

Moyles, J. (1989) *Just Playing? The Role and Status of Play in Early Childhood Education*. Milton Keynes: Open University Press.

National Advisory Committee on Creative and Cultural Education (NACCCE) (1999) *All Our Futures: Creativity, Culture and Education.* **Suffolk: DfEE.**

OfSTED (Office for Standards in Education) (2003) *Expecting the Unexpected: Developing Creativity in Primary and Secondary Schools*. London: OfSTED.

Qualifications and Curriculum Authority/Department for Education and Employment (2000) *Curriculum Guidance for the Foundation Stage*. London: QCA/DfEE.

Roberts, P. (2006) *Nurturing Creativity in Young People: A Report to Government to Inform Future Policy.* **Available at: http://www. culture.gov.uk/Reference_library/Publications/archive_2006/**

govtresponse_nurturingcreativity.htm (accessed 15 December 2006).

Root-Bernstein, R. (1991) *Discovering: Inventing and Solving Problems at the Frontiers of Scientific Knowledge*. Cambridge, MA: Harvard University Press.

Rosenblatt, E. and Winner, E. (1988) The art of children's drawing, *Journal of Aesthetic Education*, 22: 3–15.

Sternberg, R. and Lubart, T. (1995) *Defying the Crowd: Cultivating Creativity in a Culture of Conformity*. New York: Free Press.

Woods, P. (1996) 'The good times', creative teaching in primary schools, *Education 3–13*, 3–12.

Yeomans, M. (1996) 'Creativity in Art and Science: a personal view', *Journal of Art and Design Education*, 15(3): 241–50.

16 Multi-modality, play and children's mark-making in maths

Maulfry Worthington

Abstract

Growing interest in *multi-modality* is providing fresh insights into ways in which cultures, new technologies and media influence different 'texts' that children create and is informing our understanding of children's thinking in new ways, including children's meaning-making and their early explorations of symbolic languages. I consider some of the challenges and issues that practitioners have faced in teaching early 'written' mathematics and show how, through using their own mathematical graphics, multi-modal ways of representation allow children to explore significant aspects of symbols, meanings, interpretation and communication.

Multi-modality extends what we already know of children's early mark-making and the role of visual representations in supporting thinking. It links all aspects of play and representation and crosses 'subject' boundaries such as literacy and mathematics. Importantly, understanding multi-modal meanings will encourage a more generous perspective of young children as powerful and competent meaning-makers.

Introduction

In this chapter I want to explore and celebrate some of the exciting ways in which young children make multi-modal meanings. *Multi-modality* refers to the diverse ways in which children make meanings with what Kress (1997) refers to as 'lots of different stuff' and in many different ways or *modes*. The theory that underpins multi-modality is social semiotics which examines ways in which 'texts' and meanings are made, represented, communicated and understood by individuals within social contexts.

I shall also explore an area of young children's learning that has probably been one of the most misunderstood and that continues to cause considerable difficulties for young children – early 'written' mathematics. My aim is to show something of the power of young children's thinking when they are encouraged to use their own ways of representing their personal mathematical meanings.

My research evidence is of children making sense of the written symbolic 'language' of mathematics through their personal marks and symbols (Carruthers and Worthington 2006): this research meshes with the growing understanding of multi-modality and can reveal hidden depths of understanding. These two areas of research are gaining recognition and beginning to influence pedagogical approaches in early childhood settings.

Challenges

The two areas explored in this chapter are rooted in research that has a long history: developing understanding of these important aspects of learning and development will not only support young children but can also help practitioners understand and justify what they are doing. Several questions will be explored within this chapter:

- What does research show about young children as powerful meaning-makers?
- How do symbolic languages arise within children's play?
- How do young children represent their own mathematical thinking in multi-modal ways?
- What are the implications for supporting young children's meaning-making?
- What are the implications for teaching early written mathematics?

Issues

There are a number of issues for young children learning the 'written' language of mathematics:

- Standard written symbols and calculations are like a 'foreign language' for young children.
- Children often experience considerable difficulties with the standard written language of mathematics since it is unlike the informal ways of representing that they already use.
- Young children may appear to understand standard symbols and horizontal calculations but their knowledge is often superficial and will not provide a strong foundation for the increasingly standard mathematics they meet as they move through school.

- Practitioners are often unclear about official guidance on pedagogical approaches; unsure about children's development of early written mathematics and uncertain how they might assess children's own mathematical marks and representations.

How might we move to ways of learning (and teaching) early 'written' mathematics that are in tune with young learners? A multi-modal approach treats individuals 'not as language users but as language makers' (Kress 1997: xvi) – exploring children's own mathematical texts from this perspective can provide practitioners with new insights.

Young children as powerful meaning-makers

In the 1930s, the Russian psychologist Lev Vygotsky identified ways in which young children substituted alternative meanings of their own for the objects with which they played, for example, pretending that a stick was a horse (Vygotsky 1978). This work included a study of the origin of symbols and underpins much of what is now known about representation, meanings and symbolic languages such as writing and mathematics – or *social semiotics*.

Others have explored issues of 'meaning-making' in learning, including Wells (1986), Halliday (1975) and Bruner (1996), and the publication of Marie Clay's work on children's early writing in 1975 heralded a wealth of research and interest in young children's early 'emergent' or developmental writing. In the West, publication of Vygotsky's and Luria's work (in 1978 and 1983 respectively) revealed that interest in young children exploring writing though their own marks had originated in Russia in the 1930s. However, it was not until much later that interest into the multi-modal ways in which children explore meanings grew.

Multi-modality

Studies of *multi-literacies* (Cope and Kalantzis 2000) acknowledge cultural and linguistic diversity and the influence of new communication technologies and research into multi-modality grew from this context (Jewitt and Kress 2003).

Focusing on the diverse ways in which children choose to make meanings offers us new insights: it will add to our understanding of play and visual representation and is likely to engender a more holistic view of learning. For children, it supports all the complexity of their spontaneous and self-initiated play; of making things and their marks and drawings. These multi-modal ways are referred to as 'texts' and include still or moving visual images;

gesture; speech; sound; movement, spatial and print-based texts, objects, arrangements, piles of things and imaginary play. Although we are familiar with the term 'text' to refer to content that is written or printed, the various ways in which individuals communicate through these different symbol systems are also known as 'texts'.

Technologies and new texts

Multi-modal practices are influenced in part by the rapid changes in technologies and media in contemporary society (Jewitt and Kress 2003; Pahl and Rowsell 2005). Whereas previously texts printed on paper dominated, now visual images carry complex meanings. Through computer software, games, websites and mobile phones, a new visual 'language' allows fluidity of access, meanings and new ways of exploring and communicating thoughts and ideas. Texts created on computers allow different ways of representing, accessing and 'reading' meanings though graphics, layout, colour, space, fonts, sound and hypertext. As Kress emphasizes, 'the landscape of public communication is now less dominated by written language, and coming to be more dominated by visual forms' (1997: 6).

Beyond technology

Multi-modality is not only explored through new technologies but also gives rise to new ways of exploring meanings and new ways of understanding in other ways. The relationship between play and symbols may not be immediately apparent but recent research into multi-modality is revealing ever more complex ways in which children represent meanings through their play and with things they make (e.g. Kress 1997; Pahl 1999, 2003; Athey 2007).

Children explore, represent and communicate through drawings and painting (Matthews 2003; Anning and Ring 2004) and through maps (Pahl 2001). They make and transform complex meanings with junk models and cut-outs and all of these modes that highlight the extraordinary power of young children's thinking (see, for example, Kress 1997; Pahl 1999; Carruthers and Worthington 2006; Worthington 2007).

The 'creative development' section of the *Early Years Foundation Stage* (EYFS) (DfES 2006) emphasizes that children should have opportunities 'to express their ideas through a wide range of types of representation' (2006: 96). When the final version of the document is published (2008), it is hoped that the guidance makes the relationship between creativity, literacy and mathematics more explicit.

> **Reflection point**
>
> 1   The EYFS recommends that adults should be aware of 'the numerous ways in which children create and construct, and how their explorations lead to new understandings' (DfES 2006: 101).
>
> - Consider how practitioners in your setting show they value the things that children create spontaneously, including their junk models.
> - How might you emphasize more the *processes* of learning within children's spontaneous play?

Multi-modality is shaping literacy (Kress 1997): in Australia, there is a growing interest in multi-modal literacy and it is likely that a similar focus will also emerge in England (for example, QCA 2004 and 2005a for Key Stages 1–2). Science is also explored in multi-modal ways (Kress et al. 2001).

We have seen that the terms 'literacy' and 'text' go beyond the confines of written words on a page or screen (see Chapter 7). Mathematics also has its own 'literacy' – the standard written language of mathematics that children need to master as they move through school. Children's mathematical graphics allows them to explore their mathematical thinking in personal ways, to build deep meanings about symbols through their own marks and to come to understand the logic of written calculations, data handling and other aspects of written mathematics (Carruthers and Worthington 2005, 2006). This is also particularly significant in respect of continuity from the *Foundation Stage* into Year 1 (QCA 2005b). Children's mathematical graphics are also multi-modal texts.

How symbolic languages arise within children's play

In his powerful book *Before Writing*, Kress describes some of the ways in which children create multi-modal meanings through their play – building dens, role play, piles of things, cut-outs and models made with junk (Kress 1997). These meanings are mediated by how others use objects and texts and the meanings they attach to them through speech within social and cultural environments: as Kress emphasizes, 'we cannot understand how children find their way into print unless we understand the principles of their meaning making' (1997: xvii).

The emergence of symbolic languages

Using marks on paper also allows children to develop personal meanings about what they want their marks to 'mean' or represent and for young children there are no divisions between 'drawing' or 'writing'. Children gradually come to attach their own meanings to the marks they make, for example, Hannah (3 years and 2 months) drew a 'travelling loop' on paper, observing 'The bubbles are going up to the surface' (Matthews 2003: 79). Children's earliest marks on paper gradually develop (through physical actions) into differentiated marks (Matthews 2003) that are the basis of symbolic languages (Carruthers and Worthington 2006).

Some children of around 3 years of age begin to identify differences in their intentions for what their marks mean. Matt had just had his third birthday when he talked about what some of his marks 'said' as a written message; others as drawings and some marks he explained as numbers.

Nadia was 4 years and 7 months old and, on this occasion, it was the symbols themselves (their appearance and form), their potential functions and the meanings that she attached to them that interested her (see Figure 16.1). When she showed it to me, she 'read' the 'E'; several 'Js'; a star; 'T'; 'round' (gesturing with her fore-finger a circular movement); 'umbrella (*in the centre*) and 'square' (*lower right*). Thus, while some she named as standard letters, for others she focused on the shape or form of her symbols (i.e. the circle and the square), and two symbols suggested pictorial representations of things she knew (i.e. the star and an umbrella). The 'stuff' that children use to explore meanings within their play offer 'meaning-full' contexts for children's future explorations of symbolic languages such as writing.

One Saturday, Elise (4 years and 9 months) was helping her mother in the gift shop in which she worked. Elise sat near the counter 'reading' aloud from a slip of till roll on which she had written her name several times between the prices. I listened as she 'read' the till receipt, telling of a baby pterodactyl that had been captured by some 'very fierce dinosaurs'. After several alarming incidents the young pterodactyl was saved. Looking up, Elise said firmly 'The end!'

Elise understood that symbols such as letters and numerals on paper carry meanings that can be read. 'Reading aloud' or being read to, may perhaps be familiar behaviours Ellie had enjoyed at home or in nursery.

Reflection point

2   Adults working with young children need to be aware of 'the marks that children make and the meanings that they give to them' (DfES 2006: 55).

Young children use their own marks and representations in many contexts to make personal meanings and these can reveal a great deal about their thinking.

- Discuss with your team how you understand and assess individual children's own marks in your setting.
- Think about how you build your knowledge of children's early development of drawing and mark-making.

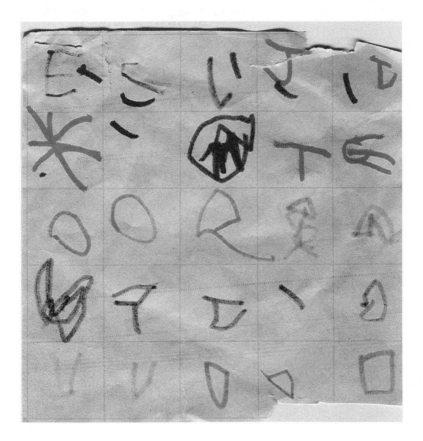

Figure 16.1 Nadia's symbols

Vygotsky identified a range of *symbolic tools* that include 'language, various systems for counting ... algebraic symbol systems, writing, diagrams, maps, technical drawings and all sorts of conventional signs' (Wertsch 1985). Used in specific ways and contexts within a culture, such tools are adapted over time and in the process, new ones are created (Rogoff 2003). Symbolic languages such as literacy and mathematics both have a specialized, written language and it has been argued that 'mathematics as a subject is really a matter of problem solving with symbolic tools' (van Oers 2001: 63).

Extending meaning within play

Young children explore mathematical meanings and concepts through play and may choose to create visual 'texts' through making models, collections and piles of things, cutting out and drawing (see Pahl 1999; Kress 1997; Athey 2007). Children also explore their own graphics within play contexts – as written props in their play and to add weight to what they mean, for example, in small world or in their role play (see, for example, Figure 16.2).

Multi-modal texts: more than at first meets the eye

Different texts offer different 'possibilities' to create meanings (Pahl and Rowsell 2005: 127). A closer focus on the examples in this chapter reveals complex layers of thinking about symbolic languages. Numerals on a shop till receipt combined with Elise's name offered her the possibility of telling a story about dinosaurs. In a different way, Nadia's choice of squared paper (Figure 16.1) suggested possible ways in which she might fill the paper that led to complex explorations of written symbols and their meanings.

Children make meanings though their own mathematical graphics

In his research, Hughes (1986) revealed some of the difficulties children have with the spoken and written language of mathematics and showed how they could represent quantities and calculations in their own ways.

Our research with children from birth to 8 years highlights the complex ways in which young children between the ages of 2 and 8 years use their own mathematical graphics to explore and communicate their mathematical thinking (Carruthers and Worthington 2005, 2006). Using their own marks and written methods – their own ways of representing – allows all children to explore their personal mathematical meanings and is, therefore, inclusive. Early years practitioners are now finding that they are able to develop their pedagogy and encourage the children in their settings to explore more open ways to exploring early 'written' mathematics.

Mathematical texts

Children use their own mathematical marks within their spontaneous play and sometimes in adult-led groups. In Figure 16.2, 4-year-old Carl decided to make some parking tickets for his small world play as he created a car park. Carl made his parking tickets from small pieces of paper that he had cut from a larger sheet. As he wrote the cost of the ticket on each, he 'read' the prices he had written: '40p, 40p, 40p, 50p, 70p, 80p, 90p'. These tickets provided new possibilities and became objects with which to play (Pahl 1999).

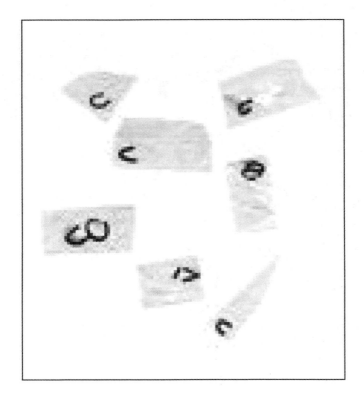

Figure 16.2 Carl's parking tickets

In a group context, some older children had been playing a game with beans and flowerpots: Barney (just 6 years old) used a number of interesting strategies to help him think about subtraction as 'taking away'. This was the first time that Barney had used paper and pen to explore his thinking about the operation of subtraction (see Figures 16.3).

At the top of the page he began with writing, '10 t 1 is p' (Ten take 1 is 9).

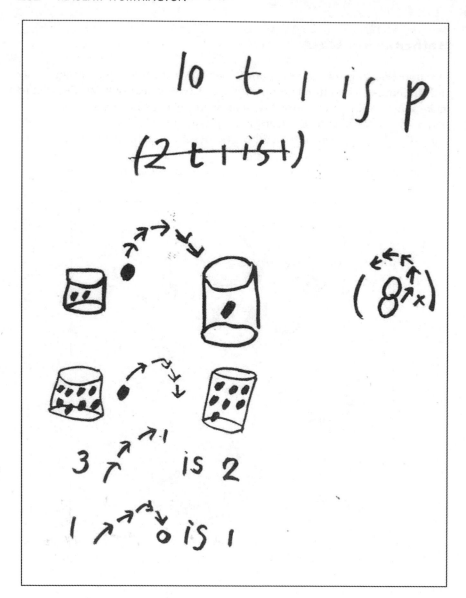

Figure 16.3   Barney's beans

He then drew the flowerpots with the beans inside and used his own way to represent the action of removing beans. He soon moved to a 'shorthand' method without pictures, using the word 'is' to stand for the '=' sign. Later in the same session, seeing another child draw a hand removing a bean to stand for the subtraction sign, he also drew a hand (not shown here). These different modes allowed him to think about the meanings of the standard symbols that he would come to understand and use.

The choices and decisions that children make in their multi-modal texts reveal a great deal about their understanding of mathematical symbols and the complex cultural influences that shape these meanings that are evident when looking closely at Barney's explorations with subtraction.

Layout, design and space

Barney considered where to place items on the page, beginning in the centre at the top where titles on screen, posters, comics, newspapers, notices and books commonly appear. He arranged most of his calculations on the left of the page, suggesting traditions from pages of 'book' text, with the reader entering on the left of the page. The calculations are set out as horizontal, left-to-right arrangements reflecting the left-to-right orientation of text in books and on screen and his writing (in English). He had also seen older children using horizontal calculations.

Barney is aware of the value of white space: here it helps the reader understand that each line of symbols is a separate calculation.

Signs of meaning

Barney's arc of arrows combines direction with the action of 'taking away', suggesting that he made an 'internalised sign' (Kress 1997: 58): this transformed the meaning of an arrow (direction) into a new sign suggesting removal or 'taking away'. He is likely to have been influenced by arrows he has seen on road signs, on a computerized, programmable toy that we had in the classroom and on other technologies at home. Arrows are symbols with distinct visual impact and are in common use in our culture.

Barney's drawing of flowerpots allows us to see the beans inside, suggesting that he had an awareness of an audience (his meaning is also transparent): without this strategy his calculations would not make sense. His use of brackets around some features reflected an aspect of our classroom culture which a number of other children used and provided an alternative to crossing something out.

I have used this depth of analysis to reveal the extent to which one child's multi-modal mathematical text is full of meanings considered; meanings he wishes to communicate and signs that are ripe with future mathematical potential. Analysing from a multi-modal perspective adds greater insights into children's mathematical graphics that are already astonishing feats of meaning-making and highlights the extent to which such a text really is much more than the 'sum of its parts'.

Reflection points

3   Collecting annotated examples of children's drawings and mark-making can help early years practitioners understand their development.

4   Do some of the examples you have of children's own mark-making through play appear to relate to children's own *mathematical* thinking? Discuss with your colleagues what these examples appear to show.

If you have not yet found any mathematical mark-making in your setting, discuss how you might encourage this.

Teaching early 'written' mathematics

Since adults can write and use the written language of mathematics, we sometimes overlook how complex learning symbolic languages such as mathematics can be for young children. With the introduction of the National Numeracy Strategy in England, guidance for teachers was provided on teaching 'mental calculations strategies' (QCA 1999a) and its companion guide *Teaching Written Calculations* (QCA 1999b). Both these publications supported flexible and individual ways of thinking about numbers, calculations and other aspects of mathematics. Teachers of 4- and 5-year-olds were advised to support children's own representations although 'at first children's recordings may not be easy for someone else to interpret, but they form an important stage in developing fluency' (QCA 1999b: 12).

Official *Curriculum Guidance for the Foundation Stage* emphasized that practitioners promote confidence in children when they begin to represent mathematics, 'asking children to "put something on paper"' (QCA/DfES 2000: 71). However, in a study with practitioners working with children aged 3–7 years, we found considerable uncertainty about how they should teach early 'written' mathematics. In some settings this resulted in emphasis on mathematics explored largely through 'practical' activities with resources such as sand, water, puzzles, counters and blocks (Carruthers and Worthington 2006; Worthington 2006). Without encouragement to also *represent* mathematical thinking in their own ways, it will be difficult for young children to begin to bridge the gap between their informal marks and standard written mathematics.

Other practitioners feel pressure to ensure that written mathematics should 'look like' mathematics with numerals written correctly and neatly and with children using standard symbols and calculations that are clearly (and horizontally) written with standard addition, subtraction and equals signs. These *products* are often then viewed as evidence of children's understanding, yet in terms of assessment they are likely to tell us only who did not understand what to write.

In the draft of the *Early Years Foundation Stage* (DfES 2006) mathematics is included under the heading of 'problem solving, reasoning and numeracy', setting out expectations for young mathematicians within the play-based EYFS curriculum. Within *communications, language and literacy*, the 'writing' section provides detailed guidance of children's mark-making. It is to be hoped that in its final form (2008) the mathematics section will give greater emphasis to children making and communicating mathematical meanings through their own marks for early 'written' mathematics.

Official advice in the UK on teaching written calculations is clear about the disadvantages of introducing and expecting standard symbols and calculations too early, emphasizing 'it is easy to be misled by children who start to use standard forms of recording too early, into thinking that they necessarily understand what they have written' (QCA 1999b: 19). Young children develop considerable informal understanding of mathematics at home (e.g. Aubrey 1997) and through their informal mathematical marks (Carruthers and Worthington 2006) although these beginnings may not always be acknowledged in their early years setting. Unless children have opportunities to build on their existing understanding when they enter an early childhood setting, there will remain a huge gulf between children's informal marks and their understanding of standard written mathematical symbols and calculations.

Concerns also persist about the lack of connection between children's mental and written methods. At the heart of children's own mathematical graphics is one of its greatest strengths – their thinking and mental methods explored on paper in ways that are personally meaningful.

Conclusion

Changes in society and the rapid pace of technological growth will, without doubt, continue to affect children's approaches: what they did in the past will not serve them well in the future; what they will need in the future is being shaped today.

Research on multi-modal texts reveals the huge variety of contexts, materials and ways in which young children explore and make meanings. In children's own mathematical texts, decisions about layout, use of space, direction, pictures, symbols and composition appear to support their early meaning-making of the written language of mathematics at a deep level. Multi-modality is not something practitioners should plan to teach as a focus of occasional activities or mathematics lessons but should be integral to the personal ways in which children make mathematical meanings.

Young children urgently need a new vision to support their learning of early written mathematics: building your professional understanding of multi-modal texts and children's mathematical graphics is likely to go a long way towards transforming learning of written mathematics.

Implications for practice

In the UK, debate and interest in the early childhood phase have been re-energized although some dilemmas remain:

1   Practitioners may sometimes find children's play – their multi-modal explorations – difficult to interpret and understand and this can lead to an over-emphasis on *products* at the expense of the child's own meanings and 'voice'.
    Suggestions:
    (a) Consider how you might give priority to children's own ways of meaning-making. How might you develop your provision for making things with junk materials, painting, drawing and mark-making?
    (b) Observing children as they play will provide you with rich insights into their meaning-making and thinking: observations should be used to plan for future experiences to further extend children's thinking.

2   Young children's early drawings and mark-making can often be difficult for adults to understand, resulting in pressure on practitioners to ensure that children produce neat drawings and 'correct', neat writing. This can restrict children's opportunities to make personal meanings about marks and symbols and limit content.
    Suggestions:
    (a) Collect the marks children make in play and in occasional adult-led groups and build a folder of each child's drawings and mark-making.
    (b) Annotate these pieces with a note of the context and anything the child said. This will help you build your understanding of each child's development over time.
    (c) Discuss children's early marks with their parents and with your team: sharing information about the children's mark-making at home and in your setting will show that you value these significant beginnings.

3   Misconceptions about the teaching of early 'written' mathematics

and a lack of official guidance mean limited opportunities for children to explore their own mathematical marks and representations. Suggestions:

(a) Develop your own professional knowledge about children's mathematical graphics to help you understand their development.

(b) Build on 'what children already know and can do' (QCA 2000: 11) as they make meanings in different ways about mathematics through their play and mathematical graphics.

(c) Develop your learning environment to support children's mathematical graphics.

(d) Build on the effective ways in which you already support children's early writing.

(e) Value children's early mathematical marks as you develop your pedagogical approaches.

(f) Assessment in mathematics should be from a positive perspective, valuing what they say and do and what their mathematical graphics show you that they understand. Many practitioners find that the taxonomy showing development of children's mathematical mark-making (Carruthers and Worthington 2006) is helpful in this respect.

Professional development

Our global society is changing at a rapid rate and we cannot afford to stand still. One of the implications of this is that practitioners working with young children need to keep abreast of educational theory and research: being up-to-date should not only be for students training to be teachers and other early years professionals, but throughout our careers. Our own research into children's mathematical graphics grew from small beginnings while we taught in settings with 3–7-year-olds: we wanted to help children better understand the beginnings of written mathematics and our interest in children's early writing suggested possible beginnings. Investigating children's learning in your own settings can provide insights that will help make a real difference and do not need to be large-scale projects.

However, concerns continue that research findings often either fail to reach settings and classrooms, or that it takes many years to do so. It is not difficult to see this leads to potential benefits for teaching and learning that are often missed: if this were to happen in the field of medicine, there would be an outcry.

One way to take ownership of your personal professional development is to find your own 'passion' in education so that you develop expertise in an area that excites and interests you. Think about something that interests you about children's meaning-making. How might you begin to explore this aspect of early years?

Building on what young children know and can do is one of the most significant ways in which you can tailor your approaches to meet young children's needs when they first begin in their early years setting. One of the more challenging aspects for early years practitioners has been to recognize children's often rich experiences of meaning-making they already explore at home in their play. Pahl's fascinating studies (e.g. 1999, 2001, 2003) allow exciting insights into children's cultural worlds while Anning and Ring's study of children's drawings (2004) also highlights some lack of continuity between their experiences at home and in early years settings. Research into children's informal mathematical knowledge at home (Aubrey 1997; Carruthers and Worthington 2006) has also highlighted the need to recognize and value young children's very considerable ability to make sense of mathematics and mark-making during the period before they enter their early childhood setting.

Consider the implications of such studies and how you might extend your knowledge of children's meaning-making and mathematics at home.

References and further reading

Anning, A. and Ring, K. (2004) *Making Sense of Children's Drawings*. Maidenhead: Open University Press/McGraw-Hill.

Athey, C. (2007) *Extending Thought in Young Children*, 2nd edn. London: Paul Chapman.

Aubrey, C. (1997) Children's early learning of number in school and out, in I. Thompson (ed.) *Teaching and Learning Early Number*. Buckingham: Open University Press.

Bruner, J. (1996) *Acts of Meaning*. Cambridge: Cambridge University Press.

Carruthers, E. and Worthington, M. (2005) Making sense of mathematical graphics: the development of understanding abstract symbolism. *European Early Childhood Education Research Association Journal*, 13(1): 57–9.

Carruthers, E. and Worthington, M. (2006) ***Children's Mathematics, Marking Marks, Making Meaning*, 2nd edn. London: Sage.**

Clay, M. (1975) *What Did I Write?* London: Heinemann.

Cope, B. and Kalantzis, M. (eds) (2000) *Multiliteracies: Literacy Learning and the Design of Social Futures*. London: Routledge.

DfES (2006) *The Early Years Foundation Stage: Consultation on a Single Quality Framework for Services to Children from Birth to Five*. Nottingham: DfES Publications. Available at: www.teachernet.gov.uk/publications (accessed 12 December 2006).

Halliday, M. (1975) *Learning How to Mean: Explorations in the Development of Language*. London: Arnold.

Hughes, M. (1986) *Children and Number: Difficulties in Learning Mathematics.* Oxford: Blackwell.

Jewitt, C. and Kress, G. (eds) (2003) *Multimodal Literacy.* New York: Peter Lang.

Kress, G. (1997) *Before Writing: Re-thinking the Paths to Literacy.* London: Routledge.

Kress, G., Jewitt, C., Ogborn, J. and Tsatsarelis, C. (2001) *Multimodal Teaching and Learning: The Rhetorics of the Science Classroom.* London: Continuum.

Luria, A. (1983) The development of writing in the child, in M. Martlew (ed.) *The Psychology of Written Language.* Chichester: John Wiley and Sons.

Matthews, J. (2003) *Drawing and Painting: Children and Visual Representation,* 2nd edn. London: Paul Chapman.

Pahl, K. (1999) *Transformations: Meaning Making in Nursery Education.* Stoke-on-Trent: Trentham Books.

Pahl, K. (2001) Texts as artefacts crossing sites: map making at home and at school, *Reading, Literacy and Language,* 35(3): 120–5.

Pahl, K. (2003) Children's text-making at home: transforming meaning across modes, in C. Jewitt and G. Kress (eds) *Multimodal Literacy.* New York: Peter Lang.

Pahl, K. and Rowsell, J. (2005) *Literacy and Education: Understanding the New Literacy Studies in the Classroom.* London: Paul Chapman Publishing.

QCA (1999a) *Teaching Mental Methods,* London: QCA.

QCA (1999b) *Teaching Written Calculations.* London: QCA.

QCA (2004) for QCA/UKLA *More than Words: Multimodal Texts in the Classroom.* London: QCA Publications.

QCA (2005a) *More than Words 2: Creating Stories on Page and Screen.* London: QCA and UKLA.

QCA (2005b) *Continuing the Learning Journey.* London: QCA.

QCA/DfES (2000) *Curriculum Guidance for the Foundation Stage.* London: QCA/DfES.

Rogoff, B. (2003) *The Cultural Nature of Human Development.* New York: Oxford University Press.

Van Oers, B. (2001) Educational forms of initiation in mathematical culture, *Educational Studies in Mathematics,* 46: 59–85.

Vygotsky, L.S. (1978) *Mind and Society.* London: Harvard University Press.

Vygotsky, L.S. (1983) The prehistory of written language, in M. Martlew (ed.) *The Psychology of Written Language.* Chichester: John Wiley and Sons.

Wells, G. (1986) *The Meaning Makers: Children Learning Languages and Using Language to Learn.* Portsmouth, NH: Heinemann Educational.

Wertsch, J. (1985) *Vygotsky and the Social Formations of Mind.* Cambridge, MA: Harvard University Press.

Worthington, M. (2006) Creativity meets Mathematics, *Practical Pre-School,* 66: 10–11.

Worthington, M. (2007) 'It's my birthday bridge': multi-modal meanings through play, in J. Moyles (ed.) *Beginning Teaching, Beginning Learning,* 2nd edn. Maidenhead: Open University Press.

17 'Hi Granny! I'm writing a novel.'

Literacy in early childhood: joys, issues and challenges

Marian Whitehead

Abstract

This chapter provides a brief overview of the complex issues and challenges surrounding the development of language and literacy in the early years of childhood. The initial section looks at the roots of literacy located in the richness of early non-verbal communication and the power of children's thinking and feeling in infancy. The main focus of the chapter is on the teaching of initial reading and the controversies and dilemmas arising from compulsory synthetic phonics instruction in early years settings. Guidance on good practice permeates the chapter while reflective questions and the concluding discussion points prompt practitioners to review their own knowledge and practices.

Introduction

This title incorporates the first words of a brief transatlantic telephone call from my grandson, Dylan, who was just one month short of his 8th birthday. His claim may still rest on the fragile evidence of scattered pieces of paper on his bedroom floor and the energetic filling of a notebook with page after page of boldly scrawled conversations and descriptions. But many adult novelists do the same and Dylan is bouncing with literary pride. He has come a long way in the years since his birth when he first shared picture books with his immediate family and learnt about the roles of readers and the significance of pictures and print (Whitehead 2002). Dylan's own literacy history can best be summed up as one of meeting joyful challenges on a passionate pilgrimage from reading people and pictures to reading words and the world (Freire and Macedo 1987). There is nothing unusual about this story and Dylan is an ordinary little boy bursting with physical energy and enthusiasm for cycling and football, skateboarding and basketball, computer games and chess. However, he does have a family who believe in him as a reader and writer, share their own literacy activities with him and have always held firmly to the view that all young children require time, confidence, interested adults and enjoyment if they are to become readers and writers – or even novelists.

These views can no longer be taken for granted, not even in schools and early years settings, and joy in early literacy has increasingly given way to stress, boredom and failure. But this is nothing new, although we might have hoped to have moved on from narrow and punitive approaches to teaching literacy to young children. In fact, literacy has always been a site of controversy and prejudice because it is bound up with social and political power and citizens have always been judged and ranked by their levels of literacy (Whitehead 2004). However, when these crass judgements filter down into early years settings and classrooms and adult prejudices and misunderstandings are treated as respectable theories of literacy, young children are caught up in some very unpleasant 'reading wars' and good sense is the first casualty. The following challenges and issues will be focused on in this chapter:

- Literacy is not rooted in letters and words, but in non-verbal communication and close relationships.
- A narrow reliance on one kind of phonic approach in the initial teaching of literacy in English will always fail many children.
- At the heart of reading is a search for meaning and understanding – stories, books and visual, technical and cultural literacies are central to this.
- There is a dauntingly high price to pay for promoting bog standard literacy in the twenty-first century.

Communication, language and living

I am enjoying my coffee and watching a baby of about 6 months with a young father just a couple of tables away. The whole period of informal observation (or eavesdropping) takes 40 minutes and the play between child and father entertains many of the coffee bar customers, as well as me!

Initially baby is sitting on dad's lap and they play a game of peep-boo with a muslin square that dad regularly drops over baby's head and then whisks away for the exciting moment of discovery and shout of 'boo!'

A second activity starts up: dad makes exaggerated facial grimaces, baby chuckles and both take turns to poke their tongues out.

This exchange continues intermittently throughout the next 30 minutes and for most of this time baby is also eating a biscuit.

Dad moves baby into a high chair and produces a rattle that he shakes rhythmically and then passes to the baby. Baby gives it a few hefty shakes before passing it back to dad and these musical exchanges continue, to the delight of both players.

From the vantage point of the high chair the baby begins to take an interest in the people sitting near by and goes in for some serious people-watching and attempts to make eye contact. Most people do respond with a smile and this elicits a triumphant answering smile from the baby. However, an elderly man at the table next to the baby is totally unresponsive and baby seems puzzled and confused, staring long and hard at this stranger who will not communicate.

This episode covered a substantial period of time and had its own rhythms of excitement, repetition, concentration and investigation. It could be described as 'getting your carer to entertain you' and, although there was a rich variety of play, communication, movement, sound, taste, texture and engaging with people, it was all done in a context of ordinary pleasures, familiar routines and a safe relationship. It should come as no surprise, then, that I wish to claim that some highly significant literacy developments start long before the early years of schooling. Literacy has its roots in the earliest interactions between babies and carers and in the play and investigations of toddlers on the move. These earliest stages of communication and language are shared with important adults, and sometimes with siblings, and coloured by powerful feelings and emotions about human relationships, identity, attachment, love and loss.

The work of Trevarthen has focused on babies 'learning in companionship' (2002: 20) and identified the prime need infants have to get to grips with the world and to do so in the course of sharing meanings with an older and wiser companion. This approach builds on the work of Vygotsky (1986) who described the optimal levels of learning and understanding reached by children when they are doing things in partnership with an older and more experienced member of the culture. This social construction of thinking highlights the importance of the rich thick textures of life and everyday experiences that make it possible for infants to get a grip on communication, relationships, objects and culture (Gopnik et al. 1999). These are complex ideas but we can bring them down to earth by reminding ourselves of the baby in the coffee bar. We can also make more sense of these ideas if we trace their links with early literacy learning:

- Literacy is communication, but communication starts with the non-verbal and verbal interactions between babies and carers and the baby partners are pro-active and skilled communicators.

- Literacy is an extension of oral culture and of our lifelong fascination with eavesdropping, gossiping, singing, dramatizing, rhyming and punning, dancing and ritual. Here are the roots of linguistic patterns, phonological sensitivity, drawing, writing and reading.
- Literacy uses signs and symbols to carry meanings and infants also sign their needs and intentions with gestures and facial expressions and make significant marks in food, mud, moisture and dust, as well as 'pretending' that they are eating, sleeping, and so forth.

Reflection point

1   If children are to build on these early literacy foundations, how can we ensure that they have ample opportunities for playful experimentation and opportunities to exercise independence in tackling the cultural conventions of literacy?

Perhaps the following observation is illuminating:

> I am observing the play of children in the large garden of a Children's Centre in an urban setting in the east of England. I decide to take a brief break to read through my notes and think about what I have seen, so I sit down in an empty willow arbour. In less than two minutes I am joined by three girls (4-year-olds) who sit close to me, take a great interest in my notebook, ask me what I am doing and ask me what I have written. They listen carefully to my answers (mainly focused on 'finding out what interesting things they can do in their garden') and then they suggest, very firmly, that they want to write about themselves in my notebook. I can hardly refuse and the results are below (Figure 17.1).

The important thing about this encounter is the children's clear grasp of what writing does, what it is for and their own roles as writers and recorders of events in their daily lives.

Trevarthen (2002) captures the richness of early communication, language and living, in a broad sweep of activities from birth to the early years of school:

> Infants play with emotional narratives long before they talk, and toddlers create dramas together before they have any demonstrable 'theory of mind'. This gives both the reason and the means for language learning. From 2 to 6 children make things, tell and listen to stories, create drama, acting fantastic parts, dance and exhibit all sorts of musical skills. Their appetite for cultural forms of life is

enormous and their perception of human roles is rich and pene-
trating. We may well ask what goes wrong!

(2002: 16–25)

We may well answer that children's own enthusiasm for communicating,
learning and investigating gets smothered beneath a deluge of unimaginative
information and unrelated facts. Children's achievements are also masked by

Figure 17.1 The little girls' drawing

a bureaucratic passion for recording what they cannot do. This arises from a worrying obsession with what comes after the early years and a failure to focus on the quality of children's lives here and now (Petrie and Apter 2004). The teaching of reading to very young children is often the chief villain in this story of lost opportunities, inappropriate educational provision and insensitive practitioners.

Phonic fibs – neither first nor fast

There is a wonderful story about teaching letter sounds in isolation that goes the rounds and, apocryphal though it may be, it has much to say to teachers, parents and communities. It was retold in a national newspaper (Mangan 2005) to great effect. The setting is a class of 4-year-olds in rural north Wales and their new, young teacher is attempting to teach the letter 'S' using a large colour photo of a sheep and demanding, with absolutely no success, that the children tell her what it is!

Eventually, one brave soul put up a tiny reluctant hand. 'Yes!' she cried, waving the photo aloft. 'Tell me what you think this is!' 'Please, Miss,' said the boy warily. 'Is it a three-year-old Border Leicester?'

The moral of the story is, never underestimate the young, thoughtful meaning-makers (Wells 1986) who are on the receiving end of such inept and grossly over-simplified approaches to the teaching of phonics. The recent 'fuss about phonics' is a case in point, and the fact that government ministers have thrown their lot in with the latest panacea for teaching reading quickly and cheaply is the worst possible reason to go along with it! Professional educators and carers have a responsibility to be thoughtful and to educate themselves about phonics and share their knowledge in accessible ways with worried parents and community groups. A confident understanding of the terms that are frequently bandied about makes a good start:

- *phonics* is a method for teaching reading that focuses on the relationship between sounds (phonemes) and letters (graphemes). A phoneme is the smallest unit of sound in a language but not necessarily a single letter, e.g. 'ee' in 'bee' is a phoneme. Linguists identify approximately 44 phonemes in English.
- *synthetic phonics* is the focus of attention in England, but it is also the oldest and most traditional of phonic methods. It assumes that simple decoding is all that is required in reading and teaches the sounds of individual letters and the 44 phonemes of English. Children are taught to sound out the letters in words and 'blend' them together. So we somehow make 'mer'- 'a'-'ter' into 'mat' and fail

dismally when we get to the more complex word patterns in a simple text, e.g. 'said', 'the', 'any'.

- *analytic phonics* is based on modern linguistic research and children are gradually taught to look at segments of words and at the frequent patterns in sounds and words. This approach begins by focusing on the beginning, or initial, sounds of words, called 'onset', and the end phonemes called 'rimes'. This involves lots of enjoyable play with the alphabet and the sounds of letters (alphabetic awareness) and children can be helped to enjoy the *alliteration* of same initial sounds in tongue twisters and the same, or similar, end rimes found in words that *rhyme* in songs, poetry and verse.

Even these simplified definitions should make it clear that perhaps using phonics in the initial teaching of reading is not going to be a straightforward and unproblematic strategy for all children and all teachers. However, there are some phonic fibs currently being promoted at the highest governmental level in the UK, namely, the insistence that there is one, and one only, foolproof method for teaching all children to read! Fibs are those rather trivial little lies that we all resort to in order to manipulate a situation, or over-simplify a case, and phonic fibs are currently doing just that.

Reflection point

2   Why do we have to go for just one kind of phonic approach, especially when it must be obvious that although the synthetic variety was used intensively in primary schools in the late nineteenth century and the early to middle years of the twentieth century, it did not instantly transform the lives and literacy skills of generations of children?

Even without historical evidence, recent professional experience and academic research, much of it from the USA, is highly ambiguous about the advantage of one kind of phonics over another (Meyer 2002; Altwerger 2005). It is more likely that different aspects of phonics are effective at different stages in young children's literacy development. Furthermore, we all get better at using a range of phonic strategies once we are able to read! There is no research support for the notion that every phoneme and every possible spelling 'rule' for English (166 and counting, plus a large number of exceptions) must be taught systematically to every child (Dombey 2006). Children really do teach themselves to read as they get involved with texts and many children who have been studied closely by academics learn to read at an early age without being taught by professional teachers (Clarke 1976). This is not to suggest that we abandon the teaching of reading, but we do have to include the achievements of such children in any respectable theory of learning to read and we have to analyse the grounds of their success. Some things are clear: the success of these children is rooted in warmly supportive homes, literacy-rich environments and experiences that help them make sense of meaningful print in the out-of-school world they share with their families and communities. They all seem to have encountered stories and printed texts, including books, as well as talk and play with language, songs, chants, hymns, rhymes and poems. Visits to libraries, places of worship, shops, clinics and offices also played a crucial role in the children's literacy, as did lots of markers and masses of scrap paper and steamed up widows! The children were supported by caring relationships with one or two special adults, as well as siblings, and their daily lives also offered opportunities to be quiet and undisturbed.

These general factors are a powerful challenge to the 'fib' that synthetic phonics must be 'first' in any approach to initial reading and, combined with the earlier discussion on communication and language development, they put paid to the notion that reading only starts when teachers 'do sounds'! The hidden, and often forgotten, mass of the literacy iceberg is beneath all the surface fuss over sounds, blending and word-building games. We must be aware of its significance and, putting 'first things first', help young children to bring their deep knowledge of language and communication to bear on the literacy of schooling.

The other 'fib' that is now permanently linked with 'first' is 'fast' and as a slogan for early education and literacy it is totally inappropriate. Those who work with young emerging readers and writers are privileged to be at the start of lifetimes of change, development, unpredictability, challenge and pleasure. Speedy solutions and quick-fix techniques are the worst possible approaches for young learners who need time for thinking, investigating, going 'off message' and playing. In the early years of care and education children must have quality experiences and their unique patterns of learning must be respected. Getting ready for the next and later phases of schooling is an unacceptable justification for nineteenth-century reading dogma and a compulsory early start to schooling! Young children are not chrysalides waiting for the ultimate stage in their educational metamorphosis: they are human beings living their lives here and now.

It is not surprising that a 'one size fits all' reading method appeals to bureaucrats and politicians. It makes the teaching of reading no more com-plex than buying socks in a department store and hides all the difficulties of individual differences in development and life experiences, complexities of language processing in the brain, or differences between the phonological system of English and other languages. Most important of all for the quick-fix advocates, the buying-new-socks theory of reading makes it possible to employ any well-intentioned adult to read the instruction books, pass on the information to the children and conduct the rote learning choruses! Thus freeing the early years of schooling from the expense of employing specialist graduate teachers!

Learning to read isn't that simple, unless adult practitioners know the one easy lesson about teaching reading: respond to what the child is trying to do (Smith 1994). This adult responsiveness involves understanding that the child must get the big picture about reading at the start: 'What's it for?', 'How does it work?', 'How do you do it?', 'What are the black marks for?', 'What are the pictures for?', 'What's it got to do with talk and telling stories?' And, What's it going to do for me? So many children are pushed through endless reading lessons without ever getting the chance to formulate, let alone ask, these initial questions about reading. Yet these are the basics for learning to behave like a reader: asking questions of the text and recreating the narrative. Young beginner readers have huge demands made on their language pro- cessing skills when they tackle text, but the more background knowledge they have of books and reading as a meaning-making activity, the better the trade- off between visual letter and phoneme decoding and constructing meanings (Crystal 2005).

Stories, books and new literacies

Stories are a timeless and universal way of making sense of experience. They are the means by which we impose order on random events and try to understand the significance of what happens to us and why people behave as they do. This is why we gossip and tell tales about our daily lives. This is why we listen to the stories of other people, or watch them narrated in plays, films and television: we hope to gain more stories, more meanings and more explanations to try out. This is why we read. It is also why very young chil- dren listen, chatter, tell tales, talk about their day, draw and make marks, dance and enact play scenarios, and mull over the puzzling world in which they find themselves. Stories are ways of thinking and are crucial to young thinkers as they set out on their daily meaning-making activities. Books give children and adults a hugely expanded resource of more stories for thinking with, and for understanding and exploring new worlds of experience. They are not optional extras in the early years, nor are they rewards for those who survive phonic training and are deemed eligible to move on to real reading. Stories and books are 'the basics' at the start of becoming literate and the only reason for doing so. The most dangerous aspect of the new synthetic phonics orthodoxy is the advice to use only approved phonically regular schemes, rather than real books written by knowable authors who share stories and facts about the human condition.

Stories and books also come with an added linguistic bonus! They use language in all its varied rhythms and patterns, including important phonic features such as alliteration, or same initial sounds, and the rhyming qualities of word endings that sound alike and sometimes look similar – but only sometimes! Stories and books offer very rich examples of new, unusual and exciting vocabulary for the emergent reader. I have seen a group of children in a nursery school so captivated by the 'sploshing' and 'squelching' of the traditional rhyme, *We're Going on a Bear Hunt*, that they rushed into the garden and created their own mud and river in a large sand tray so that they could squelch and splash through it while chanting the story word for word. Now that is the power of rhymes, stories and picture books!

Reflection points

3   Do meaning and understanding have a place in your own working definition of 'reading' and how does this shape your practice?

4   How can professional educators and carers deliver a literacy strategy that does not appear to offer an explicit definition of reading?

Our children inhabit a complex world in which many forms of literacy exist and enter into their consciousness, as we realize when they 'read' the signs on the motorway, identify the appropriate public toilet door, play a computer game, operate a DVD player and a mobile phone. Modern research into early literacy now describes the multi-modal nature of literacies and many practitioners bring these insights to bear on classroom provision and the teaching of reading (Hall 2003; Larson and Marsh 2005; Pahl and Rowsell 2005). At a time when technology is transforming literacy, it is bizarre to tackle early literacy instruction with the tools of the nineteenth century! Our youngest children can read pictures, follow digital icons, operate sophisticated ICT systems, and many can move between two or more languages and cultures. How often do we use these powerful tools for thinking to help children access the written texts that we all want them to read? The 'new literacy studies' emphasize the old truths: the teaching of literacy must be situated and meaningful and draw on the everyday literacies of homes and communities.

Bog-standard literacy: paying the price

There is considerable concern among educators and authors that if we promote a narrow, utilitarian and outdated approach to literacy, we will pay a high price in alienation from schooling and all things educational, high rates of functional illiteracy and political disengagement and passivity. These are not exactly the lessons we would wish to teach in a democracy. This new/old approach has been wittily described as bog-standard literacy, but its modest achievements are bought at an extraordinary price (Powling 2005: 6). Perhaps we should remind ourselves of the price that will be paid in the early years.

Synthetic phonics does not improve young readers' understanding of texts and this seems to be reflected in a decline in reading for pleasure, helped along by a school system that now spends far, far more on testing than on books.

Young bilinguals are short-changed if they are only trained to bark at print and discouraged from using the complex bilingual literacies, stories and symbol systems of their homes and communities. In their early days in education settings and schools they need access to a richly symbolic and playful curriculum and the chance to communicate in many different ways.

Many young boys will pay a high price if the reading experiences they are offered are passive, rote-based and seat-bound! Boys are sometimes slower to get involved with formal reading instruction and need to be physically active learners for many years, but they also thrive on adventurous texts that are factually rich as well as imaginative.

Parents will pay a high price, namely the loss of the very special contribution they can make to their children's literacy development, if they are persuaded that there is only one way to teach reading. If reading at home with mum, dad or grandma, deteriorates into imitating the worst kinds of teacherly activities like sounding out individual letters and blending them, we will have lost one of the most empowering literacy strategies to have emerged in the twentieth century.

Conclusion

It is misguided to teach children the tricks of decoding simplified print and hope that they will apply these 'rules' to genuine texts at a later stage. The quality and content of children's first reading books matter if our children are to become passionate, critical readers. Complexity is central to children's earliest communications, language development, social experiences and thinking. Young children are sensitive to subtle differences and variations in printed material if the contexts involve meaningful and emotionally rewarding encounters with people, ideas and events.

Points for discussion

- How can you work with parents, carers and the wider community to promote the joys of literacy?
- Our aim should always be to understand the individual and diverse

ways that children develop and learn. How can we achieve this while negotiating an increasingly didactic literacy approach?

- Consider the ways in which language-aware practitioners can meet all children's needs, learning styles and interests, while increasing their knowledge of alliteration, rhyme, terminal sounds and common letter strings.
- Relationships with both children and adults are at the heart of care and education – they are also at the heart of stories and literature. Discuss!

References and further reading

Altwerger, B. (ed.) (2005) *Reading for Profit: How the Bottom Line Leaves Kids Behind*. Portsmouth, NH: Heinemann.

Clarke, M. M. (1976) *Young Fluent Readers*. London: Heinemann.

Crystal, D. (2005) *How Language Works*. London: Penguin Books.

Dombey, H. (2006) How should we teach children to read? *Books for Keeps*, 156: 6–7.

Freire, P. and Macedo, D. (1987) *Literacy: Reading the Word and the World*. London: Routledge and Kegan Paul.

Gopnik, A., Meltzoff, A. and Kuhl, P. (1999) *How Babies Think: The Science of childhood*. London: Weidenfeld and Nicolson.

Hall, K. (2003) *Listening to Stephen Read: Multiple Perspectives on Literacy*. Buckingham: Open University Press.

Larson, J. and Marsh, J. (2005) *Making Literacy Real*. London: Sage.

Mangan, L. (2005) Do citizenship tests work? Ask a silly question. *The Guardian*, G2, November 2 p. 36.

Meyer, R.J. (2002) *Phonics Exposed*. Hillsdale, NJ: Lawrence Erlbaum.

Pahl, K. and Rowsell, J. (2005) *Literacy and Education: Understanding the New Literacy Studies in the Classroom*. London: Paul Chapman.

Petrie, P. and Apter, T. (2004) Will educating pre-school children in literacy and numeracy help to create a capable population? *RSA Journal*, pp. 6–9.

Powling, C. (ed.) (2005) *Waiting for a Jamie Oliver: Beyond Bog-Standard Literacy*. Reading: National Centre for Language and Literacy.

Smith, F. (1994) *Understanding Reading*, 5th edn. Hillsdale, NJ: Lawrence Erlbaum.

Trevarthen, C. (2002) Learning in companionship, *Education in the North: The Journal of Scottish Education*, 10: 16–25.

Vygotsky, L.S. (1986) *Thought and Language*. Cambridge, MA: MIT Press.

Wells, G. (1986) *The Meaning Makers*. London: Hodder and Stoughton.

Whitehead, M.R. (2002) Dylan's routes to literacy: the first three years with picture books, *Journal of Early Childhood Literacy*, 2(3): 269–89.

Whitehead, M.R. (2004) *Language and Literacy in the Early Years*, 3rd edn. London: Sage.

Endpiece

Janet Moyles

Our intention at the start of this book was to set you thinking about some of the issues incorporated into the Early Years Foundation Stage at this time. All the contributors hope that we have both given some food for thought but also significant support in making what is inevitably difficult decisions about how you will respond positively to the challenges of the EYFS and its demands on time, commitment and enthusiasm!

The really good thing about working with young children is that we KNOW they will appreciate our responsiveness, our thoughtfulness and our empathy. The joy of teaching young children is anticipating, valuing and cherishing such responses and engaging in a variety of playful and meaningful interactions with them with passion and dedication. It's somewhat hackneyed, yet nevertheless true to say, that these young people are our future – whatever we instil in them in the early years will reap its inevitable rewards on our future society: we can work and play towards ensuring that it's good.

Appendix
The scope of the book

The direct relationship between EYFS and this book are shown in this table. However, there are many areas of overlap, as readers will see once they've been through all the chapters!

EYFS contents	Chapter	Title and author
Overview	1	Changing the landscape of early childhood (*Liz Brooker*)
A UNIQUE CHILD		
Child Development		
● *Unique individual*	0	Introduction (*Janet Moyles*)
● *Skilful communicator*	2	Primary communication: what can adults learn from babies? (*Rod Parker-Rees*)
● *Competent learner*	2	Primary communication: what can adults learn from babies? (*Rod Parker-Rees*)
Inclusive Practice		
● *Children's entitlements*	3	Difference, culture and diversity: challenges, responsibilities and opportunities (*Theodora Papatheodorou*)
	4	Identity and children as learners (*Naima Browne*)
● *Equality and diversity*	3	Difference, culture and diversity: challenges, responsibilities and opportunities (*Theodora Papatheodorou*)
	4	Identity and children as learners (*Naima Browne*)
● *Early support*	3	Difference, culture and diversity: challenges, responsibilities and opportunities (*Theodora Papatheodorou*)
	4	Identity and children as learners (*Naima Browne*)

EYFS contents	Chapter	Title and author
Keeping Safe • Being safe and protected • Discovering boundaries • Making choices		
Health and Well-being • Growing and developing • Physical well-being • *Emotional well-being*	4	Identity and children as learners (*Naima Browne*)
	7	Coping with bereavement (*Rose Griffiths*)
POSITIVE RELATIONSHIPS		
Respecting each other • *Understanding feelings*	7	Coping with bereavement (*Rose Griffiths*)
• Friendships		
• *Professional relationships*	5	Working together to support playful learning and transition (*Pat Broadhead*)
	8	Vision, mission, method: challenges and issues in developing the role of the early years mentor teacher (*Jackie Eyles*)
Parents as Partners • *Respecting diversity*	4	Identity and children as learners (*Naima Browne*)
• *Communication*	6	Somebody else's business: a parent's view of childhood (*Emmie Short*)
• *Learning together*	6	Somebody else's business: a parent's view of childhood (*Emmie Short*)
Supporting Learning • *Positive interactions*	8	Vision, mission, method: challenges and issues in developing the role of the early years mentor teacher (*Jackie Eyles*)
• *Listening to children*	7	Coping with bereavement (*Rose Griffiths*)
• *Effective teaching*	9	Birth to three: the need for a loving and educated workforce (*Tricia David*)
Key Person • *Secure attachment*	7	Coping with bereavement (*Rose Griffiths*)

EYFS contents	Chapter	Title and author
● Shared care		
● Independence		
ENABLING ENVIRONMENTS		
Observation, Assessment and Planning		
● *Starting with the child*	12	Written observations or walks in the park? Documenting children's experiences (*Paulette Luff*)
● Planning		
● *Assessment*	12	Written observations or walks in the park? Documenting children's experiences (*Paulette Luff*)
The Learning Environment		
● *Children's needs*	11	Children's outdoor experiences: a sense of adventure? (*Elizabeth Carruthers*)
● *The learning journey*	12	Written observations or walks in the park? Documenting children's experiences (*Paulette Luff*)
● Working together		
The Physical Environment		
● The emotional environment		
● *The outdoor environment*	11	Children's outdoor experiences: a sense of adventure? (*Elizabeth Carruthers*)
● The indoor environment		
The Wider Context		
● *Transitions and continuity*	10	The challenges of starting school (*Hilary Fabian*)
● *Multi-agency working*	13	Food for thought: the importance of food and eating in early childhood practice (*Deborah Albon*)
● *The community*	13	Food for thought: the importance of food and eating in early childhood practice (*Deborah Albon*)
LEARNING AND DEVELOPMENT		
Play and Exploration		
● Learning through experience		
● Adult involvement		
● *Contexts for learning*	16	Multi-modality, play and children's mark-making in maths (*Maulfry Worthington*)

EYFS contents	Chapter	Title and author
Active Learning		
● Mental and physical involvement		
● *Decision-making*	14	Developing independence in learning (*David Whitebread*)
● *Personalized learning*	14	Developing independence in learning (*David Whitebread*)
Creativity and Critical Thinking		
● *Making connections*	15	What does it mean to be creative? (*Dan Davies and Alan Howe*)
● Transforming understanding		
● Sustained shared thinking		
Areas of Learning and Development		
● Personal, social and emotional development		
● *Communication, language and literacy*	17	'Hi Granny! I'm writing a novel.' Literacy in early childhood: joys, issues and challenges (*Marian Whitehead*)
● *Problem-solving, reasoning and numeracy*	16	Multi-modality, play and children's mark-making in maths (*Maulfry Worthington*)
● Knowledge and understanding of the world		
● *Creative development*	15	What does it mean to be creative? (*Dan Davies and Alan Howe*)
● Physical development		

Index